"Today, at a time when clinical work seeks to be aware of multicultural issues, desires to be more sensitive to clients' ultimate concerns and respectful of the potentially healing role of religious resources in psychological treatment, we are gifted with this groundbreaking new work. Whatever your professional background, theoretical orientation, and current views regarding the place of religious issues in treatment were before you read this book, you are sure to walk away from it with new wisdom and, hopefully, a willingness to see where your own ideas may now lead. Thought provoking, holistic, empirically based, and willing to address some of the most challenging questions surrounding the role of religious and spiritual constructs in the treatment of clients in contemporary society, it is in a word, *brilliant.*"

—**Robert J. Wicks, Psy.D.**, author of *The Tao of Ordinariness: Humility and Simplicity in a Narcissistic Age*, USA

"This is a comprehensive toolkit for understanding the empirical psychology of the numinous. It contains useful measures, an assessment guide, and suggestions for training, practice, and research. It is the essential authoritative source for all interested in the scientific study of the numinous, coauthored by the foremost expert in the field."

—**Ralph W. Hood, Jr., Ph.D.**, professor of psychology and religious studies, University of Tennessee, USA

"What is the place of the numinous in human life? How do scientists understand it, and how do clinicians work with it? Very few books offer the profound value to both scientist and practitioner that this ambitious book does. This is an uncommon, visionary, and bold work, bridging epistemology and theology, social science and clinical practice. The book's approach to understanding the numinous will challenge researchers to grow philosophically and methodologically and prompt clinicians to think more deeply and integratively."

—**Chris J. Boyatzis, Ph.D.**, professor of psychology, Bucknell University, former president of the Society for the Psychology of Religion and Spirituality, USA

"Ralph Piedmont and Teresa Wilkins have set out an ambitious task—to reconceptualize how to understand people's sense of the sacred and how mental health professionals might work with it in assessment and psychotherapy. Their concepts, practical tools, and case studies will help both practitioners and psychologists of religion and spirituality counsel more effectively and powerfully and understand why the sacred matters so much."

—**Everett L. Worthington, Jr.**, author of *Forgiveness and Spirituality in Psychotherapy: A Relational Approach*, USA

D1300372

Understanding the Psychological Soul of Spirituality

Understanding the Psychological Soul of Spirituality is a comprehensive exploration of spiritual constructs based on an empirical, evidence-based paradigm for understanding and addressing spirituality.

In a field where there is no current consensus on spirituality, this book provides a much-needed psychologically based definition and ontology that assists helping professionals in formulating their professional identities; developing effective and appropriate training models; furthering their understanding of what spirituality is and is not, from a psychological perspective; and more effectively addressing spiritual issues to support clients.

The authors provide a review of current issues in the area of spirituality, also called the *numinous*, and provide perspectives that address these concerns in ways that promote a fully scientific understanding of the construct. Ultimately, the book provides a concise definition of the numinous that places it squarely in the social sciences. Chapters outline the clear value of the numinous for psychology and detail its relevance for professionals' training.

Ralph L. Piedmont, Ph.D., is managing director of the Center for Professional Studies in Timonium, Maryland, USA.

Teresa A. Wilkins, Ph.D., is a Licensed Professional Counselor and lecturer at the Johns Hopkins University School of Nursing in Baltimore, Maryland, USA.

Understanding the Psychological Soul of Spirituality

A Guidebook for Research and Practice

Ralph L. Piedmont and Teresa A. Wilkins

Routledge
Taylor & Francis Group

NEW YORK AND LONDON

First published 2020
by Routledge
52 Vanderbilt Avenue, New York, NY 10017

and by Routledge
2 Park Square, Milton Park, Abingdon, Oxon, OX14 4RN

Routledge is an imprint of the Taylor & Francis Group, an informa business

Library of Congress Cataloguing in Publication Data
A catalog record for this title has been requested

ISBN: 978-1-138-55915-8 (hbk)
ISBN: 978-1-138-55916-5 (pbk)
ISBN: 978-1-351-16448-1 (ebk)

Typeset in Baskerville
by Swales & Willis Ltd, Exeter, Devon, UK

Dedication

I want to dedicate this book to my family (Rose, Joanna, Dominic, and Steve) who have provided me with countless insights into the nature of the numinous, to my students who have helped shape and develop my thoughts, and to my many colleagues who have always patiently listened to me, even when my ideas were not well developed, providing always encouragement and support.

—RLP

To my family, thank you for your patience and understanding during the writing of this volume and for the joy you bring to my life every day.

To the members of the Pastoral Counseling Department at Loyola University Maryland, especially the professors who were my instructors, then my colleagues, and then my good friends: Thank you for the intellectual stimulation, the superb training, the camaraderie, and the commiseration.

To my students: Thank you for your contributions, questions, strengths, and growing edges. Watching your development as budding professionals has been one of the highlights of my life.

—TAW

Contents

Foreword

Dr. Ralph Piedmont, a revered leader in the field of psychology and spirituality, and Dr. Teresa Wilkins offer mainstream psychology access to a most powerful realm of human experience: the numinous. A journey into this un-examined factor is propelled by the equally powerful force that academic psychology has to offer: rigorous science. Clinicians and counselors, academic researchers, organizational psychologists, and students alike will find confidence in the way Piedmont and Wilkins address the seemingly vast notion of the numinous with pinpoint conceptual clarity and certain science.

To fully appreciate the significance of this *field-defining* work, first it is necessary to know Piedmont for his *field-building* role. Piedmont has been a prescient "founding father," an academic statesman who was a foremost leader in building the scientific field of psychology and spirituality. I first met Ralph in 1998 at an APA Convention in Toronto. He was presenting new findings about to be published in a top research journal showing spirituality to be independent from the "Big Five," the field-defining five-factor model of personality. Ralph's innovative study said that we need a "Big Six." At that time, spirituality had been dismissed by academic psychology to be a spurious concept, assumed to be "less real," or an erroneously applied name to a more fundamental dimension of personality, such as, say, introversion. But Ralph Piedmont as an Assistant Professor had just proven otherwise. The early-career Dr. Piedmont was providing evidence about spirituality that was utterly germane to changing the core views of center-field psychology. The study was ground-shaking to anyone willing to see its implication. Still for Piedmont, this landmark study proved to be the opening of the door to a three-decade, eminent career in which he skillfully commandeered research to boldly confront, and in turn, often reformulate core tenets of academic psychology.

What I did not know in our meeting of 1998, was that Piedmont would bring along hundreds of colleagues and new scholars into this new field on this great quest, including Teri Wilkins, his doctoral assistant who became a fellow faculty member and collaborator, and who has co-authored this book with him. With excellence in research as his standard, over the past decades, Piedmont has gone on to create a scholarly field-wide "meeting space." He has inspired colleagues, students, and center-field APA leadership to collaborate in order to build the structures essential to a new academic field.

Dr. Piedmont brought forth and then served as editor-in-chief of the APA journal, *Psychology of Religion and Spirituality* for a full decade, presided as president of Division 36, the *Society for Spirituality and Psychology*, founded and led the APA *Division 36 Annual Mid-Winter Research Conference* at Loyola University Maryland for over 15 years, directed a graduate program in clinical research, and still always remained a highly prolific scholar as much as an academic statesman. Dr. Piedmont helped lead field change by building an APA home for innovation in science and practice.

In many respects, this current volume as a summative work on research on the numinous shares the principles of Piedmont's field-building statesmanship. The science speaks with the elegant rigor and clarity demanded by high-level APA research. Drs. Piedmont and Wilkins once again pragmatically position the research questions on the numinous to speak squarely to the fields of personality, research measurement, and clinical practice, and they always highlight the work that is yet to be done towards further validation, generalization, and expansion of the scope of applied questions. Piedmont is a scientist's scientist. And, as one dedicated to field-wide change, he has built the research tools that the field needs to make the numinous fully integrated into mainstream science and practice. The numinous is researched by Piedmont and Wilkins from all sides, providing a "soup to nuts" resource for researchers, clinicians, and students. The opus is thorough and totally integrated, incorporating 30 years of research, from the development of valid measures and clinical assessment tools, to models for creating meaning, and finally to a host of clinical practices for tapping and engaging the numinous.

The authors are clear to point out that numinous motivations are not exclusively the concern of psychology. They have inspired humanity throughout time in the arts and humanities; currently, the numinous is apparent as a powerful source within contemporary film and center-field culture. These needs are ever present, whether or not they are seen and acknowledged. Within psychology, it is to our own peril and that of our patients to overlook the numinous. A failure to address the numinous in patients often leads to despair and emptiness, and correlates with specific expressions in pathology. Avoidance of the numinous in a client potentially may even cause iatrogenic harm.

As a core psychological need, Piedmont and Wilkins show us that training on the centrality and identification of the numinous is the duty of all practicing therapists. They make a strong case for the necessity of considering the numinous as a "through line" in standard clinical practice, including standard assessment, strength building, and treatment for psychopathology. Indeed, they argue, that as psychological motivation, assessing and addressing the numinous is the due work of all therapists, whether or not they perceive themselves or their client to be either spiritual or religious, because infinitude, meaning, and worthiness are universal elements.

In many respects, this major work shares the principles of Piedmont's field-building statesmanship. The science speaks with the elegant rigor and clarity demanded by high-level APA research; these authors pragmatically position the research questions on the numinous to speak squarely to the field of personality theory and clinical practice, and they always highlight the work that is yet to be done towards further validation, generalization, and expansion of the scope of applied questions. Readers will see the studies from which the new measurements and assessments are refined and the data from which the conceptual conclusions are drawn. The richness of the original tables allows us to see the nuances in the findings that support the major developments in the decades of the research program.

Piedmont and Wilkins, as scientists dedicated to field-wide change, have built and delivered for the reader the tools to make the numinous fully integrated into mainstream science and practice. They lay out a groundwork for the numinous research program, and also propose a blueprint for the future. The data are presented dynamically, replete with further directions—even with a step-wise guide. The reader can feel the work gaining even more momentum in the next wave of clinical science.

I think back to Dr. Piedmont in 1998, when his study seen in earnest, revised our understanding of the classic Big Five, suggesting that we needed a Big Six, which would include the Spiritual as a new domain. Currently a highly distinguished academic statesman, it is ever more clear that he works tirelessly, but never narrowly for himself. Presented here, in all of the expanding research from his prolific lab, there is a vertically integrated structural development for the field, a place for us all to work on the numinous and use this new knowledge in current treatments, squarely in the middle of mainstream psychology.

Once again, Ralph Piedmont welcomes in colleagues and invigorates students by providing tools and showing clear direction for future work. Put simply, in the words of leadership guru Tom Peters, "Leaders don't create followers, they create more leaders."

Lisa Miller, Ph.D., Professor of Psychology and Education, Columbia University, Teachers College and College of Physician and Surgeons

Preface

Religion and spirituality (R/S) have always been important realities for all cultures, peoples, and times. People are attracted to their teachings and involve themselves in their applications (i.e., styles of dress, participation in rituals, prayer styles, etc.). Faith and beliefs provide a core sense of personal meaning that creates coherence, purpose, and direction for our lives. R/S issues are powerful components of life for many. Many professional groups are interested in examining how to include this material into their clinical practice. Social scientists, physicians, nurses, and corporate managers, to name a few, believe that including this material in their work can provide important benefits to those they serve. Introducing R/S themes into therapy, work, and medicine would help clients, patients, employees, and others develop a better sense of meaning and purpose, ultimately leading to more positive outcomes (e.g., enhanced therapeutic improvement, better health outcomes, and greater work motivation and satisfaction).

The past 25 years have seen an explosion of interest in R/S issues across a wide range of professions, with a flood of books, articles, videos, and training programs emerging to address this need. The inclusion of R/S material has been heralded as a new effort to "integrate" spirituality into the scientific process. Proponents argue that this paradigm would accommodate both the physical understandings of mental health and the higher spiritual realities that direct human endeavor. In the social sciences, a new discipline emerged to specifically address these issues: Pastoral Counseling (PC). While this term has been around for a long time in many Christian circles, only recently has the idea been expanded to move beyond strictly religious circles and enter a more mainstream social science venue. In this book, we shall refer to the concept of PC in a broader sense, as an umbrella term that describes training programs and clinicians who use R/S concepts and practices as part of the treatment process. Such individuals are not necessarily clergy, nor do they have any type of formal theological training. Rather, they represent licensed professionals who are sensitive to these ultimate concerns and issues.

Developing R/S concepts is an idea that is immensely attractive to many professionals. This perspective represents a new holistic approach to understanding the individual that focuses more on the adaptive aspects of functioning and contrasts with the more problem-centered paradigms that seem to dominate the field. This perspective transcends Cartesian dualism and offers hope that human functioning can be considered a more seamless, integrated system directed towards addressing a number of adaptive issues (i.e., physical, mental, and spiritual) simultaneously. There seem to be many points of commonality between science and theology: Both have a focus on understanding human nature; both recognize the presence of many competing, conflicting forces that drive human behavior; and both see humanity struggling to find balance in an ever-changing world. Science provides a systematic way of describing and understanding the physical mechanisms that propel behavior. Theology provides a broader cosmology for understanding human endeavor and describes the value of those spiritual dynamics that operate to give ultimate purpose to life.

This "integration" of psychology and theology has grown to be quite popular, which has led to an explosion of interest in religious and spiritual dynamics (or what we will refer to as the numinous). Numinous constructs represent those qualities perceived as being sacred, hallowed, awe-inspiring, and noetic in nature. Non-clergy interest in the numinous can be traced to two important, interconnected trends. First, the emergence of many new, non-traditional religious movements that emphasize holistic themes and recognize the interconnected, unitive nature of life has spawned interest in philosophies that cross traditional academic boundaries. These "New Age" religions strive to shake off those traditional labels that sort people into groups and to provide a more inclusive way of thinking. Many of those movements attempted to understand the spiritual process by more broadly understanding our psychological nature. The second influence has been the growing scientific research literature that empirically demonstrates the value of numinous variables for understanding the mental and physical health of people. The emerging findings show the predictive value the numinous holds; spirituality has been shown to be a significant predictor of a wide range of positive psychological outcomes such as well-being, emotional maturity, and greater physical and mental health. Thus, it is not surprising that over the past 25 years, multiple independent, educational programs have appeared to provide social science graduate degrees in this content area and to produce licensed professional therapists who are attuned to those spiritual dynamics and actively employ them in treatment.

Together those two forces have helped to make R/S issues much more of a mainstream reality than at any previous time. The rush is now on to synthesize this information in a manner that is less tied to specific denominational groups than it is concerned with developing a more universal understanding of human striving and potential. Consequently, clinicians interested in R/S issues are becoming more involved in applied settings outside of religious organizations. It is not uncommon to find spiritually oriented therapists in community mental health centers, government treatment facilities, hospitals, and independent group practices. Such therapists are increasingly being trained as social scientists to work in secular contexts aimed at providing relief to the emotional suffering of clients.

This reality is creating points of professional tension. Civic authorities (e.g., licensing boards) and professional associations seek to transcend the parochial nature of religious affiliation and to emphasize the universal aspects of theory and treatment. The infusion of numinously oriented therapists and R/S issues into secular treatment contexts raises four issues: a) To what extent is spirituality relevant to treating diverse problems? b) Can spiritually oriented counselors work effectively with people of different faith groups or with people who have no faith? Does the theological background of the counselor have implications for whom he/she can treat? c) To what extent do spiritually oriented therapists become proselytizers for religion? Is it appropriate for a clinician to suggest religiously based activities to clients as treatment options? and d) How will spiritual issues be handled in treatment: as the need to restore one's relationship to God or as a means for finding relief from the presenting psychosocial problem?

These are important issues for both practice and professional identity for those who wish to use numinous concepts in their clinical work and research. For most of those working in this area, the integration of psychology and theology is at the heart of applying the numinous. However, there is little clarity or consistency in describing exactly what this integration is and how it takes place. Another area of professional concern is the absence of any formal clinical paradigm for employing R/S constructs in ways that are appropriate for social science practitioners. The lack of resolution for these issues supports a general disdain for the numinous in many mainstream scientific circles. Too often R/S concepts are viewed as being non-scientific, fuzzy, and redundant with existing constructs.

The purpose of this book is to address these issues head on. Our goal is to outline a philosophy and method for involving R/S constructs in a manner supporting a professional identity that is firmly rooted in the social sciences. We will demonstrate how theological concepts can be developed into empirically sound variables employable in rigorous scientific research and will provide a methodological model for determining the value of those numinous constructs. A model for understanding spirituality as a psychological variable will be presented as well as a framework for conducting comprehensive assessments, including the spiritual domain. We will define what *is* and what *is not* numinous-based counseling from a social science perspective. We will provide a professional description highlighting what the use of the numinous shares in common with the other social sciences and what this approach has that is unique. We will show that the therapeutic goals with clients are the same as with other clinical professions, but the methods for change may include different, but complementary, processes.

We hope to accomplish these goals by outlining a new way of understanding R/S variables. Chapter 4 will outline the nine basic empirical assumptions we hold about the numinous that situate it clearly within the social sciences. At the heart of these assumptions are three key ideas. First, the numinous represents a unique individual-differences construct that motivates people and is a separate dimension of personality that has not been previously studied by psychology. Second, as its own nonreducible dimension, it provides incremental predictive and explanatory power to understanding a wide spectrum of important psychosocial outcomes. Finally, what is most important about the numinous is that it represents those essential psychological qualities that define the human experience. Human beings are the only species that knows from the beginning that death is the ultimate destination. Realizing this, how do people build meaning, depth, and coherence for the lives they are leading? The numinous encompasses those motivations that enable us to address these existential questions in ways that permit us to find a durable sense of abundance, purpose, and acceptance for our lives.

We see this book as a "soup to nuts" exposition about the numinous, starting with an explicitly psychological ontology for conceptualizing these qualities and their place in our mental lives. From there, we will present a scientific epistemology that outlines the empirical criteria to be used for examining and evaluating the utility of any existing R/S construct. We will present numinous-based measures that have been empirically validated as useful predictors of important clinical and psychosocial outcomes. One instrument, the *Assessment of Spirituality and Religious Sentiments* (ASPIRES) scale, which is presented in Chapter 5, captures the basic numinous motivations that drive and direct behavior. Scores from this scale have a large, developed validity literature that supports the universality of these constructs across languages, cultures, and religious status. Another instrument, the *Comprehensive Psycho-Spiritual Clinical Intake* (CPSCI) form, which is presented in Chapter 7, is designed to be used by clinicians who are interested in ensuring that a thorough assessment of a client is obtained at intake. This instrument will assess clients across the standard dimensions of clinical history, cognitive presentation, symptom experience, and personality, qualities found in most intake forms. Further, the form contains an entire section assessing the numinous qualities of the client. Also provided are conceptual models about the numinous that can help all professionals think about and understand them in empirically justified ways. A case example is presented in Chapter 8, where an actual client is assessed on these instruments. We outline how this information enabled the therapist to anticipate specific aspects of the presenting problem and to understand how the client was approaching his issues and the impact of his perspective on functioning. This example demonstrates the potential value of the numinous in treatment and what insights it can potentially provide therapists.

It is our hope that all clinicians will come away from this book with a better sense of the importance of the numinous for their own professional identities. Ultimately, we want numinously oriented practitioners and researchers to arrive at a clear sense of who they are and of their place in the larger community of social scientists. For those professionals outside of the social sciences, we wish to accomplish two things. First, we want to provide a strong assurance that R/S constructs meet the criteria for scientific rigor and empirical viability. Second, we intend to demonstrate how those constructs can be applied in ways that improve our understanding of those served and enhance treatment outcomes in different fields. Understanding the numinous from a social science perspective significantly expands current psychological models of human development and functioning and could identify potentially new intervention strategies that exploit these psychological resources. There is much to be gained by plumbing the depths of this approach, including the discovery of new types of psychological issues that are caused by dysfunctional numinous processes.

We believe that the information in this volume represents an important advancement for the field by providing well-articulated conceptual and empirical guidelines for understanding and applying numinous information. We strive to document the exceptional nature of numinous constructs as organizing psychological forces that can confer either a deep-seated sense of well-being and contentment that can create a robust sense of resilience, or a debilitating sense of dread and futility that can consume the value of one's personhood. We hope that this book provides a useful language for describing these unique numinous dynamics and to outline what clinicians and researchers working with these constructs should seek to achieve. Ultimately, we believe that the numinous represents a new direction for the sciences to pursue. Consideration of the ultimate sense of selfhood and its implications for psychological functioning that the numinous represents will expand our understanding of our mental worlds in new and exciting directions. Ultimately, we hope that you, the reader, will come away from this book with an expanded understanding of, and appreciation for, the value of the numinous for your own work.

Ralph L. Piedmont, PhD
Teresa A. Wilkins, PhD

Acknowledgments

We acknowledge the members of the Numinous Assessment Group (NAG) group who volunteered their time and talents to this project. The members of this team were: Alina Lightchaser, Angela Liddie, Anil Gonsalves, Barbara Laymon, Carol Stewart, Charles Hinz, Chun-Shin Taylor, Cynthia Canner, Diane Walsh, Jessica Haas, Mario Conliffe, Marion Toscano, Martin Burnham, Nicole Robertson, Tak Cho, Tiffany Anderson, William Flythe, and Yen Le. As the old adage goes, "many hands make light work," and through the concerted efforts of this group we were able to accomplish much in a relatively short period of time. We would also like to thank Suzanne Murray for her assistance in developing our initial prospectus and Rose Piedmont for reading and commenting on all aspects of the manuscript. Thanks are also extended to our therapist colleague (aka Claire) and her client (aka Zach) for providing us with insights and data from their therapeutic relationship. We would also like to extend gratitude to our students and colleagues who have, over the years, provided commentary on our ideas and helped us to develop them into the approaches we have included in this volume.

Figures and Tables

Figures

Tables

About the Authors

Ralph L. Piedmont received his Ph.D. in Personality Psychology from Boston University. He completed a postdoctoral fellowship at the National Institute on Aging, where he was trained in taxonomic models of personality and their relevance for understanding mental and physical outcomes. Dr. Piedmont was a full professor in the Department of Pastoral Counseling at Loyola University Maryland and is now the Managing Director of the Center for Professional Studies. His current research interests focus on the measurement of Spiritual Transcendence, a construct that represents a broad, nondenominational, motivational measure of spirituality. He has demonstrated the predictive value of this construct in both normal and clinical contexts, using both American and cross-cultural samples. Dr. Piedmont is extensively published in the scientific literature and is on the editorial boards for *Measurement and Evaluation in Counseling and Development, Assessment, and Journal of Personality Assessment.* He was the founding editor of the new APA journal, *Psychology of Religion and Spirituality.* He is a fellow of the American Psychological Association and a member of the American Counseling Association (ACA). He is also very much involved in Division 36, the Society for the Psychology of Religion and Spirituality for the APA and ACA's Association for Spiritual, Ethical, and Religious Values in Counseling.

Teresa A. Wilkins, Ph.D., L.C.P.C., L.P.C., N.C.C., A.C.S. is a professor, board-certified counselor, researcher, and supervisor. She is a recipient of the Joseph W. Ciarrocchi Research Award and the Cardinal's Award for Teaching Excellence. Her background is in community mental health, and her interests include the numinous domain, personality, and the development of young adults. She has taught at Loyola University MD, Johns Hopkins School of Nursing, Fordham University, and Goucher College. She has provided professional development seminars for psychotherapists and educators. Her work has been published in the *Journal of Social Research & Policy, Research in the Scientific Study of Religion,* the *Handbook of the Psychology of Religion and Spirituality,* and the *APA Handbook of Psychology, Religion, and Spirituality.*

1 A Brief Overview of the Current Status of Religiousness and Spirituality in the Social Sciences

Where We Are and Where We Need to Go

If you are interested in learning how theology can be used to shape and direct the counseling process, this book is *not* for you. However, if you are a professional in the social, physical, or medical sciences and want to learn how to understand and manage spiritual issues as psychological constructs, then please read on. Our goal for this book is to demonstrate that the spiritual and religious dimensions of the individual represent the psychological qualities that uniquely define the human experience. This book is not about theology but rather our human nature.

Religiousness and spirituality (R/S) have increasingly been recognized as important aspects of psychotherapy and medical care, and professionals in these areas have been eager to learn the best methods for addressing these issues in ways that are consistent with their professional training. This movement to understand R/S constructs has created a demand for journals and clinical texts that can be helpful in developing competencies to work with this material. However, this process has generated a number of professional and ethical issues and has also raised concerns about the need for a professional paradigm(s) that can be broadly useful across disciplines.

The purpose of this book is to review current issues facing the scientific field in its treatment of R/S issues, both from research and clinical perspectives, and to present scientifically based models that can help professionals better understand the underlying psychological issues surrounding R/S concepts. Our focus is on professionals in the helping sciences who engage with this material and to address the many concerns that these experts have raised regarding the use of R/S constructs. We hope to capture some of the points of tension that exist in the field and to provide an internally consistent, empirically verifiable model for professionally engaging this material in the scientific community. Ultimately, we wish to provide scientists with a data-driven paradigm for comprehending this material that can prove useful for expanding their understandings of people and for enhancing their therapeutic efficacy. Our intent is to provide a new way of thinking about R/S issues that is consistent with and supportive of researchers' and therapists' professional training. This chapter will provide an overview of some of the basic issues that currently exist in the field in the hope of providing perspective on where we are, so that we can outline the directions in which we need to move in order to progress.

How We Got Here

Something very interesting and exciting has occurred in the field of the psychology of religion and spirituality: R/S constructs have become a mainstream topic of scientific interest. This has not always been the case. R/S issues have been with psychology since its founding over 125 years ago. Perhaps the most foundational work was provided by William James, who noted in his classic work, *The Varieties of Religious Experience*, "Evidently, then, the science and the religion are both of them genuine keys for unlocking the world's treasure-house to him who can use either of them, practically" (James, 1902/1994, p. 138). He clearly laid out from the beginning that R/S issues are important and relevant for study to anyone with an interest in psychological issues. Yet, despite such a compelling presentation of the importance of R/S issues for the mental life of people, the field mostly ignored his urgings. In fact, the social sciences initially proved very resistant to taking R/S constructs seriously (e.g., Ellis, 1980; Freud, 1927/1961). As such, interest quickly faded away as attention turned towards understanding the basic animal instincts that were driving human behavior.

Nonetheless, psychologists who immersed themselves into understanding the human condition would intermittently return to this topic and once again herald its value. Jung (1957) outlined how our species carried certain archetypes that captured important aspects of our evolutionary experiences as well as racial memories. While his work was engaging and interesting, he failed to harness much general notice. Coming afterwards was Allport (1950), a trait psychologist who may be considered one of the founding fathers of the modern field of the psychology of religion. He viewed religiousness as a *master motive*, a force at the core of personality that was responsible for organizing all other motivations. For Allport, religiousness was firmly rooted in personality and was considered by him to be:

> the portion of personality that arises at the core of the life and is directed toward the infinite. It is the region of mental life that has the longest-range intentions, and for this reason is capable of conferring marked integration upon personality, engendering meaning and peace in the face of the tragedy and confusion of life.
>
> (Allport, 1950, p. 142)

However, his work with religiousness never moved into the mainstream.

Humanists took a more positive perspective on understanding human aspirations, seeing people as having higher order needs that move beyond simple drive reduction paradigms. Maslow (1971) noted that self-actualizing people seek to enhance their being, to expand self-knowledge, and to operationalize their personality in any activity. This process of growth is guided by a larger set of values that stresses the goodness, beauty, and wholeness of life. These themes were further elaborated and extended by the work of Frankl (1959), who focused on the *noölogical* dimension of humankind: Our innate motivation is to find ultimate meaning and purpose for life that directs us towards goals of vital, personal importance. All of these major theoreticians saw and appreciated the capacity of people to transcend their immediate experiences in order to find a more wholistic, synthetic understanding that would provide overall coherence and resilience to life.

Still, the larger field of psychology was unresponsive to these persistent insights and did little to include this material in the mainstream literature. The reasons for this are complex and move beyond the purview of this book (see Kugelmann, 2011 for an interesting historical perspective). However, several forces can be seen at work supporting this separation. There is little doubt that the natural tensions that have existed between theology and science go far back historically and continue to reverberate today. The social and physical sciences have been loath to include R/S material because of their theological foundations, which preclude the type of open discussion preferred by science, as well as the intrinsic inability for these ideas to be falsified. Perhaps the most important issue driving science's avoidance of religious issues was the lack of any compelling data that supported its scientific utility. In short, it is one thing to conceptually discuss R/S and its potential role in the mental life of people, and it is another thing entirely to have empirical data that meet the standards of science and provide evidence for the value of such concepts.

In an early review of the field, Dittes (1969) overviewed issues that were contributing to problems in the study of R/S, and his comments remain fresh and timely today:

> The field has been marked largely by brief flurries of interest as one investigator after another is attracted to it, then bewildered by the difficulties of study. There has been no sustained development of theory, empirical findings, or research techniques. . .the chief problem appears to be in the realm of theory and in the theoretical relevance of data. The critical psychological questions and the categories of data by which they can be answered simply have not yet been specified.
>
> (Dittes, 1969, p. 603)

Problems existed with how to measure R/S constructs; frequently this was done with single items that assessed frequency of religious attendance.

Allport was the first to develop a specific scale that captured essential aspects of religiousness, what he termed "Intrinsic and Extrinsic Religiousness" (I/E Scale; Allport & Ross, 1967). This scale was a standard for many years, despite its many flaws (e.g., Donahue, 1985; Gorsuch & McPherson, 1989), because it was a psychometrically useful instrument that was able to provide the kind of data the social sciences would understand as well as a useful psychological definition of these complex R/S concepts. Yet, the psychology of religion and spirituality remained mostly a boutique concept on the fringes of science.

It was not until the mid-1990s that this all changed. The interest in R/S issues increased dramatically, and a surge of research studies appeared in the scientific journals and were supported by a flood of books. This enthusiasm for the field has not abated. The question is "Why?" We believe that the reason for this sustained interest has been the development of a wide array of psychological scales that address important R/S concepts and constructs in ways that are amenable to scientific analysis. Data emerged from not only psychology but medicine, sociology, nursing, and other fields that demonstrated the value of these constructs for promoting understanding and treatment from these different perspectives. It seems like the genie is out of the bottle and cannot be put back. Despite the many weaknesses and limitations to the field (see Batson, 1997; Piedmont, 2014), the sheer volume and consistency of findings seem to have shifted science's view of R/S issues.

Despite all of these data, there is still a lack of comfort that has led to some ironies in the field. The first significant problem is that the study of R/S constructs seems to be theologically based. This is reflected in many research papers that focus on how religious commitments influence important psychosocial outcomes, or a focus on the characteristics of clergy, or specific denominationally related techniques impacting behavior (e.g., meditation, gratitude, gratefulness, etc.). Constructs are developed that refer to particular theological concepts (e.g., the Ego Grasping Scale: Knoblauch & Falconer, 1986; the Christian Moral Values Scale; Francis & Greer, 1990). Having a grounding in a particular theology or denomination seems to convey an advantage to users of these instruments, who would be able to truly understand the larger metaphysical aspects of these constructs. From a clinical perspective, Pastoral Counseling (more is presented on this in Chapter 3) represents a specific attempt to integrate theology and psychology in the treatment of psychological problems (Townsend, 2009). Originally, most individuals in this area were clergy themselves, who were trying to find a way to exploit current psychological insights for use in traditional efforts at helping believers live out the precepts of their faith.

Such an explicit theological element has created a conundrum for the helping sciences, especially for those professionals who are not religiously committed to, familiar with, or even interested in theological concepts.

Further complicating matters is the issue of training. To what extent are typical social science professionals trained in theologically related issues? How much training does one need to acquire in order to practice in an ethical manner? Given that many professionals are not religiously affiliated or even theists, how do they engage clients in these topics? A final ethical concern centers on whether licensed clinicians ought to even discuss such topics for fear that they may be perceived as proselytizers or shills for religion (Sloan, Bagiella, & Powell, 2001). While in the past these issues may have been sufficient to warrant the ongoing apathy for all things religious, the weight of the quickly accumulating data continues to force social scientists, and their professional organizations, to address these issues directly.

One place where the resulting stress lines over these matters is seen is in how R/S issues are currently understood by the various helping professions. As we will outline in multiple chapters, organizations like the American Psychological Association (APA), the American Counseling Association (ACA), and others have come to view R/S constructs as multicultural variables. Religion represents a style of being and interacting in the world similar to race, class, and sexual orientation. Just as the clinically competent therapist ought to be aware of their clients' cultural heritage and knowledgeable about the related styles of dress, eating, and social behavior, so too must one be cognizant of the styles that are associated with specific religious groups. Therapists need to be able to productively engage clients in an intimate, personal relationship. To successfully accomplish this requires the therapist to have a sensitivity to the nuances of the worldview of their clients. This perspective is a comfortable one for social scientists. Yet, when research examines R/S constructs, it views them as intrinsic individual-differences variables that have a significant motivational impact on behavior. Many of the how-to clinical treatment books in this area (e.g., Cashwell & Young, 2011) focus on using R/S content explicitly in the treatment process to bring about desired clinical outcomes. Examining issues such as *spiritual bypass* (Harper & Gill, 2005), a defense mechanism in which people avoid personal responsibility for their feelings and actions because they allow R/S beliefs to dictate their movements, reflects a belief that R/S issues are psychological dynamics inherent to our mental operations. These R/S dynamics represent active internal agents rather than markers reflecting clients' worldviews.

This is an important disconnect to note. Understanding R/S constructs as multicultural variables is an easy sell for the social sciences. There is no need for therapists to learn or be schooled in theological traditions, models, or practices. There is no need for therapists to be concerned over interpreting religious or spiritual material in treatment, because these qualities refer more to the stylistic actions of their clients rather than reflecting something more substantive that may require an understanding of a possibly metaphysical concept. While this multicultural orientation helps to allay any fears therapists may have about their competence in managing religious issues and/or conflicts, it does not prepare therapists for managing clients' perceived religious and spiritual conflicts and questions.

This awkwardness is due to the lack of any developed psychological understanding of what R/S variables represent. Psychological theories have not traditionally developed a role for R/S constructs and how they operate in the mental lives of people. Such theories are important because they identify the inner workings of the mind, both the structures and processes that influence the expression of behavior. Theories also outline the types of issues and problems that may develop in this system and articulate what needs to be done to address and resolve these difficulties. Without any clear definitions of what spirituality is, it is difficult to include it in any systematic theory for treatment. While R/S variables may be important aspects of the psychic world, exactly what type of variable are they? Cultural? Organismic? Something else? Where do they fit in the mind? It would also be important to determine whether managing R/S issues is something a therapist should proactively seek to do with clients in treatment, or is it preferable to delay such investigating until, or if, clients bring it up?

The lack of answers for these questions makes for a level of discomfort in those fields that seek to engage R/S issues in their work. While science may have come to recognize the value of R/S constructs, there are few resources for assisting in the understanding, development, and application of these variables in a scientific context. This is the purpose of the current volume. Our interest is in providing scientists of all kinds with an explicitly scientific paradigm for conceptualizing the nature of R/S constructs (what we will refer to and define below as the numinous) that is clearly psychological in nature. There is no theology being presented in this work, nor is our focus on trying to help individuals live out their faiths. Rather, we will provide an empirical epistemology for developing, testing, and applying R/S constructs in ways that are consistent with current scientific standards.

This is a completely data-driven approach, and our goal is to demonstrate the value of constructs emerging from this paradigm for both research and clinical applications. This paradigm was developed to address explicitly the questions we raised above and to provide satisfying answers that will make sense to social scientists. The tools and techniques we offer here are based on a secular perspective of R/S and should fit comfortably within any social science-based training model. It is our hope for this book that our paradigm will provide convincing evidence of the importance of R/S constructs for understanding our mental world. Further, we believe it will be made clear that including R/S content in both research and practice will ensure that professionals are being comprehensive in their models and assessments. R/S constructs need to be examined in all clients, regardless of whether they are denominationally connected or not, whether they are theists or not. We hope to show in this book that the spiritual and religious dimensions of the individual represent psychological qualities that uniquely define the human experience. So, when considering these qualities, one is engaging with the most intimate aspects of our nature: our humanity.

Identifying the Issues Confronting the Field Today

An extensive research literature has accrued over the past 20 years demonstrating the relational fertility between R/S constructs and a variety of important physical and psychological outcomes (e.g., Pargament, Exline, & Jones, 2013). Much of this research has shown the value R/S variables have for promoting a more developed and expanded understanding of our psychological systems. While the full impact of this work has yet to be abundantly harvested, there are still some key questions that remain to be answered. These issues include: 1) agreement on terminology; 2) a psychological ontology for R/S constructs; 3) a scientific epistemology for developing and testing R/S constructs; 4) evidence of uniqueness; and 5) evidence of causal impact on behavior. Each of these concepts will be discussed in turn. These are the basic issues that the field needs to directly address. Before beginning, it is important to review the various ways R/S constructs can be understood. There are three different levels of analysis for considering R/S variables, and each level has important implications for both research and practice.

R/S Levels of Analysis

R/S constructs reflect very broad categories of functioning that impact behavior in various direct and indirect ways. Such complexity requires a framework for outlining the levels that R/S constructs can engage one's larger mental world. These levels represent broad categories that reflect how these variables are understood and the dynamics they embody. Understanding the level one is examining is key to determining the types of conclusions that can be drawn from R/S data. Also, it is important that when evaluating research findings, the data are organized within each of these levels. Only data from the same level can be directly compared. Comparing data from different levels results in confusion because what the R/S constructs represent is different in each level, and their interpretation correspondingly varies. Further, the goals of research at each level are similarly different. Much like the levels of measurement for numbers (e.g., nominal, ordinal, interval, and ratio), each level has something important to contribute but care needs to be taken when combining multi-level information. The three levels of analysis for R/S constructs are: demographic, cultural, and organismic. Each will be discussed in turn.

Demographic

This is the most basic level of analysis, with R/S constructs representing group membership and patterns of behavior. For example, one can examine the shifts from one religious group to another or movement away from more liberal theologies to more conservative ones. This level examines particular behaviors and their frequencies that each religious group performs. It is most relevant to sociologists and anthropologists, who are interested in examining broad shifts in interests and practices. For example, current research has shown a distinct increase in the number of *Nones*: individuals indicating no religious affiliation (Pew Forum on Religion and Public Life, 2012). Such demographic shifts may have important implications in terms of socio-political attitudes and economic performance.

Cultural

This is perhaps the most frequently used level across the social sciences. It is how most clinical professionals understand and employ R/S variables in their work. At this level, the goal is to understand how an individual's commitments impact participation with his/her world. This would include interpersonal styles, language usage, dress, food choices, and gender roles, to name a few. Being sensitive to these cultural forces enables one to better engage with religious/spiritual individuals in a manner that facilitates communication and the development of a therapeutic rapport. The religious dimension is an important part of being a multiculturally sensitive professional, because it makes clear the various rituals and doctrines that most directly impact behavior. From this perspective, no assumptions are made regarding the psychological role of R/S constructs within the mental life of the individual. Instead, the focus is on how religious/spiritual commitments influence a person's style of living.

Organismic

This level of analysis examines R/S constructs as internal psychological motivations. More than a worldview or style of living, at this level R/S constructs represent something that is intrinsic to people and compels them to move in particular life directions. Religiousness and spirituality are understood as components of the mental world of everyone, just like other temperamental qualities, such as personality. This approach characterizes much of the research done with R/S constructs, which seeks to link these qualities to important psychosocial outcomes, such as well-being, coping ability, health status, and maturity levels. This approach considers R/S constructs as variables that have, ultimately, a causal connection to behavior. As psychological entities, R/S constructs should not be considered as theological concepts. R/S variables must be seen as empirical constructs that can meet the accepted standards of reliability and validity. Thus, they are falsifiable variables that address psychosocial processes and outcomes and are not intended to either support or disprove any particular theological or denominational belief system. Efforts at measuring metaphysical concepts such as grace, heaven, sin, and soul are misplaced, and constructs designed to measure such qualities are inherently nonscientific and have no place in the psychology of religion and spirituality.

This book will be taking the organismic perspective in its discussions of R/S constructs. As social scientists, our approach is in identifying important individual difference qualities that have important consequences to behavior. Our goal is to provide a comprehensive model of the psychological world of the person. We believe that R/S variables are basic temperamental dispositions that drive individuals towards specific outcomes. Understanding R/S constructs as organismic variables provides intriguing possibilities for the field. First, because traditional psychology has not really included R/S constructs in its work, bringing in new constructs that do not overlap with more established variables raises that potential for expanding our understanding of people. New constructs make predictive models more accurate and efficient. New temperamental dimensions open the possibility for identifying innovative therapeutic modalities and intervention techniques. If we are to consider R/S constructs as master motives, as we do, then unpacking their relevance and influence on behavior can profoundly reshape our understandings of who we are. In order to realize such outcomes, research in this area needs to address the five basic scientific issues raised at the beginning of this chapter and provide satisfying answers to each issue. We now turn to addressing these concerns.

Basic Scientific Issues for R/S Research

Terminology

Taking the organismic perspective, the goal of our work was to create a psychological measure of spirituality. As such, it was important that any construct we developed needed to meet relevant empirical standards. Our approach was to expand our understanding of human psychology, not to support (or deny) any particular theology or denominational perspective. This endeavor is all about psychology. Unfortunately, the terms we currently use in this field (e.g., spirituality, religiousness) are frequently intertwined with theological perspectives and terms (see Gorsuch, 1984; 1990). Too frequently, mainstream Christian theology is infused into measures and inferences in this area. For example, the Faith Maturity Scale (Benson, Donahue, & Erickson, 1993) includes the item, "my life is committed to Jesus Christ," which reflects a specific theological approach. Such infusions add confusion to the research by making scales with limited applicability and relevance, as well as undermining efforts at identifying nomothetic processes. Because the current terminology flows so directly from theological sources, it is difficult to separate the two because much of how spirituality is understood has been shaped and defined by theology. This helps explain why many scales are infused with specific theological perspectives. In fact, some (e.g., Moberg, 2002) have argued that the only effective means of understanding spirituality is to do so from the perspective of each religious denomination. There is no one single spiritual motivation; rather, there exists a plethora of spiritualities, each with their own nuances and dynamics. While there may be value to this perspective, we believe that at the organismic level of analysis new terms need to be used that are meaningful for the social sciences and do not lend themselves to theological parochialism.

When discussing the psychological aspects of spirituality, we prefer to use the term *the numinous*. It has many advantages over current terms. First, it has clear religious value. It was originally used by Otto (1923/1958) to reflect aspects of the mystical experience: the awe, wonder, emotional integration, and essential ineffability of encountering a divine reality. The numinous was the relationship between the individual and that which was considered sanctified and ineffable. Second, it is a term that has been used psychologically by Erikson. The numinous represents one of the positive outcomes experienced at the first stage of psychosocial development: Trust vs Mistrust. For Erikson, a child develops feelings of the numinous (awe-some, hallowed) as a result of a mother's care and reliable concern for the needs of her child. She promotes and supports her child's beginning sense of self-identity while also supporting the ability to transcend fears of aloneness and separateness (Erikson, 1977). This usage reveals that our spirituality has its roots in the very beginning of our psychological lives and its presence influences all future development. Finally, the term includes several different elements to it and underscores the reality that there are many diverse parts to our spirituality. Therefore, the numinous represents a useful descriptive term for the *domain* of R/S functioning: There are elements of transcendence, spirituality, religiousness (e.g., the prayers we say and the rituals we perform), and mysticism, among others. New terms can be added as the research identifies. The psychological pedigree of the term makes it more amenable to social scientists and does not, in such an obvious manner, involve any theological or metaphysical concepts. Relying only on the terms "religiousness" and "spirituality" is just too limiting and does not do justice to the large literature that has identified so many numinous constructs. As such, this term will be used to refer to all things R/S.

The term "numinous" helps to clarify the basic question that is being asked at the organismic level of analysis: "What are the psychological qualities inherent to the human mind that make religion and spirituality so important to us?" While theology attempts to outline the nature of God and what our ultimate nature is, psychology attempts to understand why the idea of a god and an eternal time perspective are so compelling to us as a species.

Psychological Ontology

Perhaps the greatest weakness in the study of R/S constructs is the absence of any developed ontology for the field. Ontology is concerned with understanding the nature of things: their origin, developmental process, and influence on functioning. While there is a great interest in the numinous, no one can really say what these constructs represent psychologically. Are they behavioral variables? Are they cognitive, emotional, personological, or stylistic qualities? Some (e.g., Paloutzian & Park, 2013) argue that they are all of these qualities and should be evaluated from each of these perspectives. While R/S constructs have been associated with a wide array of bio-psycho-social outcomes and have been evaluated from various perspectives and levels, these findings remain ungrounded in the field, making their relevance and value uncompelling (e.g., Buss, 2002; Funder, 2002).

Without an ontological model, there is no scientific reason why R/S variables should be included in any social scientific research program. Why should these variables be examined? What value do they hold for expanding our psychological understandings? Very little has been put forth to address these most fundamental of questions. Without understanding what a spiritual construct is, it then becomes difficult to interpret the research findings that have accrued. Noting that spirituality is related to well-being (e.g., Piedmont, 2009) is, in and of itself, not a very important finding. Why should spirituality even be related to this outcome? What psychological processes are involved in its expression? In short, having an ontological explanation for R/S constructs provides the *raison d'être* for their inclusion in the scientific arena and will provide greater interpretive depth to the obtained findings. It will also enable more a priori hypothesis development and testing.

Currently, there are at least two semi-ontological perspectives dominant in the field. The first is outlined by Barrett (2004; 2013), who understands R/S constructs as cognitive variables that shape how we understand ourselves and our roles in the world. R/S cognitive activities find their basis as an evolutionary *spangle*. A spangle is an unintended consequence of some evolved ability. For example, flight is considered a spangle in that this behavior did not directly evolve. Rather, it was a consequence of reptiles' need to regulate temperature. As cold-blooded animals, obtaining and retaining heat for energy is paramount to survival. One evolved mechanism to help in this was the development of feathers. Feathers are lightweight insular material that keeps animals warm. In conjunction with lighter bodies and extra skin flaps, feathers helped animals to glide purposefully in air.

Similarly, religiousness was also a consequence of another evolved behavior: our tendency to interpret activity in the environment as the result of some other actor's behavior. Barrett (2004) termed this a *hyperactive agentic detection device* or HADD. HADD refers to our evolved bias to interpret actions in the environment to be due to the behaviors of some other organism than merely the result of some random process. It certainly is in our best interests to assume that the rustling in some bushes is caused by the presence of some predator and to run away, rather than to assume that it is only the result of a breeze. Thus, it is an easy generalization to see how larger events in our environment that we may not understand (e.g., heavy rain, earthquakes, illness) may be the consequence of some larger being's involvement. The value of this approach is that it situates R/S constructs within our own evolutionary process and contains distinct survival value for our species. This evolutionary pedigree provides significance and importance to R/S constructs. However, while there may be no doubt that there is some evolutionary foundation to humans' religious and spiritual activities, it must be pointed out that other species also share this similar interpretive bias, but no other species can be considered religious or spiritual.

Another approach that is very consistent with the organismic perspective taken here is championed by Pargament (1999), who sees R/S constructs as representing a *search for the sacred*. Simple and elegant, this approach highlights an ongoing process in which individuals are engaged in a course of action that is directed towards attaining some transcendent reality. There are two good points of interest in this perspective. First, it recognizes R/S activities as being intrinsic to the individual and seemingly motivationally based. To search for something implies that one has a lack or a need for an object. Second, this object, the sacred, is an outcome that individuals are moving towards. If the sacred is an eternal, transcendent reality, understanding it should shed light on the motivations driving people towards it. However, this model does not provide any details or specifications into the underlying motivations defining this search, what their nature is, and why they exist.

The lack of a fully developed scientific ontology for R/S constructs is perhaps the most significant weakness in this field. Without understanding the underlying nature of these constructs, their putative origins and influences, it becomes difficult to develop inclusive definitions (i.e., definitions that state what R/S constructs are and what they are *not*). The lack of such definitional clarity poses substantial problems for the field, not the least of which is the inability to define measurement models that can be used to develop such measures and to test their reliability and validity.

Scientific Epistemology

The scientific method represents a set of rules and procedures that are designed to structure our observations of the world in order for us to discern, ultimately, causal relations among variables. Underlying these rules and procedures is what is known as disconfirmatory reasoning: a process by which we learn not by identifying what is true, but by ruling out all that is untrue. This process of falsification has operated very well and has provided humanity with a tremendous amount of knowledge and insight into how things operate in the world. While the scientific method may not be able to tell us everything about the universe, it has provided a tremendous amount of useful information. Science has proved itself very flexible and adaptive in its ability to address a wide array of questions and subject areas.

Some believe that science is not a useful way for studying numinous constructs because science is unable to get at the underlying metaphysical mysteries that are at the core of spiritual and religious functioning (Kugelmann, 2011; Slife, Reber, & Lefevor, 2012). While there is no doubt that science is not able to address metaphysical issues, to the extent that spirituality and religiousness have physical correlates (e.g., feelings, beliefs, behaviors, etc.), science can provide useful information. What is imperative is that researchers in this area will need to identify, define, and interpret aspects of religious and spiritual functioning as *physical* constructs. Without an established psychological ontology, this can be challenging because we have no articulation of what the physical components to numinous functioning are. Where do we draw the line between understanding spirituality as a physical construct (and potentially measurable) versus its nonphysical elements (e.g., grace, sin, heaven) that are beyond science's purview?

Such decisions have to be made if one wishes to apply the scientific method to understanding numinous qualities. Clinicians and researchers in this area need to address this issue clearly so that as social scientists, they will be able to identify their professional scope of practice. While this issue will be more clearly discussed in Chapter 4, it is important that social scientists clearly identify the psychological boundaries surrounding R/S constructs/processes and to operate within them accordingly. As such, professionals in this area must develop clear definitions of their numinous constructs in ways that are amenable to the scientific process of disconfirmation.

Our approach, as noted above, is to understand numinous constructs as important, individual-difference constructs. There are several assumptions that flow from this position. First, numinous constructs represent psychological qualities that are present, to varying degrees, within all people. Individuals do not need to be religiously committed to a faith tradition in order to be spiritual. We believe that it is individuals' underlying numinous motivations that lead them to a faith community; being part of a religious denomination does not create numinous needs but rather fulfills them. Second, as a psychological quality, numinous constructs can be measured in ways consistent with the demands of the scientific method. Those developing numinous constructs need to demonstrate the underlying scientific value of their variables in terms of the current standards of reliability and validity. To accomplish this, professionals need to identify a priori the scientific models appropriate for accomplishing this process. Questions to be addressed would include "Is the numinous a multidimensional or multifaceted construct?" and "What is the best way to assess these motivations, with a self-report measure or projective test or a behavioral index?" Ultimately, these tests will need to work out of some larger conceptual/empirical model that will provide interpretive context for these results as well as a barometer for evaluating the utility of the numinous constructs. Currently, there are conceptual models being employed. For example. Rizzuto (1979; 2009) takes a psychoanalytic approach to the numinous, seeing these motivations serving as a permanent transitional object for the individual. Others, like Kirkpatrick (1998) employ attachment theory as a framework for evaluating the numinous: It impacts our ability to connect with the eternal as well as setting a template for our relationships with family, friends, and co-workers.

Such efforts are important because they establish how the numinous is to be measured, evaluated empirically, interpreted, and ultimately its ecological validity and utility for the field determined. The one limitation to many current efforts at folding the numinous into larger conceptual models is that these models themselves are not well established empirically. Our goal is not to review the evidence for these various models but to outline our approach and articulate its advantages. Given that we take an organismic perspective to the numinous, we believe that a very powerful method for developing and testing the significance of numinous constructs is to examine them within the context of the Five Factor Model (FFM) of personality (Costa & McCrae, 1992; Digman, 1990; McCrae, 2010; McCrae & John, 1992; Piedmont, 1998).

The FFM is a comprehensive, empirically derived, robust taxonomy of individual differences relating to qualities traditionally associated with personality. These dimensions are labeled: *neuroticism (N)*, the tendency to experience negative emotions such as anxiety, depression, and hostility; *extraversion (E)*, the quantity and intensity of one's interpersonal interactions; *openness (O)*, the proactive seeking and appreciation of new experiences; *agreeableness (A)*, the quality of one's interpersonal interactions along a continuum from compassion to antagonism, and finally, *conscientiousness (C)*, the persistence, organization, and motivation exhibited in goal-directed behaviors (Costa & McCrae, 1992). Research has found strong cross-observer, cross-instrument convergence indicating that these dimensions are not a product of any self-distortion or rater bias (e.g., Piedmont, 1994). FFM research is one of the few areas where we do not see the so-called "replication crisis" in psychology. Jarrett (2019) has reported that patterns of findings between these personality domains and life outcomes have been shown to be quite robust.

These dimensions were also found to be extremely stable over the adult life span; 25-year stability coefficients indicate that 80% of the variance in these traits is unchanging, and 60% is estimated to remain constant over a 50-year adult lifespan (Costa & McCrae, 1994). Finally, these dimensions have a strong genetic basis (Heath, Neale, Kessler, Eaves, & Kendler, 1992), indicating that they are not mere summary descriptions of behavior but rather genotypic tendencies of individuals to think, act, and feel in consistent ways. The value of this model is twofold. Empirically this model is well-defined, emerging even cross-culturally (McCrae & Costa, 1997). As such, it can provide an assessment of the universality of numinous constructs. Conceptually, these domains are well-validated and provide clear definitions of very circumscribed constructs. Therefore, the FFM can serve as a useful reference point for developing and evaluating religious variables (see Piedmont, 1999, 2005). Correlates with the FFM domains can help to understand and anticipate the kinds of outcomes numinous scores should predict as well as assisting in the interpretation of the personological qualities that are subsumed by these scales.

Incremental Validity

We believe that measures of the FFM should be included in all research studies using numinous constructs that are designed to capture the personological aspects of the individual. The empirical integrity of the model, its relative comprehensiveness, and its current acceptance as the dominant personality model make it an important component to research. While understanding how numinous constructs fit within the FFM (see Saroglou, 2010) can help to identify the personal qualities that are contained by a construct, ultimately the value of numinous constructs will be found in what they contribute that is new to the field.

Science hates redundancy. Its focus on parsimony means there is no room for developing multiple measures of the same construct. Redundancy adds unnecessary hubris to the field that ultimately impedes progress. One major criticism of the research in this area has been that the numinous constructs really do not add anything new to the field (Smith, 2001; Funder, 2002). Buss (2002, p. 203) noted that spiritual constructs are simply the *parasitization* of already existing psychological constructs. Van Wicklin (1990, p. 36) asserted that numinous variables are merely the *religification* of already existing constructs. What these criticisms imply is that while there are those who like to speak about spirituality and its value for the individual, ultimately this construct does not really add anything new to our psychological understandings. Simply put, spirituality is just a stand-in for other psychological variables. For example, what does a measure of religious well-being tell us about a person over above what more established, secular measures of well-being already tell us? What is the value added of the "spiritual" component to well-being?

Sechrest (1963) long ago noted how important it is to demonstrate the incremental validity of new scales. For a construct to be useful, it must show what additional contribution it makes to the field. Demonstrating incremental validity for numinous constructs is an essential, key endeavor for three reasons. First, this field has generated a tremendous number of constructs (see Hill & Hood, 1999 for a small sampling) purported to relate to a large number of physical and psychosocial outcomes (e.g., Koenig, McCullough, & Larson, 2001; Pargament et al., 2013).The presence of so many constructs naturally begs the larger questions of what do these constructs represent and how are they organized? Second, there is an intrinsic resistance to R/S constructs in the larger scientific fields. While this tension has a long history and its discussion moves far beyond the scope of this volume, suffice it to say that science has difficulty in accepting spiritual constructs because of a perceived belief that these concepts are not amenable to scientific scrutiny or falsification and are outside of the professional scope of social scientists (e.g., Sloan et al., 2001). Thus, it is imperative to demonstrate a scientific pedigree of our constructs that includes some demonstration of their added empirical and interpretive value. Finally, the incremental validity paradigm provides a more rigorous methodological process for developing and testing numinous constructs that will provide a wealth of information about what these constructs represent and how and where they impact the psychological life of the individual.

We believe that the FFM provides a wonderful empirical platform for testing the incremental validity of numinous constructs. Our efforts in creating scales that capture numinous motivations are based on a belief that they are distinct from those already identified and classified by the field. To be valuable, numinous variables must show predictive value over and above the dimensions of the FFM. Conducting such a test can be done quite simply, using basic multiple regression techniques. Showing that the numinous scale adds predictive power over the FFM domains provides strong empirical evidence that the scale does have something new, not contained by these other personality dimensions.

This is the crucial pay-off for this approach. Showing incremental validity means that numinous constructs are necessary variables for anyone interested in developing a comprehensive predictive model. Incremental validity gives substantive, empirical value to numinous constructs by demonstrating both their uniqueness from already established personality constructs and their individual value for predicting important outcomes. We believe that any purported numinous scale that does not demonstrate incremental predictive validity over the FFM cannot be considered a valid measure of spiritual or religious functioning. Such a scale is simply a stand-in for an already existing construct and holds no ultimate value for the field.

Causal Impact

The scientific literature examining the role and value of numinous constructs is wide. To some extent this is a product of the lack of any psychological ontology and established epistemology. Without conceptual clarity surrounding definitions of the basic constructs and the absence of any established methods for developing and testing new constructs, what results is a vast collection of unconnected studies, examining an array of constructs and their impact on diverse outcomes. On the one hand, this literature and the identification of so many significant associations underscores the potential value of numinous constructs. R/S variables link up with other important physical and psychosocial outcomes. It is not surprising that there is such a sustained, multidisciplinary interest in this area. What is lacking, though, extracts a significant scientific toll from these endeavors.

Without a larger, consensual understanding of the nature of the numinous, it becomes very difficult linking the results of studies together. The literature in this area has a very limited cumulativeness to it because there is no agreed-upon definition of constructs of interest. Thus, one cannot have much confidence in how the results of different studies can be organized. Further, much of the research in this area is comprised of studies that examine the direct relations between numinous constructs and outcomes, with little or no controlling for covariates and potential mediators. Further, there are no statistical controls for multiple comparisons or redundancy among predictors (see Sloan et al., 2001). Given that the great majority of the current research is based on self-report measures, there is no control for common method error. Perhaps most lacking are model-building or model-testing approaches. How do numinous constructs fit in the larger psychological world of the individual? How does the numinous fit in with other constructs, both independently and interactively? Answers to these questions require the use of multivariate paradigms that can systematically control for experiment-wise Type I error rates and examine for more complex effects.

Given that most quantitative research in the field is correlationally based, the most important question is "Do spiritual and religious constructs represent causal inputs into the mental world of people, or are they merely outcomes of other psychological systems?" This is a central question for the field to answer. If numinous activities are merely the consequence of one's cultural context/upbringing, or a desire for being part of a group, or a useful heuristic in managing life stressors, then the domain is of little value for science. Science is more interested in identifying the causes of behavior then in documenting their consequences. Science seeks understanding in order to predict behavior and, ultimately, to control it. If manipulating someone's numinous motivations has no impact on behavior, and is merely the consequence of other processes, then should not the focus of study be on those predictors rather than their consequences? If numinous variables do act as the prime movers of behavior, then they become important constructs to be understood. Knowing how, when, and under what conditions these motivations can be aroused and their impact on other, more important outcomes is the heart and soul of the scientific endeavor. While many implicitly assume that spirituality is a causal agent (e.g., pastoral counselors, spiritual advisors, religiously oriented therapists: Townsend, 2009), there are precious little data addressing this topic and no scientific statement as to why one would expect this type of causal process in the first place.

Research needs to move beyond the univariate, correlational level to explore more complex, multivariate questions. The goal needs to be directed at understanding if, and how, numinous constructs impact the texture and timber of one's inner psychological world. Answering this question carries important weight. If the numinous is a causal input, then its role as both a protector and as a risk factor in other processes needs to be understood. The potential would then exist for identifying new intervention techniques and strategies that can be useful in managing psychological issues.

Considering the numinous may open new insights into current issues. For example, with the war on terror dragging on, many military personnel have seen combat and are experiencing negative emotional consequences. While post-traumatic stress disorder (PTSD) is a common diagnosis, not all seem to respond to established treatments for the disorder. Efforts at identifying potential mediating variables have resulted in some veterans being seen as experiencing moral injury, a condition that phenotypically resembles PTSD symptomologically but with different underlying dynamics (see Hodgson & Carey, 2017). Feeling that one has compromised ultimate ethical and moral values due to military involvements creates a larger existential dread within these sufferers, as opposed to those with PTSD. Perhaps a consideration of numinous dimensions may open up another modality for viewing and understanding individuals with moral injury. Perhaps the high level of existential conflict and dread stems from a battle between one's actions in the line of duty with one's higher order, transcendent-oriented motivations that drive us to find connection, nurturance, and constructive engagement with others. Articulating these numinous qualities, developing empirically sound measures to assess them, and constructing relevant modalities for engaging therapeutically these motivations would help to address the underlying causes of moral injury.

There is much potentially to be gained by studying the numinous in a systematic, scientifically sound manner. Ultimately, it may be discovered that some of the current psychological problems that have proved resistant to conventional treatment efforts (e.g., moral injury) may be a consequence of numinous dynamics. The use of multivariate experimental techniques, such as structural equation modeling (SEM), holds the potential for determining the uniqueness of numinous constructs from more established psychological ones and outlining their potential causal role on human functioning (e.g., Piedmont et al., 2009). Such a determination would help to further differentiate the underlying forces that help to construct our mental worlds, providing science with new potential avenues for positively intervening in individuals' efforts at building meaning, worthiness, and abundance for their lives.

Direction for this Volume

There is certainly much more work that needs to be done in the scientific study of spirituality and religiousness; in many ways, the field is still in its infancy. The five issues outlined here serve as the core framework for this book. These are the essential issues currently impacting the field. Without addressing these concerns, we believe that interest in numinous issues will fade, out of necessity, because the data will be unable to support their empirical value (e.g., Dittes, 1969). Our goal is to prevent this from happening by providing perspectives that directly address these five issues. While we concede that our perspective is but one of potentially many and that there is some partisanship in our views, we hope that the content of this book will do three things: a) it will articulate the fundamental issues that need to be addressed; b) it will provide a first attempt at addressing these issues; and c) it will provide a point of departure for a more systematic, rational discussion for developing key ideas about the nature, functioning, and value of numinous constructs.

To accomplish this, we will do two things. First, we will provide an overview to the conceptual frameworks we employ in guiding our own research and clinical work. Second, we will provide research-based examples of how these ideas can be applied and the empirical yields we have experienced. We hope that readers will find this material stimulating and relevant to their own interests and pursuits in this area. We believe that the empirical strategies we outline here will be followed and built upon. Ultimately, we wish to help facilitate a process that will form a more nuanced and articulated sense of what the numinous is (and is not) so that a more consolidated and cumulative research database can be established.

References

Allport, G. W. (1950). *The individual and his religion.* New York, NY: MacMillan.

Allport, G. W., & Ross, J. M. (1967). Personal religious orientation and prejudice. *Journal of Personality and Social Psychology, 6,* 423–443.

Barrett, J. L. (2004). *Why would anyone believe in God?* Lanham, MD: AltaMira Press.

Barrett, J. L. (2013). Exploring religion's basement: The cognitive science of religion. In R. F. Paloutzian & C. L. Park (Eds.), *Handbook of the psychology of religion and spirituality* (pp. 234–255). New York, NY: Guilford Press.

Batson, C. D. (1997). An agenda item for the psychology of religion: Getting respect. In B. Spilka & D. N. McIntosh (Eds.), *The psychology of religion: Theoretical approaches* (pp. 3–10). Boulder, CO: Westview Press.

Benson, P. L., Donahue, M. J., & Erickson, J. A. (1993). The Faith Maturity Scale: Conceptualization, measurement, and empirical validation. *Research in the Social Scientific Study of Religion, 5,* 1–26.

Buss, D. M. (2002). Sex, marriage, and religion: What adaptive problems do religious phenomena solve? *Psychological Inquiry, 13,* 201–203.

Cashwell, C. S., & Young, J. S. (Eds.). (2011). *Integrating spirituality and religion into counseling: A guide to competent practice* (2nd ed.). Alexandria, VA: The American Counseling Association.

Costa, P. T., Jr., & McCrae, R. R. (1992). The five-factor model of personality and its relevance to personality disorders. *Journal of Personality Disorders, 6,* 343–359.

Costa, P. T., Jr., & McCrae, R. R. (1994). "Set like plaster"? Evidence for the stability of adult personality. In T. F. Heatherton & J. L. Weinberger (Eds.), *Can personality change?* (pp. 21–40). Washington, DC: American Psychological Association.

Digman, J. M. (1990). Personality structure: Emergence of the five-factor model. *Annual Review of Psychology, 41,* 417–440.

Dittes, J. E. (1969). The psychology of religion. In G. Lindzey & E. Aronson (Eds.), *Handbook of social psychology* (pp. 602–659). Reading, MA: Addison-Wesley Publishing Co.

Donahue, M. J. (1985). Intrinsic and extrinsic religiousness: Review and meta-analysis. *Journal of Personality and Social Psychology, 48,* 400–419.

Ellis, A. (1980). Psychotherapy and atheistic values; A response to A. E. Begrin's "Psychotherapy and religious issues." *Journal of Consulting and Clinical Psychology, 48,* 635–639.

Erikson, E. H. (1977). *Toys and reasons.* New York, NY: W. W. Norton.

Francis, L. J., & Greer, J. E. (1990). Catholic schools and adolescent religiosity in Northern Ireland: Shaping moral values. *Irish Journal of Education, 2,* 40–47.

Frankl, V. E. (1959). *From death camp to existentialism.* Boston, MA: Beacon Press.

Freud, S. (1927/1961). *The future of an illusion* (J. Strachey, Trans.). New York, NY: Norton.

Funder, D.C. (2002). Why study religion? *Psychological Inquiry, 13,* 213–214.

Gorsuch, R. L. (1984). Measurement: The boon and bane of investigating religion. *American Psychologist, 39,* 228–236.

Gorsuch, R. L. (1990). Measurement in psychology of religion revisited. *Journal of Psychology and Christianity, 9,* 82–92.

Gorsuch, R. L., & McPherson, S. E. (1989). Intrinsic/Extrinsic measurement: I/E-Revised and single item scales. *Journal for the Scientific Study of Religion, 28,* 348–364.

Harper, M. C., & Gill, C. S. (2005). Assessing the client's spiritual domain. In C. S. Cashwell & J. S. Scott (Eds.). *Integrating spirituality and religion into counseling* (pp. 31–62). Alexandria, VA: American Counseling Association.

Heath, A. C., Neale, M. C., Kessler, R. C., Eaves, L. J., & Kendler, K. S. (1992). Evidence for genetic influences on personality from self-reports and informant ratings. *Journal of Personality and Social Psychology, 63,* 85–96. doi:10.1037/0022-3514.63.1.85

Hill, P. C., & Hood, R. W., Jr. (1999). *Measures of religiosity.* Birmingham, AL: Religious Education Press.

Hodgson, T. J., & Carey, L. B. (2017). Moral injury and definitional clarity: Betrayal, spirituality and the role of chaplains. *Journal of Religion and Health, 56,* 1212–1228. doi:10.1007/s10943-017-0407-z

James, W. (1902/1994). *The varieties of religious experience.* New York, NY: The Modern Library.

Jarrett, C. (2019, February 6). There's another area of psychology where most of the results do replicate—Personality research. *British Psychological Society Research Digest.* Retrieved from https://digest.bps.org.uk/2019/02/06/theres-another-area-of-psychology-where-most-of-the-results-do-replicate-personality-research/

Jung, C. G. (1957). *The undiscovered self: Present and future.* In Vol. 10 of *The collected works of C. G. Jung.* Princeton, NJ: Princeton University Press.

Kirkpatrick, L. A. (1998). God as substitute attachment figure: A longitudinal study of adult attachment style and religious changes in college. *Personality and Social Psychology Bulletin, 24,* 961–973.

Knoblauch, D. L., & Falconer, J. A. (1986). The relationship of a measured Taoist orientation to Western personality dimensions. *Journal of Transpersonal Psychology, 18,* 73–83.

Koenig, H. G., McCullough, M. E., & Larson, D. B. (2001). *Handbook of religion and health.* New York, NY: Oxford University Press.

Kugelmann, R. (2011). *Psychology and Catholicism: Contested boundaries.* Cambridge, England: Cambridge University Press.

Maslow, A. H. (1971). *The farther reaches of human nature.* New York, NY: Viking Press.

McCrae, R. R. (2010). The place of the FFM in personality research. *Psychological Inquiry, 21,* 57–64.

McCrae, R. R., & Costa, P. T., Jr. (1997). Personality trait structure as a human universal. *American Psychologist, 52,* 509–516. doi:10.1037/0003-066X.52.5.509

McCrae, R. R., & John, O. P. (1992). An introduction to the five-factor model and its applications. *Journal of Personality, 60,* 175–215.

Moberg, D. A. (2002). Assessing and measuring spirituality: Confronting dilemmas of universal and particular evaluative criteria. *Journal of Adult Development, 9*(1), 47–60. doi:10.1023/A:1013877201375

Otto, R. (1923/1958). *The idea of the holy.* Oxford, UK: Oxford University Press.

Paloutzian, R. F. & Park, C. L. (Eds.). (2013). *Handbook of the psychology of religion and spirituality* (2nd ed.). New York, NY: The Guilford Press.

Pargament, K. I. (1999). The psychology of religion *and* spirituality? Yes and no. *International Journal for the Psychology of Religion, 9,* 3–16.

Pargament, K. I., Exline, J. J., & Jones, J. W. (Eds.). (2013). *The APA handbook of psychology, religion, and spirituality.* Washington, DC: American Psychological Association.

Pew Forum on Religion and Public Life. (2012). *"Nones" on the rise: One-in-five adults have no religious affiliation.* Washington, DC: Pew Research Center.

Piedmont, R. L. (1994). Validation of the NEO PI-R observer form for college students: Toward a paradigm for studying personality development. *Assessment, 1,* 259–268.

Piedmont, R. L. (1998). *The Revised NEO Personality Inventory: Clinical and research applications.* New York, NY: Plenum.

Piedmont, R. L. (1999) Strategies for using the five-factor model of personality in religious research. *Journal of Psychology and Theology, 27,* 338–350.

Piedmont, R. L. (2005). The role of personality in understanding religious and spiritual constructs. In R. F. Paloutzian & C. L. Park (Eds.), *Handbook of the psychology of religion and spirituality* (pp. 253–273). New York, NY: The Guilford Press.

Piedmont, R. L. (2009). The contribution of religiousness and spirituality to subjective well-being and satisfaction with life. In L. J. Francis (Ed.). *International handbook of education for spirituality, care and well-being* (pp. 89–105). New York, NY: Springer.

Piedmont, R. L. (2014). Looking back and finding our way forward: An editorial call to action. *Psychology of Religion and Spirituality, 6,* 265–267. doi:10.1037/rel10000014

Piedmont, R. L., Ciarrocchi, J. W., Dy-Liacco, G. S., & Williams, J. E. G. (2009). The empirical and conceptual value of the Spiritual Transcendence and Religious Involvement Scales for personality research. *Psychology of Religion and Spirituality, 1,* 162–179.

Rizzuto, A.-M. (1979). *The birth of the living God.* Chicago, IL: University of Chicago Press.

Rizzuto, A.-M. (2009). Sacred space, analytic space, the self, and God. *Journal of the American Academy of Psychoanalysis and Dynamic Psychiatry, 37,* 175–188.

Saroglou, V. (2010). Religiousness as a cultural adaptation of basic traits: A five-factor model perspective. *Personality and Social Psychology Review, 14,* 108–125.

Sechrest, L. (1963). Incremental validity: A recommendation. *Educational and Psychological Measurement, 23,* 153–158.

Slife, B. D., Reber, J. S., & Lefevor, G. T. (2012). When God truly matters: A theistic approach to psychology. *Research in the Social Scientific Study of Religion, 23,* 213–238.

Sloan, R. P., Bagiella, E., & Powell, T. (2001). Without a prayer: Methodological problems, ethical challenges, and misrepresentations in the study of religion, spirituality, and medicine. In T. G. Plante & A. C. Sherman (Eds.), *Faith and health: Psychological perspectives* (pp. 339–354). New York, NY: The Guilford Press.

Smith, T. W. (2001). Religion and spirituality in the science and practice of health psychology: Openness, skepticism, and the agnosticism of methodology. In T. G. Plante & A. C. Sherman (Eds.), *Faith and health: Psychological perspectives* (pp. 355–380). New York, NY: The Guilford Press.

Townsend, L. (2009). *Introduction to pastoral counseling*. Nashville, TN: Abingdon.

Van Wicklin, J. F. (1990). Conceiving and measuring ways of being religious. *Journal of Psychology and Christianity, 9,* 27–40.

2 A Psychological Ontology for Understanding Spirituality and the Numinous

With the great interest in religious and spiritual (R/S) constructs, with literally thousands of such variables available for analysis and the veritable number of related scales, multiple concerns about their uniqueness, psychometric integrity, and utility for the field have emerged (Buss, 2002; Funder, 2002; Kapuscinski & Masters, 2010; Piedmont, 2014). While there may be many legitimate technical issues surrounding measurement in this area, there is a larger question that overshadows these other concerns and represents a key, mostly overlooked, area of inquiry: "What *psychological* aspects of the individual do R/S scales represent?" Do such measures simply reflect the ways people adapt, or do R/S constructs reflect specific, unique psychological processes? Few measures of R/S have outlined how they relate to larger psychological models or identified the specific psychosocial processes/dynamics they represent (see Rizzuto, 1979; Rizzuto & Schafranske, 2013). This lack of a developed psychological understanding of the nature of R/S constructs makes interpretations of their linkages to psychosocial outcomes of limited value. The purpose of this chapter is to provide a useful psychological framework that outlines the mechanisms and processes that underlie R/S strivings. Most importantly, we will argue that R/S constructs reflect those aspects of our psychology that are unique to, and defining of, our own humanity.

The Tension between Social Science and Theology

The failure to create a psychological ontology for R/S constructs keeps the study of the psychology of religion and spirituality in a state of professional tension. This tension is the natural resistance that is present in the larger scientific field about the inclusion of R/S constructs into the research process. The domains of religion and spirituality have long been the purview of philosophy and theology, fields that have epistemologies that are quite different from science. As such, it is difficult to reconcile these perspectives into a single understanding. The eschatological nature of theology makes many metaphysical assumptions that science cannot test. Science focuses on the examination of physical events and attempts to postulate physical processes that can describe, control, and explain those events. Reaching beyond the physical is out of bounds. Thus, there is a need for conceptual models that outline how R/S variables can be constructively used scientifically. While researchers may use R/S scales to predict outcomes, the practical issue is how to interpret the role of these variables on the outcomes of interest. Scales such as the Faith Maturity Scale (Benson, Donahue, & Erickson, 1993), Christian Moral Values Scale (Francis & Greer, 1990), and Christian Fundamentalist Scale (Gibson & Francis, 1996) may represent important aspects of the spiritual experience, but how is one to understand or interpret the findings psychologically? How much theology (and whose theology?) does one need to include in the interpretation of these variables' effects? Fully recognizing that metaphysical constructs cannot be used as explanatory variables in scientific models, how does science need to understand R/S variables in order both to preserve their intrinsic integrity and to plumb their empirical value?

The intrinsic incompatibility between these two disciplines should be obvious. Attempts at integrating these two approaches too often result in approaches that are essentially dualistic in nature and only serve to compromise the values each field offers. For example, scientific formulations can too easily be used to simplify spiritual issues (e.g., reductionism) while theology may attempt to (mis)use science to acquire the veneer of empirical justification for its views. Like oil and water, the substances of these two fields have no natural compatibility. While some may choose to walk away from any intersection of these two disciplines, such a course seems to leave an important aspect of the human condition unexamined. There is something special about our religious and spiritual selves, about the higher nature theistic approaches attempt to outline and to which we are called to explore. Because religion and spirituality are unique to the human species (Baumeister, Bauer, & Lloyd, 2010), and these qualities impact all cultures, peoples, and civilizations, it seems myopic for science not to want to investigate the ineluctable qualities associated with these wisdom traditions and to avoid mining what insights they may hold for better understanding who we are.

Rather than an integration, we believe that science and theology can engage in a collaboration. Figure 2.1 outlines the nature of this complementarity. Both fields are very much interested in human nature and our ultimate potential. Both disciplines strive to outline the qualities, conditions, and actions necessary for humans to take in order to have lives of depth, meaning, and connection. It is this common interest that will always cause science and theology to be in close proximity to one another and suggests that each perspective may enhance the other. Theology understands ultimate meaning as something arising out of the presence of a metaphysical, eternal reality. A nonphysical place, we

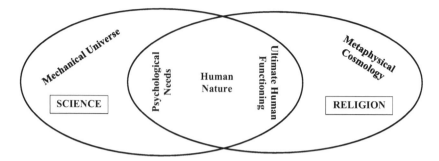

Figure 2.1 A Collaborative Model for Understanding the Relationship between
    Science and Theology. Copyright 2014 by Ralph L. Piedmont,
    reprinted with permission. All rights reserved. This figure may not
    be reproduced in whole or part in any form or by any means without
    written permission of the author.

strive to reach this through a personal commitment to certain behaviors, beliefs, and practices. The social sciences can complement theology by helping it better understand the natural human condition, its basic needs and intrinsic drives. Such a psychological understanding helps religions avoid placing people into unsustainable emotional positions that will impede their ultimate growth. For the social sciences, theology can help outline humankind's essential nature and make evident aspects of our character that can build resiliency, creativity, and compassion in ways heretofore not considered by science. Theology can help the social sciences look beyond the obvious and discern the inner forces that define uniquely the human experience.

This type of dialogue has the most utility for both fields. For science, the value of this engagement would be to help expand the social sciences' understanding of the individual. Insights and understandings from theology can be harvested in ways that promote new testable insights into human character. Such an approach would not be reductionist because the process results in the development of new constructs for science, rather than trying to explain theological insights with existing psychological variables. However, doing so would entail a trade-off. For science to operationalize a theological construct, it would need to remove its metaphysical qualities. It would be like passing a three-dimensional object through a two-dimensional space. Imagine moving a ball through a world where there was no sense of depth. If we were in that two-dimensional space, we would see an object coming through it; it would be seen as a circle. Certainly, there are important similarities between a ball and a circle; both share the concepts of roundness. However, in the two-dimensional world, the depth is gone. The question to be asked is, "Does the loss of depth preclude the experience of a circle from having any meaning for those in the two-dimensional world?"

This would be an important question for the social sciences to address. If one removes the metaphysical aspects of theological constructs, do those constructs lose their interpretive and predictive value? For example, a theist may ask, "What role does the Holy Spirit play in promoting change in psychotherapy?" Science cannot answer this question because the concept of the Holy Spirit is an empirically non-testable concept. This idea that extra-physical entities can help clients better respond to therapeutic interventions can be reconfigured to be testable by examining the role of personal inspiration. To what extent does a client or therapist believe that God is active in the counseling room? This construct can be measured and its value clearly tested (e.g., O'Grady & Richards, 2010). One could argue that inspiration and the Holy Spirit are two different concepts, or that inspiration misses important metaphysical realities and as such has no value. While operationalizing R/S constructs from different wisdom traditions will necessitate losing some important aspects of the original concepts, it is the potential predictive value of what is left that holds the key for science. If these new, redacted constructs reflect insights non-redundant with existing scientific variables, then there is a potential for expanding our psychological understandings.

Research has already shown that some R/S constructs do indeed evidence incremental validity in predicting important psychosocial outcomes over existing personality constructs (e.g., Piedmont, Ciarrocchi, Dy-Liacco, & Williams, 2009; see Chapter 5). This is the potential value of the field of numinous psychology. Exploring wisdom traditions for new insights into our humanity holds the door open to finding new psychological resources and dynamics intrinsic to our inner worlds as well as associated techniques for developing and harnessing these qualities. The opportunity exists for a paradigm shift in the social sciences, one that can more explicitly identify, access, and enhance those essential qualities that are unique to the human species. It can open a dimension for psychological exploration. To do this will require a conceptual framework for orienting and interpreting this type of work from a scientific perspective.

Ontogeny Recapitulates Phylogeny

This basic phrase was a cornerstone of my (RLP) Introduction to Psychology class back in 1975. Impressive phraseology, it was a statement that played a pivotal role in how we interpreted human experience. What this statement means is that any examination of human development, from conception to death, will reflect the morphology of our evolutionary history. Especially in embryonic form, it is clear to see the complex route of evolution humans went through. Evidence of a vestigial tail is seen in our coccyx bone; during gestation, structures that resemble gills appear and then transform into our hearing system; the segmented quality of our "six-pack abs" reflects a time when we had more of a worm-like form. We share much in common with other animals, having many common ancestors. Even today, we know that we share over 90% of our genes with our pet cat, and over 96% of our genes with the Great Apes and other related simians (The Chimpanzee Sequencing and Analysis Consortium, 2005; National Academy of Sciences, 2018).

It is interesting to see how much our species shares in common with other animals. In fact, the early days of science were spent showing that humans operated in ways very similar to others in the animal kingdom, aiming to de-throne man from his narcissistic self-image as being special in the universe. Our instincts were animal instincts; our passions, our morphology, and our evolution were all the same as every other animal on the planet. In psychology class we studied the *fight or flight* instinct, we noted the group herd mentality, and we saw how animal models could accurately reflect complex human processes. Our nobility was shattered in the face of these revelations about our common ancestry.

However, over time this view seemed oversimplified and unfulfilling intellectually. Certainly, we cannot dismiss the fact that we evolved like all other life forms, being shaped by the same physical processes and historical events. Similarly, one cannot overlook the fact that there is also something very special about our species. A simple thought experiment highlights this. Imagine the world 50,000 years ago. What were squirrels doing then? No doubt they were scurrying around finding berries and nuts, living in openings in trees, and trying to stay alive. What was man doing 50,000 years ago? Pretty much the same things, gathering nuts and berries, hunting squirrels, and living in openings wherever they could be found. Today, what are squirrels doing? Essentially their lives are unchanged. And ours? Well that is an entirely different story. The world has been altered and shaped by our existence, our inner and outer worlds growing in ever-increasing complexity. We have intentionally molded the world to fit some larger plan or vision about how we wished it to be. We have learned about the universe, and that knowledge has influenced how we think about the world and our role in it and how we wish to modify it to meet our needs. Our involvements continue to help us develop and accumulate new capacities. Unlike every other species, we live in all environments from high mountains to low valleys, from wet and humid terrains to arid and dry landscapes. As a single species we have adapted to and shaped all the different environments of this planet (and are now moving beyond into space!). We have eradicated diseases, increased our life expectancy, and harvested the bounty of the earth's natural resources. The trajectory of our behavior over time is not static and unchanging as it is for every other species (like squirrels).

There is no doubt that the center of what is unique about who we are is our brain. It has evolved features and capacities that no other animal's brain has. It allows us to learn, know, and understand the universe in ways that not even the nearest of our evolutionary cousins can imitate. Our brain power is enormous, and it is exploited by an even more important quality: that of self-awareness. Humans not only live in the world, but they have their own worlds. We are aware of ourselves as existing while simultaneously realizing the reality of nonexistence. Our brains have created this unique reality: an internal mental space that can envision that which is not and that which can be. More than just surviving, we need to thrive as well. We create art, literature, and philosophy both to capture the human experience and to model it back to ourselves. Our methods aim to enhance our experiencing of the worlds, both inside our minds and in the physical reality we inhabit. We fashion communities and societies to provide context and meaning to the things we do. It is our intellect that has allowed us to grow over time; our history is one characterized by increasing differentiation and sophistication.

The fundamental, ontological question has always been, "What are the qualities of this unique mental space that defines who we are?" These qualities serve to unbind our species from a blind adherence to instinctual scripts, providing for a creative flexibility in engaging the world. From here we need to determine what capacities and dynamics arise from this space and shape and direct the flow of human endeavor. Toward what goals are these forces taking us? This species-defining space is where we find our ultimate concerns. In this space we find that which organizes and provides defining meaning to our existence. It is the place that is most intimate to our existence and most important to our assertion of ourselves; it is the place that we refer to as the numinous. The numinous is the foundational psychological space for our existence. It contains those intrinsic, unique qualities that define both our species and our individual identities. It is the space that provides the guiding meaning for our lives and the essential resources for living that life. Being self-aware, humans are the only animals that know, from early in their lives, that they are going to die someday. Understanding this, the essential human task is how to make meaning, bring depth, and forge coherence for this transient life.

Of course, the social sciences are not the first to address these concerns. This aspect of our essential identity has long been the purview of philosophy and theology. These fields have already developed for themselves a sophisticated vocabulary that can articulate the personal dynamics that characterize this space and provides archetypes that capture its essential motivations in ways that are readily accepted and understood (see McCauley, 2011). The social sciences are new to this area, because our research has only now taken us towards this space. We have much to learn from what these other traditions have found.

While our methods may seem awkward and inefficient in this terrain, they do offer a way for understanding what is occurring in the numinous space and for harvesting these insights in ways that stress their universal application. The social sciences have yet to fully construct an ontology for spirituality that is compatible with the models and understandings inherent to the field. Rather than usurping the role of these other disciplines, through collaboration science can utilize their information as a platform for launching its own expeditions.

A Psychological Ontology for the Numinous

This section will examine and define the unique psychological space that defines the human experience. We refer to this aspect of functioning as *the numinous* because, as we noted in Chapter 1, the term has both theological and psychological meaning. In developing this term for capturing our unique psychological nature, there are two qualities that need to be emphasized. First, this space is foundational to who we are. It is not something that emerges later in life or as a product of other aspects of growth and development, although our numinous capacities do mature and develop over time in response to both internal and external experiences. It is present at birth and is operating even in the first year of life. Its influence underlies all later development. Second, this space is ultimately relational in nature. More than just our level of sociability, the numinous is where the individual constructs his/her ultimate sense of self and establishes its relational engagement with the totality of the universe as conceived by the person. The nature of this cosmological enmeshment influences all other aspects of functioning, the master motive as Allport (1950) refers to it. Thus, the numinous represents a domain of functioning independent of all other aspects of our mental systems and, as such, defines a category large enough to contain many other smaller qualities that exist in this space (e.g., spirituality, religiousness, mysticism). The following two sections will outline what the essential numinous space is and the dynamics intrinsic to it.

Defining the Numinous Space

The mental space that uniquely defines the human experience is a consequence of natural evolution and the emergence of our cerebral neocortex. This new, neuroanatomical structure has created an experiential dimension that is not a consequence of other psychological systems in the human mental world. The mental operations that occur in this space operate in ways that are not dependent upon the psychological dynamics that are mediated by other neuropsychological systems. This space contains its own dynamics that motivate behavior. Essentially, the numinous is irreducible to more basic tendencies or drives: It is *sui generis*. Yet, the numinous and the other psychological systems are always constructively engaged, although they do not interfere with one another. Tillich (1952/2000) provided a useful metaphor from geometry for understanding this seeming paradox. Imagine a box: It has length, width, and depth. Each of these qualities is essential for understanding the box, each of them impacts the others at every point, yet none of them ever interferes, defines, or limits the others in any way.

The numinous impacts our more fundamental drives and motivations, can direct them, over-ride them, or acquiesce to them. Our basic drives can influence the qualities of the numinous although can never extinguish them. The numinous can be a source of support and a healing force when more basic emotional systems may be dysfunctional. In a similar manner, when the ultimate existential issues become overwhelming and are in crisis, the other psychological qualities can also be resources to be exploited for restoring equilibrium. While there are two different systems operating, they are seamlessly coupled and collaboratively produce a unified agentic capacity, much like the two different hemispheres of our brain working conjunctively to create the perception of a singular experience.

There is no doubt that our intellectual capacities enable and support the uniqueness of our personhood. The abilities to think abstractly, to remember, and to find patterns are essential properties of our numinous nature. However, intelligence itself is not the essential or necessary element of our unique nature. There is something exclusive in our own genetic description that carries and creates this aspect of our nature. There are three elements that are the defining essences of this psychological space: self-awareness, self-consideration, and self-integration. Each will be examined in turn.

Self-Awareness

The most salient aspect of the human experience is that we are all aware of our existence. We recognize that we are self-animated, sentient, and self-aware. This capacity to understand ourselves as an executive agency is developed in four ways. First, we recognize that we exist in ways that many other objects do not (e.g., rock, tree, water). Self-awareness provides the capacity to operate as an agentic organism: to choose, select, and determine the directions of movement in time and space. Second, inherent to self-awareness is an apperception of an "other." While one can determine personal self-hood, there is also recognition of additional psychophysical agencies: understood as the "not self." These other external entities, both real and imagined, provide opportunities for defining (and refining) the personal self. Third, promoting the sense of personhood is an awareness of the psychological environment that one occupies. We create an inner representation of the world and our place within it. This self-constructed diorama is a creative, unique template that organizes and defines our knowledge of ourselves and our actions in the world. The qualities and events of that space and their impact on the individual work to enhance self-awareness and personal agency. Finally, implicit to our understanding that we do exist is the recognition of nonexistence or nonbeing. The recognition of our self as being something is contrasted with the understanding that the self can also not exist. Humans are the only animal who are aware of their mortality. It is against the backdrop of nothingness that the self is always aware and from which it seeks to define itself.

Self-Consideration

The human mind contains seemingly unlimited processing capacity and diverse skills for applying this analytical power. This tremendous resource is at the disposal of one's selfhood and enables one to imagine the self in different ways, unfettered by time and place. No other species shares the capacity for creating such a broad perception of the environment, and the self's involvement in it, for understanding one's life against an eternal time frame. As Baumeister et al. (2010, p. 76) noted:

> The capacity to think about the future and orient behavior toward it, beyond the press of the immediate stimulus environment, is arguably one of the most important advances in human cognition, and it may be an essential step in making culture and civilization possible.

The human mind's seemingly unlimited capacity to imagine possibilities, to manipulate the environment, and to seek outcomes that enhance the self's engagement with its environment provides for a high level of creativity, spontaneity, and negative entropy in human striving. The human person seeks not only to survive but to prosper and grow. Action from this source is non-consummatory in nature, in that it is invested in creating and adding value rather than taking value away.

The process of construing the self also takes place in consideration of, or in relation to, some social context. Inherent to our species, more than just being a social animal or having advanced social skills, is a relational capacity to human functioning within which we embed ourselves. There is an intrinsic, self-defined connection to others in our world. These communities that provide a basis for defining the self can be real or imagined, but they provide a sense of context for understanding ourselves, for finding an ultimate sense of acceptance or belonging, and for representing the beneficiaries of our efforts. Simply put, all of us need to find our self-defining place within humanity.

Self-Integration

Having the capacity to process tremendous amounts of information, both real data from the senses to psychological data relating to our imaginations, creates a need for heuristics that can organize and channel this knowledge. Humans have an enhanced ability to synthesize information and build frameworks for cohesively organizing data. These cognitive structures in turn provide meaning: scripts that promote understanding of information and allow humans to focus and direct their energies towards specific outcomes. From the perspective of the numinous, this capacity enables individuals to create for themselves a sense of organization and continuity in their lives. Human beings are the only animal who not only live in the world but also have their own, unique worlds. These constructed realities include personal cosmologies: the context that people build for understanding their lives and the processes by which those lives need to unfold over time. Self-integration is the process by which information, taken in through the senses and experience, is seamlessly interwoven into patterns from which inferences about the external world are drawn. These provide the basic architecture for how the self understands itself in relation to the constructed universe the self perceives. Humans need to create patterns and purposes in their lives to find meaning and value for the self and its strivings.

These three capacities are responsible for creating the psychological space that defines the human species. There are no animal models for these qualities, and they do not conform to the expectations of theories that are based on needs-based aspects of functioning (e.g., drive reduction, learning systems, and psychodynamic models). We can be confident that this space exists by noting how humans behave in ways different from all other animals. For example, humans can act independently from their basic instincts and motivations and, in some circumstances, they can act in ways directly at odds with them (e.g., self-sacrifices individuals make for larger values). Humans also demonstrate a consistent ability for increasing differentiation and sophistication in their environments: Human civilization is characterized by growing complexity in its systems and methods. Perhaps most unique is humans' need to create broad cognitive-emotional frameworks for articulating ultimate meaning: cosmologies that give depth, purpose, and coherence to the self even while realizing that it is finite.

Defining the Basic Motivations of the Numinous Space

The ways in which individuals respond to the dynamics that originate in the numinous space represent the processes by which people construct and express their essential humanity. While the numinous motivations may be independent of other needs and drives, coping with these demands requires the full participation of the entire psychic system. Yet, there are strong individual differences regarding how people manage these intrinsic motivations. Positive adjustment to numinous motivations enables people to live authentic lives, capable of being present to, involved in, and moved by the universal context within which the self construes itself to occupy. Such individuals find gratification of their needs within a relational context. They embrace freely their membership in specific communities because such involvement allows them to create a sense of ultimate meaning and wholeness in a manner in which the dimension of time, while acknowledged, is no longer relevant. Negative adjustments can impair individuals' abilities to constructively engage others in ways that promote personal authenticity and growth. Inadequate management of numinous motivations may lead to destructiveness, expressed in many forms, oriented both internally and externally. When this essential space is compromised, individuals seek to find meaning not through their own efforts but through conformity to other ideals and standards. In addition to assuming the meaning of others (e.g., people, institutions, philosophies), such conformity helps assuage feelings of worthlessness and diminished personal value. The paradox here is that dysfunctional numinous motivations create vulnerabilities and fears that are inconsolable by these external agencies.

As noted above, the fields of theology and philosophy have for centuries addressed the essential questions of our being and ultimate nature. Perhaps the most insightful, perceptive, and psychologically relevant description of the essential numinous motivations was presented by Tillich (1952/2000). With precision and clarity, he captured the indispensable elements of the human experience. For Tillich, the fully functioning individual needs to find the courage to be oneself. Courage, for Tillich, "is the self-affirmation of being in spite of the fact of nonbeing" (1952/2000, p. 155). Having the capacity to assert our existence and our actions in the world in the face of nonexistence is the essential existential task (what is referred to above as relational engagement). He presented how this process occurs in consideration of the three numinous human capacities noted above. As such, the following is my (RLP) interpretation and extension of Tillich's ideas on courage and the dynamics that constitute our necessary numinous motivations in a manner that is congruent with the thrust of this volume. While the social sciences are relatively new to this area, researchers have begun to ask and investigate these types of questions and are finding success in identifying aspects of functioning that are numinous in nature (e.g., spiritual struggles, Exline & Rose, 2005; relational spirituality, Mahoney, 2013). What is exciting is that moving from different directions and using varying assumptions, the wisdom traditions and psychology have identified common constructs.

There are three basic motivational dynamics that constitute the numinous: infinitude, meaning, and worthiness. Tillich cast these constructs as basic existential anxieties that relate to nonbeing, meaninglessness/

chaos, and condemnation. Regardless of whether humans are motivated to avoid certain potentialities or if we are impelled by our nature to create particular outcomes, human life is significantly influenced by these forces. These motivations have created a set of archetypal-type themes that characterize our existential strivings and resonate deeply in our being. The presentation to follow will attempt to define both the positive and negative polarities of each motivation. While independently presented, these motivations are all interrelated and have overlapping and mutually supporting functions.

Infinitude vs Nonbeing

The most important characteristic of the human experience is self-awareness. As noted above, concomitant to this realization is the awareness of nonexistence. Knowing that we are alive is in contrast with the opposite of this, which is recognizing our own mortality. What can we do with the knowledge that eventually our existence will end? How do we create meaning, coherence, and depth to the lives we are leading, knowing that we will die? For Tillich, this is the most basic of motivations for humans, and it is the most fundamental drive. As he noted, "Man as man in every civilization is anxiously aware of the threat of nonbeing and needs the courage to affirm himself in spite of it" (Tillich, 1952/2000, p. 43). The awareness of our finitude impels us to find security for ourselves in a changing and time-limited world. We create security in many ways. I (RLP) hypothesize that the source of human spirituality is found here. For me, spirituality represents a way of conceiving the universe, and our place in it, in terms that exclude a consideration of time. A full sense of spirituality is developed when individuals understand the context of their lives against an eternal time frame (see Chapter 6 for a fuller discussion on how meaning is made). Conceiving our lives as being one stage in a larger ontological process enables individuals to act with the greatest freedom and involvement. Whether using the term "heaven," "collective unconscious," or "brahmaloka," people create an ultimate eternity for their selves that supports their abilities to become enmeshed in their communities. Spirituality enables individuals to sacrifice themselves for others, to commit their lives to service, and to forego advancement in lieu of a greater good for the community. The joy and freedom of spirituality are found in its belief of eternal existence. As Tillich (1952/2000, p. 170) stated, "He who participates in God participates in eternity." Whether such states exist or not is irrelevant; the personal belief of spiritual immortality can allow a greater engagement with life and with others. This description does not exclude those who do not believe in a spiritual eternity. Such people can find their sense of infinitude fulfilled in a transpersonal orientation that understands the repercussions of individual behavior vibrating across generations.

A second area where infinitude finds expression is in the development of security. From a corporate perspective, humans bind together to create social structures and institutions that capitalize on their numbers to leverage more safety and provide resources for their own care and nurturance. The essential relational nature of humanity finds succor and support in the interrelationships it creates. The history of human civilizations shows the ongoing development of social, economic, political, and legal institutions (among others), whose focus is to provide for the common good. While many philosophies of government exist, they all focus on the question of how to best provide for the integrity of the populace. One characteristic of our collectivistic enterprise is increasing levels of development and sophistication that define human existence. Humanity is always harnessing its abilities to learn and understand the world in ways that will develop and improve the institutions and structures we have created to nurture our existence. Negative entropy is an intrinsic quality of human experience and characterizes us from the individual to the societal levels.

The two positive qualities of the motivation of infinitude are its relational quality and growth function. Feeling secure in ourselves, being able to accept the inevitable fate of our physical destiny, we are capable of fully involving our talents and passions in the lives we lead. We take risks, make sacrifices in the here and now for advantages later in time or to others, and assert our ideas in order to benefit our groups. Negative aspects of this motivation lead to the opposite outcomes. When finitude overwhelms people, they are forced into more circumscribed situations that are more reactive than proactive. Safety concerns are met when individuals feel "protected" by something, whether it be membership in a particular group, belief in an ideology, or retreat into a more solipsistic reality. The key here is a state of being that does not actively engage with the larger community, is defensive, and is ritualistic. By creating a smaller and more limited sense of self, individuals overwhelmed by the sense of nonbeing attempt to find a manageable psychosocial structure that can insulate them from those threats that aggravate their insecure sense of self. Tillich (1952/2000, p. 66) succinctly characterized this state as, "the way of avoiding nonbeing by avoiding being." Failure to actualize this motivation results in a more limited sense of self, a restricted personal freedom of choice, and a more passive and uncreative perspective on life.

Meaning vs Chaos

As active agents, we need to create a context for our activity. Purpose and direction are key elements of our agency. However, like sensation is to perception, we live in an objective world but operate within the confines of our subjective understanding of it. We create meaning to give depth, coherence, direction, and purpose to the lives we lead. It is within this web of meaning that we find pleasure, joy, and fulfillment to our endeavors. We do things to accomplish ends that are of consequence and importance to us. We develop values, priorities, and morals to organize and direct our energies in ways that will maximize their impact in the relational context within which we exist. The meanings we create help to amplify our efforts at negative entropy by providing the specific impetus for increasing diversification and sophistication. It is within this motivation that we find the capacity to thrive as well as ultimate fulfillment. As Tillich (1952/2000, p. 46) noted:

> Everyone who lives creatively in meaning affirms himself as a participant in these meanings. He affirms himself as receiving and transforming reality creatively. He loves himself as participating in the spiritual life and as loving its contents. He loves them because they are his own fulfillment and because they are actualized through him.

For Tillich, meaning is what spirituality is about, and spirituality is the essence of our humanity. All spirituality involves meaning making.

More than just personal scripts or preferences, the sense of meaning created within this numinous space represents the ultimate values to which people commit their lives. Emmons (1999) pointed out that this ultimate level of meaning, and its related goals, is different in nature than other types of strivings more commonly studied in psychology. It includes the principles, morals, and tenets that form the foundation of being as well as serving as the definitive goals to which people devote their lives towards obtaining. It is what people put their ultimate trust in and what is used to organize and support all other values. It is their essential character.

The natural consequence to creating a meaning network is doubt and questioning, the necessary tools for building meaning. The value of acquired meanings needs to be re-evaluated for continuing significance and relevance. As situations change and our understanding evolves, the need always exists for enhancements in our meaning systems. Such self-reflection promotes growth and differentiation in our thinking and understanding. Being free to pursue new understandings and to enhance our construal of our agentic experiences leads to greater involvement of people in our lives. However, the danger does exist for our meaning system to come up as being inadequate or incorrect. Our meanings and values may be found to be solipsistic or artificial. The patterns we discern may not be patterns at all! The breakdown in our meaning capacity results in feelings of chaos and unpredictability. When properly managed, this anxiety around chaos can lead to enhanced meaning creation. When not managed well, the fear of chaos can bring high levels of emotional dysphoria to people. Without a valid sense of meaning, then the created world of our existence falls to pieces creating paralysis and despair. Ultimately, the despair of meaninglessness is a psychologically untenable and intolerable reality. Tillich pointed out that any threat to our meaning making (or spirituality) is a threat to our whole personhood and can result in suicidal thoughts and actions. A less extreme response would include a flight to fanaticism: a self-surrender to some system that imposes meaning authoritatively and preempts our own efforts at questioning and doubt. The world of fanatics is restricted to fit the confines of the new philosophy, and they fight vehemently against and persecute those whose ideas question or vary from their own.

Worthiness vs Condemnation

As noted earlier, an intrinsic aspect of spirituality is its relational nature. We create meaning within a social context: a collage of relationships, commitments, and obligations that helps define our awareness of self and directs how we create meaning. We need to have a "center of being," an ultimately transpersonal perspective of our origins that provides meaning and insight into our sense of self. It is the simultaneous understanding of our lives in an expanding series of communities of increasing size. We are members of a family, town, faith group, profession, nation, race, and species. It is in these contexts that we strive to create a sense of positive affirmation for who we are and the value we offer these communities. In return, these communities, through the agency of our selfhood, require of us a statement of our value and worth. Have we conducted ourselves in ways that have empowered and enhanced these centers of being? The drive for worthiness finds in it the quest for moral action, to engage the world in ways that promote the goodness contained within the humanity of those we meet. Our worthiness is bound intrinsically to our sense of infinitude and the ultimate sense of reality with which we seek to connect ourselves. While we may seek such affirmation in awards, accomplishments, and accolades from others, ultimately we find self-worth within our own capacity to apperceive acceptance from the totality of our entire sense of ultimate meaning.

The challenge in establishing this sense of worthiness is found in our own self-examinations and judgments. Our foibles, imperfections, and personal failures hobble our efforts at creating acceptance; we recognize some level of unacceptability in who we are. Imperfect beings act imperfectly, and actions may bring immoral or negative consequences, intended or not, that taint our sense of being. Thus, the intrinsic tension of this motivation is how to find acceptance when we believe we are unacceptable. I (RLP) posit that this dynamic is a pervasive characteristic for most people. Issues of self-esteem may appear similar, but they do not really capture the dynamic in action here. However, differentiating between condemnation and (low) self-esteem is important. The latter relates to an ongoing sense of impaired personal well-being that is a facet of negative affect. Such individuals feel inadequate and inferior to others and may experience shame. The former represents aspects of existential distress (or nöological crisis; Frankl, 1997) independent of shame and inferiority (and of the larger personality domain of Neuroticism), and it is based on a perception that one's entire sense of self-agency, meaning, and action is being rejected or deemed unsuitable by one's framework of ultimate meaning.

The positive resolution of this tension is found in people finding the capacity to accept themselves as being acceptable in spite of their unacceptability. This is not to mean that we find the ability to accept ourselves as ourselves. Rather, it reflects an ability to perceive in the face of the transcendent, acceptance of our individual selves. What is essential here is the idea of ultimate forgiveness. Wisdom traditions around the globe all highlight the need to find forgiveness and reconciliation with the divine. This sense of "being right with God" has important implications for the global stability of our psychic worlds. As Tillich (1952/2000, p. 164) described it, "The courage to affirm oneself in spite of this anxiety is the courage which we have called the courage of confidence. It is rooted in the personal, total, and immediate certainty of divine forgiveness." Even for those whose meaning does not include an eternity, the need for acceptance is present and solved when this sense of unconditional acceptance is found in the communities they value and is received by them. This sense of worthiness is not provided by any person or agency but is received and accepted by us from the totality of our own created meaning. Such acceptance does not remove our limitations, failures, or weaknesses. Rather we become confident that despite them, we are worthy.

A negative resolution of this tension results in a powerful sense of existential condemnation. Despite whatever values, talents, and skills we possess, we are seen as insufficient and/or unaccepted. We as a personal agency are deemed worthless and find ourselves rejected by the very fiber of things that give us meaning. The result of this is utter despair. This lack of acceptability undermines our purposes and meanings and leaves our sense of being without value or worth. This is a tragic reality that leaves us with few options. When not addressed, this despair leads to self-destruction, either through suicide or by self-destructive behaviors aimed at injuring those communities we value most. In this way, individuals engage in injurious behaviors that also maximize the emotional injury, insult, and hurtfulness that can be directed at those "others" from whom we seek acceptance but from whom we feel rejected. For example, substance abusers may engage in these activities to both punish the self for being rejected by parents or loved ones and to punish those same people for making them feel inadequate and unworthy. Two strategies individuals can use to restore a sense of worthiness are by service to some larger purpose (e.g., military, humanitarian organization) or by embracing and enacting a strict moral persona (e.g., assuming religious vows, ascetic lifestyle). Our ability to manage this motivation will determine whether these strategies have a beneficial or detrimental impact on us.

The Research Evidence

There is a tremendous amount of research examining R/S constructs from a variety of perspectives. While the purpose of this section is not to overview this body of work, its focus is to identify briefly, and selectively, some programs of research whose findings resonate with the themes presented here. It is exciting to note that there exists empirical work, developed from specific psychological perspectives, that has identified aspects of intrapsychic functioning that reflect the basic numinous issues outlined here. Their data provide validation to these concepts and their clinical value. Concerns over finitude and nonbeing take center stage in Terror Management Theory (TMT; Solomon, Greenberg, & Pyszczynski, 1991). This theory asserts that thoughts surrounding death provoke great psychological upheaval (e.g., terror) requiring individuals to find ways to manage or minimize. When subjects' mortality is stressed (e.g., by asking them to tell you what they think will happen to them after they die), individuals take very clear steps to manage their terror by becoming more focused on their cultural values, to enhance personal meaning. Meaning is enhanced when beliefs in an afterlife are stressed, or even when national values/identity are affirmed. When the threat of nonbeing is raised, individuals seek existential reassurance and protection through enmeshment in larger groups and their reaffirming values. TMT acknowledges the uniqueness of this phenomenon for humans and links this dynamic to important psychosocial outcomes including self-esteem, coping ability, and health.

Meaning and ultimate concern have been long recognized as being important. Frankl (1997) clearly outlined that a personal sense of meaning creates more resilience and coherence in personality. When meaning is compromised or not well established, individuals are at risk for an existential, or nöological, crisis. The lack of meaning impairs individuals' ability to thrive. Hood, Hill, and Williamson (2005) have identified four criteria by which religion can uniquely provide global meaning: comprehensiveness, accessibility, transcendence, and direct authoritative claims. The ability of religions to connect meaning to such higher-level systems gives it, according to these authors, an unmatched ability to provide and maintain a high level of meaning. Park (2013) provided a model outlining the processes by which individuals construct meaning in their lives and the role of religion in that system. Ultimately, religion impacts how individuals appraise stressful events, which in turn influences how people create global meaning. Emmons (1999) noted how the ultimate concerns individuals create to organize their lives have implications for stress management, resilience, and direction. Examining theistic/spiritual strivings, Emmons noted that people with more spiritual goals experienced less conflict around their goals and more personal integration.

Finally, more recent research examining spiritual struggles and religious crisis (Exline & Rose, 2005; Piedmont et al., 2007) demonstrated how beliefs of being rejected by God and faith communities creates large amounts of emotional dysphoria that is independent of personality constructs related to negative affect. Further, this existential sense of condemnation also leads to larger psychological difficulties. Finally, my own research seeking to construct a universal dimension of spirituality resulted in the development of the Spiritual Transcendence Scale (Piedmont, 1999, 2012). This unidimensional construct contains three correlated facets: prayer fulfillment, universality, and connectedness. These scales line up well with the motivations of infinitude, meaning, and worthiness, respectively. Further, Spiritual Transcendence has been shown to represent aspects of motivation independent of the Big Five personality domains, to generalize cross-culturally, and to generate scores that are reliable and valid across a variety of faith groups, including atheists. Such data underscore the utility and psychological importance of numinous constructs for expanding our understanding of human behavior.

The Psychology of the Numinous

The basic tenet of the psychology of the numinous is that it is concerned with the internal, essential psychological space that defines the human experience. The mental capacities and the motivations they generate drive us to engage the world, in all its facets, relationally and creatively. These inner numinous qualities inform our social constructions and cultural expressions and ultimately impact the types of behaviors we enact and the choices we make. A scientific examination of the insights, texts, and stories of the wisdom traditions offers a fertile ground for harvesting new ideas and understandings about the essential human experience and the role of the numinous in directing our ultimate concerns. Wisdom traditions outline salient archetypal issues that resonate deeply within the human condition (e.g., worthiness, forgiveness, suffering, and guilt). Empirical analysis can remove the denominational-specific, metaphysical elements from these concepts and facilitate the identification of universal dynamics from which the theoretical and practical value can be readily determined (Piedmont, 1999).

Aside from being a source of new psychological constructs, the wisdom traditions have also spent centuries developing techniques, practices, and methods for accessing and developing these essential numinous motivations. Such processes hold the potential for the identification of new types of therapeutic interventions. Already several such techniques have been explored, such as meditation, mindfulness, and gratitude. Their psychological value has been noted, and research continues to find ways to improve their efficacy. However, these methods are just the surface, with potentially many more such techniques waiting to be discovered. Coupling these techniques with a more developed sense of our numinous nature may provide a powerful approach to helping people manage their personal problems and struggles with adaptation. This is a key point to emphasize. While numinous psychology collaborates with other disciplines and wisdom traditions, its goal is not to replace them. Constructive engagement among these different disciplines will bring a more integrated and holistic understanding of the individual. Assisting people to move productively through their lives will necessitate the skills of an interdisciplinary team.

A psychology of the numinous should provide therapists with a more developed treatment plan for the inclusion of R/S constructs and interventions in their practice. The theory of the numinous provides a rationale for why R/S techniques are included in treatment and the psychotherapeutic goals they are directed towards. Understanding spirituality as something more than just a cultural context necessitates an understanding of spiritual interventions as more than just a way of making a client feel comfortable with the therapeutic experience. Such interventions are directed towards accessing important numinous qualities that are impacting and/or relevant to the psychological status of the client. Accessing the ultimate sources of meaning, worthiness, and infinitude clients use to define themselves can be diagnostically revealing and offer potential resources for change. Promoting adaptation and mental health requires more than just symptom reduction, it necessitates a consideration of our ultimate levels of well-being. Treatment ought to include an effort to enhance an individual's numinous self that includes both an improved sense of worthiness and a life-enhancing sense of ultimate meaning and personal abundance (see Piedmont, 2004a, 2004b).

The psychology of the numinous is both a recognition and formalization of the interest of the social sciences in understanding the essential nature of humanity. The last 25 years have seen an explosion in research interested in identifying numinous constructs and charting their psychological value. The preponderance of research begs the larger question of how to organize and understand these findings. Social scientists need a conceptual context for aligning their variables with other psychological constructs in order to promote continuity and cumulativeness to their findings. It is hoped that professionals interested in R/S constructs will find that this exposition provided enhanced clarity for their own efforts in terms of the nature of their constructs.

References

Allport, G. W. (1950). *The individual and his religion.* New York, NY: MacMillan.

Baumeister, R. F., Bauer, I. M., & Lloyd, S. A. (2010). Choice, free will, and religion. *Psychology of Religion and Spirituality, 2,* 67–82.

Benson, P. L., Donahue, M. J., & Erickson, J. A. (1993). The Faith Maturity Scale: Conceptualization, measurement, and empirical validation. *Research in the Social Scientific Study of Religion, 5,* 1–26.

Buss, D. M. (2002). Sex, marriage, and religion: What adaptive problems do religious phenomena solve? *Psychological Inquiry, 13,* 201–203.

The Chimpanzee Sequencing and Analysis Consortium. (2005). Initial sequence of the chimpanzee genome and comparison with the human genome. *Nature, 437,* 69–87. doi:10.1038/nature04072

Emmons, R. A. (1999). *The psychology of ultimate concerns: Motivation and spirituality in personality.* New York, NY: Guilford Press.

Exline, J. J., & Rose, E. (2005). Religious and spiritual struggles. In R. Paloutzian & C. Park (Eds.), *Handbook of the psychology of religion and spirituality* (pp. 315–330). New York, NY: The Guilford Press.

Francis, L. J., & Greer, J. E. (1990). Catholic schools and adolescent religiosity in Northern Ireland: Shaping moral values. *Irish Journal of Education, 2,* 40–47.

Frankl, V. E. (1997). *Man's search for ultimate meaning.* New York, NY: Plenum Press.

Funder, D. C. (2002). Why study religion? *Psychological Inquiry, 13,* 213–214.

Gibson, H. M., & Francis, L. J. (1996). Measuring Christian fundamentalist belief among 11–15 year old adolescents in Scotland. In L. J. Francis & W. S. Campbell (Eds.), *Research in religious education* (pp. 249–255). Leominster, UK: Fowler Wright.

Hood, R. W., Jr., Hill, P. C., & Williamson, W. P. (2005). *The psychology of religious fundamentalism.* New York, NY: Guilford Press.

Kapuscinski, A. N., & Masters, K. S. (2010). The current status of measures of spirituality: A critical review of scale development. *Psychology of Religion and Spirituality, 2,* 191–205. doi:10.1037/a0020498

Mahoney, A. (2013). The spirituality of us: Relational spirituality in the context of family relationships. In K. I. Pargament, J. J. Exline, & J. W. Jones (Eds.), *The APA handbook of psychology, religion, and spirituality* (Vol. 1; pp. 365–389). Washington, DC: American Psychological Association.

McCauley, R. N. (2011). *Why religion is natural and science is not.* New York, NY: Oxford University Press.

National Academy of Sciences. (2018). Putting DNA to work. *Marian Koshland Science Museum.* Retrieved from www.koshland-science-museum.org/sites/all/exhibits/exhibitdna/intro03.jsp

O'Grady, K. A., & Richards, P. S. (2010). The role of inspiration in the helping professions. *Psychology of Religion and Spirituality, 2,* 57–66. doi:10.1037/a0018551

Park, C. L. (2013). Religion and meaning. In R. F. Paloutzian & C. L. Park (Eds.). *Handbook of the psychology of religion and spirituality* (pp. 357–379). New York, NY: The Guilford Press.

Piedmont, R. L. (1999). Does spirituality represent the sixth factor of personality? Spiritual transcendence and the five-factor model. *Journal of Personality, 67,* 985–1013.

Piedmont, R. L. (2004a). Spiritual Transcendence as a predictor of psychosocial outcome from an outpatient substance abuse program. *Psychology of Addictive Behaviors, 18*, 213–222.

Piedmont, R. L. (2004b). The logoplex as a paradigm for understanding spiritual transcendence. *Research in the Social Scientific Study of Religion, 15*, 263–284.

Piedmont, R. L. (2012). Overview and development of a trait-based measure of numinous constructs: The Assessment of Spirituality and Religious Sentiments (ASPIRES) scale. In L. Miller (Ed.), *The Oxford handbook of psychology of spirituality and consciousness* (pp. 104–122). New York, NY: Oxford University Press.

Piedmont, R. L. (2014). Looking back and finding our way forward: An editorial call to action. *Psychology of Religion and Spirituality, 6*, 265–267. doi:10.1037/rel0000014

Piedmont, R. L., Ciarrocchi, J. W., Dy-Liacco, G. S., & Williams, J. E. G. (2009). The empirical and conceptual value of the Spiritual Transcendence and Religious Involvement Scales for personality research. *Psychology of Religion and Spirituality, 1*, 162–179.

Piedmont, R. L., Hassinger, C. J., Rhorer, J., Sherman, M. F., Sherman, N. C., & Williams, J. E. G. (2007). The relations among spirituality and religiosity and Axis II functioning in two college samples. *Research in the Social Scientific Study of Religion, 18*, 53–73.

Rizzuto, A.-M. (1979). *The birth of the living God.* Chicago, IL: University of Chicago Press.

Rizzuto, A.-M., & Schafranske, E. P. (2013). Addressing religion and spirituality in treatment from a psychodynamic perspective. In K. I. Pargament, J. J. Exline, & J. W. Jones (Eds.), *APA handbook of psychology, religion, and spirituality.* (Vol. 2; pp. 125–146). Washington, DC: American Psychological Association.

Solomon, S., Greenberg, J., & Pyszczynski, T. (1991). A terror management theory of self-esteem. In C. R. Snyder & F. R. Donelson (Eds.), *Handbook of social and clinical psychology: The health perspective* (pp. 21–40). Elmsford, NY: Pergamon Press.

Tillich, P. (1952/2000). *The courage to be* (2nd ed.). New Haven, CT: Yale University Press.

3 A Social Science Paradigm for Making Numinous-Based Clinical Interventions

From the Integration to the Collaboration of the Social Sciences and Theology

Religious and spiritual (R/S) issues are important concerns for many people as they struggle to live lives that are meaningful and ethical. R/S concepts are frequently associated with personal strivings and emotional conflicts as they relate to the more intimate aspects of an individual's mental life. There are several reasons for this. First, in many Western cultures, especially the US, many people consider themselves to be religious/spiritual. These concepts therefore provide a framework of meaning and an ethical structure for living. Second, whether religiously involved or not, R/S concepts and values permeate society. In the US, religious holidays like Christmas, Easter, Yom Kippur, Hanukkah, and Ramadan, to name a few, impact our calendar year, advertising, work and school schedules, movies, TV shows, and our cultural ethos. These themes impact and influence our meaning-making apparatus in both direct and indirect ways. Whether one is a religious believer or not, most people know something about Santa Claus, the Easter Bunny, Jesus, and Allah. One would be hard pressed to live a life that is perfectly secular; R/S concepts seep into much of the fabric of our culture and influence our thinking.

It is not surprising then to know that when confronting a serious physical and/or emotional problem many people seek out a clergy member for help. In fact, clergy are a first line of defense in addressing psychosocial problems. Sperry (2012) noted that a 1992 Gallup poll indicated that for two-thirds of the respondents, when experiencing a significant emotional problem, they preferred to see a therapist who personally held spiritual values and beliefs. It is also clear why helping professionals across multiple disciplines are interested in learning more about R/S issues because their clients bring these issues up in secular treatments as well (Post & Wade, 2009; Rose, Westefeld, & Ansley, 2001). While involving R/S issues in contemporary psychosocial treatments is relatively new, clergy have been doing this for ages. Spiritual Direction, Spiritual Formation, and Pastoral Counseling are fields that have developed within religious traditions and are concerned with helping the faithful apply their religious beliefs towards living a life of righteousness.

Life is messy, and there are many issues, problems, and conflicts that seem endemic. All wisdom traditions rely on scriptural texts that, to varying degrees, address many of these issues and provide a template for believers to follow to overcome these emotional challenges in ways that promote spiritual growth and personal holiness. With time, the development of psychological theories and treatments offered clergy new resources to employ in their own spiritual guidance work. Clergy sought psychological training to augment their pastoral skills and to recognize when an issue was more relevant to psychological treatment, to spiritual guidance, or to a combination of the two.

There are multiple ways that R/S concepts are brought to bear with clinical work. Generically, this is referred to as *pastoral integration*, the process by which the psychological and theological are brought together to provide insight and growth for the client. For the purpose of this volume, we will use the term *Pastoral Counseling* (PC) to refer to this wide range of disciplines that seek to provide this integration. Curiously, there exists no real framework for integrating the use of R/S concepts into the management of psychosocial issues. As such, this area is very broad and contains a wide array of perspectives and modalities. For some (e.g., Snodgrass, McCreight, & McFee, 2014), PC, like any counseling approach, involves a specific "way of being" (Cheston, 2000, p. 256). For PC, this refers to a therapist's personal orientation to the God of their understanding and its resulting spiritual dictates for the process and goal of engaging clients in a collaborative spiritual journey. For others, it may include a scriptural-based approach that encourages individuals to re-examine their religious beliefs and to involve themselves in specific rituals and activities (Snodgrass et al., 2000). Whatever the approach, there is an explicit component to the modality that believes science and theology work together, synergistically, to enable change. In reviewing the literature, we have identified five different ways that PC attempts to integrate psychology and theology into a treatment approach: a) the reductionistic; b) bilingualism; c) post-hoc or contingency based; d) spiritual direction; and e) theistic psychology.

Before overviewing each of these approaches, two points need to be made. First, while all PC therapists will define their approach as "integrative," there is no definition of what that integration means (Townsend, 2009). The lack of definition creates a vacuum in the field, undermining therapists' ability to define their professional scope of practice in a manner consistent with their training and credentialing. For example, in using R/S concepts in treatment, at what point would a counselor, social worker, or psychologist stop being a social scientist and start being more of spiritual guide or director? Where is the boundary between the psychological and theological aspects of this integration? This is a very important issue because it speaks directly to therapists' ability to operate in an ethically appropriate manner. As Sloan, Bagiella, and Powell

(2001, p. 348) have noted, "When doctors depart from areas of established expertise to promote a nonmedical agenda, they abuse their status as professionals." So, when a therapist advises a client to attend religious services more frequently, or to read scripture and pray, this may be part of an effort at integration, but it may also be a step outside of his/her scope of practice. Conversely, spiritual directors need to recognize that while there may be R/S facets to aspects of a client's emotional distress, there are limits to what a guided spiritual exchange can do to help with serious psychological impairment (e.g., substance abuse, sexual paraphilias, schizophrenia). Applying R/S issues in any type of counseling requires the explicit need for a set of internally consistent boundaries appropriate for the professional training of the therapist.

Second, it is not clear what the "integration" component really represents. While we have noted in Chapter 2 that it is impossible to integrate science and theology because they represent two very diverse intellectual systems, we recognize that this statement contradicts what many PC professionals claim to accomplish in their clinical practice. We hope that a review of these different ways of conducting PC will serve to make our point clearer. We start by providing a definition of what the term *integration* means. The *American Heritage Dictionary* (2019) defines the term *integrate* as, "The organization of the psychological or social traits and tendencies of a personality into a harmonious whole." Implicit to this definition is the assumption that these different parts can be seamlessly tied together, that there is an innate compatibility to the diverse elements that enables them to be linked together and their functions complementing. An example of such integration is found in the area of cognitive-behavioral psychology (CBP).

Originally, there was the field of behaviorism, which was concerned with the identification of the processes that influenced the acquisition and expression of behaviors by organisms. Initially, behaviorism was focused solely on external events, like learning curves, reinforcement schedules, and stimuli distinctiveness. The focus was not on internal events and the role of the mind was greatly diminished, being referred to as the *black box*. Behaviorism originally did not concern itself with what went on mentally, which was seen as too unsystematic for scientific scrutiny. Researchers like Skinner and Pavlov were successful in demonstrating the power of environments for controlling what is learned and what is forgotten. However, cognitive psychologists also believed in the power of mentation for influencing the learning of behaviors. Theorists like Freud and Frankl believed that the inner motivations, beliefs, and understandings that people held directly influenced the kinds of behaviors that people would learn and the actions they would take. The inner mind, which may appear chaotic and contradictory on some levels, had its own logic and systems that could be understood and manipulated. For some time, these two approaches seemed inimical to one another.

Fortunately, Bandura's Social Learning Theory (Bandura, 1977; Bandura & Walters, 1963) helped to bring these two seemingly incompatible paradigms together. Bandura was able to show how cognitions acted in the behavior acquisition process: They could serve as both stimuli and reinforcers to learned behaviors. Rather than a black box, Bandura demonstrated how the inner mind can operate in logical ways consistent with the rules of behavioral learning theory. Thus, the two fields were neatly integrated because the elements of both shared similar qualities that enabled them to be fitted together into a larger, more economical and predictively powerful, system. The point to be considered in examining the different PC approaches below is the extent to which R/S concepts can be fitted together with specific psychological processes so that the combination of the two sets of constructs can operate collaboratively under a common rubric.

Current Paradigms for Psycho-Spiritual Integration

The following five approaches are summarized in global ways that capture their intrinsic perspectives. We will demonstrate how each system understands the interplay between science and theology. These approaches will see the interrelationship as being symmetrical, asymmetrical, or ordered in nature. We will note the different implications for each perspective as well.

Reductionistic

Early psychological approaches to understanding numinous issues viewed them through the lens of psychological theories. In other words, when considering issues of spirituality and its related theology, social scientists would work to find ways to connect these putative metaphysical concepts with specific psychological dynamics. In this manner, social science could find a way to understand the esoteric ideas of theology in scientific terms. For example, Edinger (1972) attempted to contextualize Christianity as being an analogy for the more important Jungian process of individuation. Edinger outlined how Christian values and ideals could be understood as representations of concepts developed by modern psychology. It is then through this psychological framework that one can understand the theological emphases of religion. Freud (cited in Bischof, 1970), on the other hand, saw religious strivings and behaviors as merely the expression of underlying psychological processes aimed at managing more basic primal needs. Rather than seeing religious activities as being isomorphic with psychological processes, Freud understood theological content as just another expression of, and attempt at gratifying, underlying unconscious tensions.

The reductionistic approach characterized early efforts by psychology to understand the R/S sentiments of people. Like other activities of life (e.g., relationships, mental health, vocation), religious aspirations reflected the known psychological system of the individual at work. This approach made religion seem understandable to social scientists, although frequently this understanding saw such activities as representing unhealthy or immature psychological strivings. The value of this approach is that it allowed science to see that R/S strivings included very strong amounts of psychological material. There were clear psychological processes driving individuals to seek out transcendent realities, and these endeavors, regardless of whatever putative metaphysical incentives or rewards, provided people with psychological satisfaction and helped maintain their sense of personhood. An advantage of embedding R/S concepts within established psychological models is that it offers an ontological basis that provides useful interpretive depth to the constructs. This perspective lingers in the field even to this day. Critics of the psychology of religion (e.g., Buss, 2002; Funder, 2002) have argued that R/S constructs really do not identify any new motivations or processes. Rather, they are merely the *religification* (van Wicklin, 1990) of already existing psychological constructs. Current social science already provides sufficient ground for understanding anything related to the numinous.

However, there are serious limitations to this perspective. A reductionist platform can hardly be considered "integrative" in nature. Simplifying the numinous into something else loses the very character of the element being reduced. Reductionism fails to appreciate the unique, non-reducible perspectives that theology presents concerning the ultimate nature of humanity. While this approach may be satisfying to some social scientists, to theologians and those interested in the kinds of questions theology focuses on, reductionism is overly simplistic and presents a naïve optimism about scientific understanding:

> For Barth, psychological concepts could not possibly exist on the same levels as theological concepts because psychology by definition pertains only to a creaturely level of reality ... there is a specificity to theological content which has no anthropological or psychological counterpart.
>
> (van Deusen Hunsinger, 1995, p. 93)

Bilingualism

If reductionism can be understood as science's default position towards R/S concepts, then bilingualism can be seen as the preferred position of helping professionals who take a much more theological perspective to treatment (e.g., Spiritual Directors, Religiously-Oriented Therapists). The underlying perspective here is that both theological and psychological concepts are clearly intertwined and, depending on the perspective, cannot be readily separated. Despite such close bonding, each set of concepts has its own characteristics and functional agenda in the mental life of people. To appreciate this fully, one would need to have training in both areas. By having such dual expertise, a pastoral counselor can understand inner distress on different levels and can design interventions that solve issues on both levels. Pastoral counselors (i.e., those skilled in both psychology and theology) can have both a therapeutic and a pastoral conversation with the client:

> The pastor, however, *uses* the tools of psychology in a way that is understood to be quite different from their use by a psychotherapist. The psychotherapist used them directly to help resolve psychic conflicts and heal neurosis. The pastor is concerned, however, not with neurosis but with a deeper disturbance, that of sin. Sin is understood to be the ground out of which neurosis emerges but as something quite distinct from neurosis. Because the pastor is more focused on sin than on neurosis, he or she brings other tools to the counseling task.
>
> (van Deusen Hunsinger, 1995, p. 79; italics in original)

While this perspective strongly appreciates the multidisciplinary and holistic nature of psychological treatments, it really cannot be considered integrative in nature. This approach argues that theological issues are at the core of all psychological problems and must themselves be solved before the presenting psychosocial issues can be overcome. To accomplish this, one needs to be well versed in the methods of both psychology and theology. While not impossible to do, developing such skills is very daunting. Developing expertise in psychotherapy takes many years of training and experience, as does preparation for ministry. To attempt both professions would require many years of study.

The bilingual approach has its primary emphasis on the underlying theological issues confronting the person, with the psychological being a related, though secondary, aspect of the presenting problem. Therefore, this approach really does not provide any integration of the two fields, as we have defined it above. There is no unity because psychology and theology are treated as separate levels of functioning, requiring counselors to develop multiple types of skills. Further, given the preeminence of theology in this process, the natural question is, "Whose theology?" What the Pastoral Counseling situation represents would vary across different theological models, as the underlying metaphysical concepts would be different. In the above quote it was noted that sin is the ground from which neurosis emerges. However, this idea is a very Western and Christian perspective that would not generalize to other faith groups for whom a different theology is followed (e.g., Buddhism, where there is no concept of sin). Thus, how science and theology combine to impact functioning would be very different across denominations. Finding a universal pattern that integrates these two concepts is impossible from this perspective. At best, the bilingual approach exits at the cultural level of analysis, providing explanations that make sense from the theological perspective of the particular client; there are no universal processes being identified and explained. As such, the frequent goal of this approach is to help individuals more fully live out the values of their faith commitments.

Post-hoc or Contingency Based

Two questions frequently asked by professors in clinical supervision courses are: a) "Why did you do that?" and b) "Why did you do that, now?" Psychotherapy is an ongoing process by which a counselor and client connect. The counselor's role is to understand the client's story and to work collaboratively with the client in his or her efforts at coping and adapting to the demands of life. As this process unfolds, moments appear when the counselor needs to make an intervention: a general response to an emerging issue in the client's life experience. While these interventions may appear at seemingly random moments, what to do and when to do it are usually determined by the overarching therapeutic model or theory that the counselor espouses. Supervision courses are designed to examine the clinical judgment of future counselors and their ability to put their models into action appropriately in the therapeutic process.

From this perspective, the inclusion of R/S concepts into the counseling process would be a reaction to issues raised by the client. Sperry (2012) noted that most clients expect their counselor to integrate their spiritual values and beliefs into the therapeutic process. Weld and Eriksen (2007) noted that many Christian clients prefer that prayer be part of the counseling process. Thus, at some point in treatment, the likelihood that a client will raise R/S-related issues is highly probable. When this occurs, the counselor is put in a position to respond to this request by including this material in the process. This is one reason why clinicians from across disciplines are actively seeking to develop basic skills in this area in order to feel competent in addressing these issues when they occur (see McMinn, 2009). Does the inclusion of a spiritually based intervention into counseling at the client's request constitute a type of integration?

We think not. Application of R/S constructs on a case-by-case basis is really no foundation for any type of integration. Such a post-hoc approach does not seem to reflect the need for unifying diverse elements as outlined in our earlier definition of the term. For integration to be considered present in a therapeutic process, we believe that certain conditions need to be met. First, there needs to exist, on the part of the counselor, an a priori understanding of what R/S constructs represent psychologically and their value in the clinical process. Second, given the value of numinous constructs, the therapeutic process is designed to actively capture, include, and involve such constructs. The timing of this involvement is determined by the model of treatment the counselor is employing and the client's readiness. Finally, the deployment of numinous-based techniques and concepts is done mindfully to attain pre-determined therapeutic goals (see Pargament, 2007, p. 177). There is an intentionality to using numinous constructs in an integrative manner that is just lacking from this perspective.

Providers need to be very careful in using numinous techniques in such a post-hoc manner. There is an important ethical issue at stake here. Hathaway and Ripley (2009) have outlined a set of ethical guidelines for the conduct of a spiritually based practice for psychologists, and the Association for Spiritual, Ethical, and Religious Values in Counseling (ASERVIC, 2009) has published competencies for addressing R/S issues for counselors. These guidelines represent specific treatment approaches that one must develop *prior to* deploying them in therapy. Such training prepares therapists for managing these types of issues before they occur. Helping professionals need to avoid being caught off-guard by client requests for specific spiritual interventions that may lie outside of a therapist's experience, training, and/or value system. This would place the therapist in an awkward position of having to affirm the client request but being unable to accommodate it. Therapists need to frame their therapeutic process in a manner that exploits their competencies. It is essential that therapists have an a priori model that contextualizes the numinous within the treatment process.

Spiritual Direction

This method of integration represents a more extreme version of the bilingual approach reviewed above. What distinguishes it from bilingualism is its singular treatment focus as the clients' stronger connection to the God of their understanding. It is a recognition that whatever psychosocial conflicts are being experienced, it is the ultimate spiritual reality that is the overarching context within which any psychological efforts are placed (see van Deusen Hunsinger, 1995). This is where contemporary Pastoral Counseling finds its origins. All religious faiths are concerned about the spiritual/religious health of their members. Striving to live a fulfilling and meaningful life within the context of a religious set of values can provide challenges. Helping people manage these crises is the essential element of Spiritual Direction. At the heart of this process is what is termed *pastoral reflection*, the process of examining the role of the divine (or personal sense of ultimacy) within a person's life. This process dates back to the 3rd century within, most notably, the Catholic Church (although other faiths also employ similar techniques: see Bhikku, 2003; Leech, 1977; Sperry, 2012).

What characterizes this approach is a utilization of the techniques and rituals identified by a wisdom tradition as being associated with spiritual growth and health. While most social scientist-oriented therapists are not likely to fall into this category, there are clergy who are also licensed therapists for whom this may be an issue. Clergy therapists are usually individuals who are first trained as clergy and then later acquire their clinical skills. These individuals are well-versed in spiritual techniques and pastoral care. Thus, when spiritual issues arise in counseling, the clergy member may quickly move to address these concerns from their baseline theological training, instead of from the perspective of empirically supported interventions. Trying to use only spiritual techniques to address issues such as depression, substance abuse, marital conflict, and victimization cannot be considered an integrative approach. Re-establishing clients in their denominational homes and energizing their faith is not what we consider the integrative use of the numinous in psychotherapy. What distinguishes the spiritual direction approach from a more integrative, psychological approach is the goal of the treatment: In integrative therapy, the goal is to help individuals better manage the psychosocial demands of their life. With the Spiritual Direction approach, the treatment goal is clearly focused on improving the spiritual health of the individual. Simply put, the social science perspective is concerned with overall adaptation, while the theological approach is concerned with grace. These two goals are incompatible with one another, and therapists need to stay focused on the originally established goals of the treatment. If a client comes to receive psychotherapy, then that must be the focus of treatment. Moving into a spiritual direction modality creates a dual role for the therapist (one as counselor, the other as spiritual director), which can become confusing for the client.

Theistic Psychology

This approach is the most recent school of thought that finds its origins within the social sciences. The underlying assumption of this view is that science is not a neutral epistemology but reflects a very specific perspective with its own underlying, untested assumptions. The epistemology of science centers on a naturalistic perspective that espouses two major assumptions: a) that the world has an intrinsic orderliness to it; and b) that God has no role in this process (Slife, Reber, & Lefevor, 2012). These assumptions create a *negative bias* in science (James, 2004) that leads to an a priori rejection of anything that is not physical or replicable. Per theistic psychology, without any inclusion of God as an active participant in the ongoing unfolding of creation, one cannot claim to have developed a complete understanding of the world. As Slife et al. (2012, p. 218) noted, "theism will attend to other aspects and explanations for psychological phenomena that conventional methods may overlook, making it a potentially valuable supplement."

The inclusion of a theistic perspective brings into the scientific enterprise a new set of assumptions that will impact how science will think about and assess the processes of the physical world. What changes for science is a new and revised epistemology that accepts the presence of nonmaterial metaphysical realities that influence human behavior. Consequently, the inclusion of a theistic perspective opens the door to employing religiously based spiritual practices as potential techniques for therapeutic interventions (e.g., Nelson & Thomason, 2012). The central goal of a theistic-based treatment approach is to "Help clients experience and affirm their eternal spiritual identity and live in harmony with the Spirit of Truth" (Richards & Bergin, 1997, p.116).

We believe that the scientific study of spirituality and religiousness is an important undertaking for social scientists. We further believe that a consideration of the numinous will significantly expand our understanding of human functioning. However, the theistic approach is just not the method for accomplishing this. Theistic psychology has serious problems that preclude its use in the social sciences (see Helminiak, Hoffman, & Dodson, 2012 for a comprehensive critique). At the heart of the issue is that the theists do not really understand what the scientific model is about. As we defined in Chapter 2, science is an epistemological model, a set of rules and procedures that determine what phenomena will be studied and the procedures and rules to be used in gathering relevant information, analyzing that information, and drawing conclusions. Science is singularly concerned with understanding physical phenomena. What science does not examine are metaphysical processes. Science does not have techniques and tools for conducing metaphysical analyses. These constructs are just beyond the purview of science. Piedmont (2014) has clearly stated that one cannot employ metaphysical concepts as explanatory variables in scientific models. Yet, this is exactly what theists wish to do. An examination of metaphysical concepts such as grace, God, and God's laws are not appropriate fodder for scientific work.

The reason for this is simple: metaphysical constructs are not falsifiable. Falsification is at the heart of science. Science cannot prove anything correct; it can only prove that something is incorrect. The reasoning behind science is that once you have ruled out all the incorrect explanations, whatever is left must be true! Unfortunately, the basic assumptions of theism cannot be falsified. If one assumes that God created the universe, how does one prove that wrong? How does one show that God did not influence some historical event or outcome? If God is not a physical being, how does science study this? Science is secular (or naturalistic) by nature, and it does not include God as either a hypothetical construct or an intervening variable. The idea of God falls outside of its scope of practice. Trying to make theistic ideas equal to physical ideas is impossible and just will not work because metaphysical concepts cannot be falsified. To expand the definition of science to include theistic constructs (e.g.,

Slife et al., 2012) would change the very nature of science's epistemology, making it something else entirely.

As with bilingualism, the larger issue becomes, "whose theology do we use?" The Christian perspective is mostly behind the theistic movement. While there are some (e.g., Richards & Bergin, 1997) who believe that there should be a universal theistic approach that is inclusive and applicable to all religions, others are firmly rooted in the trinitarian Christian notion of God (e.g., James, 2004). Yet, across and within religious faith groups there exists a great variability in beliefs, and many of these beliefs may be at odds with one another (e.g., non-trinitarian Christians do not see Jesus as God; Buddhists and Confucianists may not believe in an eternal soul or an afterlife). There is no method for discerning the value of these different constructs and their validity in terms of influencing human behavior. Mindlessly considering metaphysical constructs as being part of the scientific process is naïve and simplistic, because it avoids the hard truth of having to discern the relative values of different theistic concepts. We believe that at the heart of this perspective is an agenda that seeks to find scientific proof for someone's specific religious beliefs and to prove that a particular faith is actually the one "true" faith.

Science may not be the be all-end all epistemological model, capable of explaining everything in the universe and beyond. However, it is an exceedingly powerful method for accurately discerning the nature of physical phenomena. While it cannot address metaphysical issues, it has been responsible for significantly improving the human condition. While science cannot address the putative metaphysical aspects of spirituality and religiousness, it does address the physical side of the equation: how we perceive God. As we hope to demonstrate in this volume, this work can have important implications for the social and physical sciences.

Moving Beyond Integration

The phrase "integration of theology and psychology" is frequently used in the field, not to denote that a way has been found to seamlessly tie together these two areas but to indicate that theological terms, concepts, and techniques are being used in a traditional therapeutic process. Despite the lack of any psychological ontology for spirituality or any consensual definition of the constructs, the social sciences have moved forward promulgating this integrative approach (e.g., Aten, O'Grady, & Worthington, 2012; Pargament, 2007; Richards & Bergin, 1997) without much concern for the larger epistemological and scientific issues that were noted earlier. Nonetheless, the success of these works and the growing interest in all things spiritual/religious underscore the reality that numinous constructs are being recognized as valuable aspects of individuals and that their utilization in treatment can have positive outcomes for clients. There is no doubt that the numinous is important and useful for the social sciences.

From this review of the various modes of integration, it is clear that the field has not been able to provide any true integration of psychological and theological constructs. Therapists use the numinous because: a) they are spiritually/religiously oriented individuals themselves and want to express their faith commitments in their work; or b) their training in other fields gives them a sensitivity and proclivity to address these issues either in response to client concerns or in an a priori manner because this is something more comfortable to them. As we have showed, though, there is no way to bring these two fields together; they are very different and provide competing perspectives to treatment. This is what creates potential problems for the field, not the least of which are ethical in nature. Therapists cannot practice outside of their sphere of training and competency. Because religious training is not part of the educational experience of many therapists, addressing numinous concerns can prove challenging. Without any formal training in different religious traditions (or even in one's own denominational perspective), the complexity of theological issues may quickly overwhelm the therapist's ability to effectively manage these client concerns. It is not surprising then that the most frequent perspective on the numinous for clinicians is to view it as a cultural variable. This is a simpler perspective that most clinicians are comfortable with: It is more about understanding style than content.

Even if a therapist has expertise in both pastoral care and psychotherapy, it may still be unethical or problematic for him/her to work with R/S content. The underlying issue here concerns the development of a dual relationship. It is important that therapists clearly provide potential clients with information regarding the anticipated treatment and what it entails. Such consent for treatment forms help keep the therapeutic context transparent by outlining the procedures, obligations, and expectations for success that are relevant for the work. While clients may be religiously oriented, they go to a therapist because of psychosocial issues that they want to address from a psychological perspective. As part of that process, clients may wish to include their religious beliefs and examine how they may be contributing to their emotional problems and how they may potentially be used to help overcome those issues. Through it all, clients may have the expectation that their therapist will always be operating as a therapist and not as a clergy person promoting a religious agenda. These two roles maintain different perspectives on treatment; sometimes they are conflicting perspectives.

The therapist therefore needs to wear one, and only one, hat in the counseling situation. A therapist moving back and forth between being a clinician applying psychological knowledge (i.e., empirically supported interventions) and being a spiritual director using scriptural text and denominational orthodoxy to manage the religious issues can create confusion in the client. How will the client know when the therapist is acting as a social scientist and when he or she is acting as a pastoral or spiritual director? It would be important for the client to know when the therapist is speaking as a counselor and when the therapist is speaking as a spiritual director. There needs to be an interpretive context for the client when processing the information received in treatment. Presenting theistic information under the guise of psychological treatment is unethical. Merely using the term "integrative" as a treatment label is inadequate for addressing these ethical issues.

The question then becomes, "How do we propose avoiding these issues?" Our solution is simple: Pick a discipline! We have used the term Pastoral Counselor broadly to denote those who are interested in using numinous concepts in treatment. While the term is integrative in nature, we recommend that therapists need to decide whether they want to be a pastor or a counselor. You cannot be both. Determining which professional category is appropriate can be accomplished by considering your training program's accreditation and the board that is licensing your practice. Today, many therapists are accredited by state-sponsored professional licensing boards that set and oversee their members' standards of practice. It is to these professional groups that practitioners are accountable. These boards outline the standards and expectations that practitioners need to fulfill in their work. Clergy are licensed by their denominations to practice; therefore, taking a spiritual guidance perspective is appropriate. If one is licensed as a counselor or psychologist, then it is important that the clinical work is compatible with the professional standards of that board. To do anything outside of that defined scope of practice will create serious liabilities. This issue is most pressing for those professionals who are endorsed by both a religious denomination and licensed by a secular mental health board; it is imperative that such individuals select only one professional orientation for each client. This orientation needs to be made explicit to clients at the beginning of treatment.

Thus, the purpose of this volume: to provide a comprehensive, social science-based paradigm for the understanding, development, and application of numinous constructs and to present a framework for social scientists on how to use the numinous in ways that are consistent with their training and accreditation. One does not need to become theologically informed, or to be a theist personally, or to have to develop expertise in a different discipline. We are not theologians or spiritual directors. Thus, our work, which may seem similar in some ways, is not redundant with these more religious approaches. We orient ourselves to this content matter as social scientists, which means that our goals are different from other practitioners. Our focus as therapists is not to help build and develop a client's relationship with the God of his/her understanding. Rather, it is to help the client become better able at managing the psychosocial stressor(s) in his or her life. Our orienting question about the numinous is not how religion and spirituality provide solutions to our problems; rather it is to determine what it is about us as individuals that makes religion and spirituality important to us. There is no integration needed here; the social sciences have all the necessary tools to accomplish this goal.

By keeping this psychological focus, therapists can confidently use a panoply of techniques commonly found in spiritual direction and pastoral care interventions: scripture reading, prayer, meditation, pastoral reflection. Social science practitioners can engage in these endeavors without fear of moving beyond their competency and scope of practice because the goal is to address the basic psychological issues of infinitude, meaning, and worthiness (the basic numinous motivations). Familiarity with well-developed, empirical numinous constructs allows therapists to use these techniques, regardless of their own theological sophistication, competently because they are guiding the client psychologically, not theologically. Using religious materials is not an end in itself, as it may be for a more theistically oriented practitioner. Rather, religion is a medium through which psychotherapists can access more basic psychological motivations, a subtle but important distinction. We believe our framework allows for a high level of professional precision because we are operating from only one epistemology, which clearly denotes what we are doing and what we are not doing. Despite such a unifocal perspective, our approach does allow for a wide range of techniques that theists and clergy would be comfortable in employing. When asked, "Why did you do that?" the answer is clear: Because I am addressing essential numinous motivations that focus clients on the ultimate aspects of who they are and how they understand their place in the world.

The following sections provide a cursory overview of the development of Pastoral Counseling and its evolution from a theological discipline to a social science. We will present our definition of numinous-oriented social science and contrast it with more theistic approaches. Our goal is to show what the field is and includes in its professional core as well as what the field is not and what is not part of its work. Creating such clear boundaries will help provide professional focus, scientific direction, and therapeutic clarity to those scientists working in this field.

Understanding Pastoral Counseling as a Social Science

Brief Historical Overview

Pastoral Counseling (PC) is a field that has a long past but only a short history. Because there are many good reviews of the history and development of PC (e.g., Townsend, 2009), this chapter will only provide a cursory review. Essentially, PC arose as a specific, denominationally endorsed endeavor that had the aim of helping individuals live the righteous life with regards to their theological beliefs. The goal of PC was to outline the behaviors, practices, and lifestyle patterns that were in accord with the basic tenets and principles of an individual's religious beliefs. Clergy were the focus of this endeavor, and PC was an essential component of their ministries (see Lesser, 1999). When individuals encountered problems in living or new developmental challenges (e.g., marriage, parenthood, care of elderly), clergy were present to help identify and orient people to the appropriate methods, actions, and beliefs, based on the theological teachings of the faith, that were relevant to the situation. Over time, it became clear that it is frequently difficult to delineate between religious and emotional problems. While clergy can deal with the spiritual issues, managing the more clinically salient psychological issues associated with living (e.g., mental illness, substance abuse) presented more of a challenge. With the rise of the psychotherapy movement, an opportunity appeared for clergy to avail themselves of the new insights of modern psychology to help facilitate their PC endeavors. By learning basic counseling skills, clergy would be able to manage better their spiritual work with constituents as well as being able to identify real psychological issues that would benefit by referral to secular therapists. During this time, some clergy developed more advanced therapeutic skills that would enable them to provide both the spiritual and psychological guidance their followers required.

In order to provide some oversight to clergy training and professional accountability, the American Association of Pastoral Counselors (AAPC) was founded in 1963. AAPC provided professional practice standards for clergy interested in providing Pastoral Counseling services. AAPC would help in the training of clergy in psychological knowledge and clinical skills. Originally, to be a member one had to have the official endorsement of a larger religious organization. PC was still clearly situated within the clerical domain as evidenced by the fact that the overwhelming majority of PC degrees are offered by seminaries and schools of theology (see Snodgrass, 2018 for a historical overview of the organization). From this perspective, PC is an element of applied theology. However, starting in the early to mid-1980s, a paradigm shift began to occur. Leading the way in this evolution was the PC program at Loyola University Maryland, which changed the focus of its training from clinically preparing clergy operating within a religious context to a more secular-based, professional counseling program that was directed towards licensure. Including both lay and clerical students, the PC program at Loyola became a freestanding program preparing students to work in all types of counseling situations. With accreditation provided by the Council for Accreditation of Counseling and Related Educational Programs (CACREP), and graduates receiving state licensure as Licensed Clinical Professional Counselors (LCPCs), Loyola's program moved away from its originally deep theological roots, to a more social science-oriented curriculum that attracted mostly lay students interested in including spiritual issues in the counseling process. Our graduates compete with social workers, psychologists, psychiatric nurses, and other social scientists for jobs, clients, and professional standing. By virtue of our accreditation and training, we are social scientists (see Townsend, 2009, pp. 64–65). Today there are at least four such programs that offer, through PC departments, degrees that are accredited by CACREP. PC is becoming an appealing option for emerging, non-clerical, clinical professionals. We therefore need to structure our training, formation, and clinical work in ways that conform to the expectations of the social sciences.

While a compelling idea that has attracted much interest from students and professionals, an ongoing issue that continues to plague secular approaches to PC is how to define this new professional ground. Townsend (2009) surveyed a number of pastoral counselors and asked them to define PC. The most common answer was: "I integrate theology and behavioral sciences" (p. 75). When pressed to define what this integration represents, respondents became vague and nonspecific. Townsend stated, "integration is a nontechnical and sometimes ambiguous idea for most pastoral counselors" (2009, p. 98). He asserted that among his respondents, they all could describe why integration was important, but they could not describe how they did it. The reason for this is simple: there are no paradigms for linking R/S constructs with psychological processes. For all the reasons outlined in Chapter 2, it is impossible to merge theological models with psychological processes. Instead of trying to bridge two worlds, it would be easier if PC opted to live in just one of them. The presented psychological ontology of spirituality does provide a conceptual framework for understanding, accessing, and utilizing numinous qualities in ways consistent with the scientific perspective. It can provide a useful assumptive clinical model for engaging aspects of ultimate meaning in ways that are therapeutically useful for promoting psychological change. The following section will examine what PC would look like from this perspective.

PC as a Social Science

There is no doubt that within PC, broadly defined, there are multiple professional models that involve, to varying degrees, theological-related issues and reflect the heritage of the field. Thus, it is important that our understanding of R/S constructs be consistent with the theories, practices, and methods of the social sciences. Failure to do so will create difficult ethical issues to manage as we try to explain how specific theological practices and rituals complement and support the counseling process to our secular accreditors. While the term "PC" has been well established, we are using the term in a more general manner. For us, PC represents an empirical approach to understanding and treating individuals in which the numinous represents an essential component. The numinous would be the organizing praxis for clinical work. It is critical, therefore, that we define the scope of PC practice to be clearly contained within the bounds of therapists' training and accreditation standards. Thus, we propose the following definition:

> Pastoral Counseling (i.e., addressing the numinous in psychotherapy) is the operationalization of theological and spiritual concepts within a social scientific paradigm. Our aim is to identify the ultimate qualities of personhood that uniquely define the human experience. Our clinical interventions seek to harness the intrinsic, transformative power of these constructs for promoting personal coherence, well-being, and durable change in the lives of our clients.

This definition of PC formalizes the psychological ontology outlined in the previous chapter for spirituality. Our methods are scientific, our constructs empirical with demonstrated interpretive and predictive utility. We utilize theological and spiritual concepts only to the extent to which they encourage a better understanding of our clients' essential psychological nature. Our goals are to promote improved psychosocial adaptation and wellness in those who receive our services. This approach does make some very clear distinctions from PC as understood from a theological perspective. A comparison between the two approaches is outlined in Table 3.1.

As can be seen, PC from a theologically oriented perspective involves a very different experience, contains different assumptions and expectations, and seeks a different goal than PC from a social science orientation. The theologically oriented approach is staffed by a chaplain-type professional; this could be an ordained clergy member, lay minister, or other religiously trained person. Theological competence and many times ecclesiastical endorsement are essential qualifications. Their goal is to help individuals create ultimate meaning in their lives as it pertains to a relationship with the God of their understanding.

Table 3.1 Comparison of PC from Theological and Social Science Perspectives

Functions	Pastoral Counseling Perspective	
	Theological	*Social Science*
Who	Chaplain	Therapist
Goal	Ultimate Metaphysical Good	Ultimate Psychosocial Adaptation
Method	Options Presented (judgment)	Options Explored (discernment)
Consequence	Being Right with God	Being Right with Self and Others

Exploration of essential human psychological space is done as a venue for reaching out towards metaphysical realities, where ultimate fulfillment and meaning are found. As such, the engagement with a client surrounding his/her personal struggles and conflicts entails the search for solutions that will promote a better relationship with the ultimate transcendent reality. Thus, the pool of solutions (and interventions for that matter) will always be constrained by a consideration of what is deemed theologically appropriate or suitable. Implicit to this process is a sense of judgment, where selecting non-appropriate solutions may be condemned while opting for "approved" solutions will be encouraged and supported. Counseling techniques are used to facilitate this process. The consequence of this process is to make an individual "right with God." Establishing a connection with the divine that is consistent with the practices and understandings of the faith is the immediate byproduct of the clinical work.

The social science approach is very different. Therapists are licensed clinical professionals. Whether or not they have formal theological training is irrelevant to their level of competency. Rather, it is their psychological acumen and clinical skills that are most important. Because clients seek out the therapist for assistance in managing personal struggles and problems in living, the goal of treatment is to enhance their levels of psychosocial adaptation and improve wellness. This is consistent with the ACA approved definition of counseling, which is, "a professional relationship that empowers diverse individuals, families, and groups to accomplish mental health, wellness, education, and career goals" (Kaplan, Tarvydas, & Gladding, 2014, p. 366). The therapeutic process involves helping clients in an open-ended search of potential solutions for their problems and identifying those that are synchronous with their needs. The therapist is there to assist in this discernment process and to support clients in their efforts to apply them. The consequence of this process is to enable clients to be "right with themselves and others." Responding to God-related issues may be included in this process, but it is not the focus of treatment. The exploration of the essential human space is the focus, with the primary goal being to help clients construct a more inclusive, embracing, and self-affirming sense of ultimate meaning that promotes enhanced adaptive abilities and improved well-being.

The goals of "integration" are very different for these two perspectives. The goal from the theological perspective is to develop and strengthen people's relationship with the God of their understanding. In many ways there is a very strong spiritual direction component to this approach: helping individuals better apply their faith and its teachings to the management of their personal conflicts and issues. The social science approach is primarily concerned with enabling individuals to cope better with the psychosocial issues they confront (e.g., emotional, occupational, intellectual, and spiritual; see Substance Abuse and Mental Health Services Administration, 2016). This is accomplished, in part, by helping clients to reframe their self-understandings and personal archetypes in ways that promote a more positive engagement with the different aspects of their lives. R/S material is used to facilitate a dialogue regarding clients' sense of ultimate meaning, not as the ultimate outcome of the treatment.

These two approaches contain diverging implications. From the social science perspective, the theological approach presents several potential problems. First, the practitioner frequently assumes a dual professional identity: On the one hand, he or she is the "counselor" who engages the client in discussion of the underlying issues, facilitates dialogue, and develops therapeutic rapport; on the other hand, he or she is the "pastor" who is responsible for maintaining the theological integrity of the process. It may not always be clear to clients which hat the practitioner may be wearing at any given moment or when the practitioner may switch hats in the process. Second, this approach may limit the types of treatment options presented to clients, thus limiting potential opportunities to find a workable solution to their difficulties. From the theological perspective, the social science approach presents its own set of limitations. First, the lack of any consideration of ultimate metaphysical realities makes the approach seem limited and incomplete. Without an eschatological context for grounding the dynamics of our unique inner space, any constructed sense of meaning will ultimately be flawed and not provide a durable solution for clients' problems. Second, the focus on only personal meanings and physical realities could lead to interventions that might be considered immoral or sinful. While ameliorating problems in the short run, such solutions could prove to be useless in the longer run. It is therefore important that counselors have a clear sense of what their professional identity is. Counselors need to wear only one hat in treatment sessions; clients need to know what to expect from the services they receive.

Understanding PC as a social science provides a powerful approach to engaging clients in a very personal and intimate manner and offers techniques for making substantial transformations in their lives. While availing itself of the insights and understandings gleaned from the wisdom traditions, PC works to articulate these understandings in ways that are applicable in a more universal manner. How does the pastoral counselor fit within the social sciences? What is it that pastoral counselors bring to the discipline that is new?

Who Is the Pastoral Counselor?

A clear professional identity entails knowing who one is and who one is not. Within this distinctly defined boundary, it is important to delineate those qualities one shares in common with similar professionals as well as characteristics that are unique to one's practice. As an emerging profession, this is particularly important for PC and its practitioners.

There are four qualities that define the pastoral counselor. The most fundamental quality is that they are social scientists and not theologians. This means that it is the epistemology of science that defines how information is obtained and understood. Science is concerned with physical events. This does not mean that metaphysical issues do not exist or are not important. Rather, they are outside the purview of science. Pastoral counselors focus on material aspects of R/S and their impact on the psychological status of the individual. Unlike the theologian who sees ultimate fulfillment found in one's connection to the metaphysical, pastoral counselors are concerned with the client finding personal fulfillment in the physical world. The second defining quality of pastoral counselors is that they are counselors, not spiritual directors. As such the goal of their interventions is to enable clients to resolve their problems in living and to facilitate psychosocial adaptation. The primary goal of PC is not to help clients create and maintain a better relationship with the God of their understanding. Rather, pastoral counselors work with clients to identify solutions to their problems that are personally meaningful, and they provide support as clients implement these changes in their lives. There are few preconceived notions as to what types of solutions are appropriate or relevant as well as the processes by which these solutions are applied. The hallmark of the counselor is a sensitivity to and respect for the integrity of individuals and their freedom to choose.

The third quality characteristic of pastoral counselors is that they are spiritually grounded and engage in pastoral reflection. Being spiritually grounded entails three components: First, pastoral counselors have explored their inner, essential numinous space. They have a developed sense of the dynamics, themes, and archetypes that resonate within them and carry their own ultimate meaning. Second, pastoral counselors are students of the wisdom traditions and are interested in knowing how the essential numinous dynamics are characterized and understood. How do conflicts surrounding finitude, meaning, and worthiness become expressed in living; how are they managed and resolved? Not only do the wisdom traditions maintain well-developed understandings of all these numinous qualities, they have also developed a useful language for discussing them. Pastoral counselors acquire expertise in knowing these different systems and languages. This is distinct from the bilingual approach noted earlier because the goal of this training is not to acquire theological expertise but rather to develop an awareness of how the essential numinous motivations are represented in these texts. The knowledge of these different theistic systems helps clinicians better understand and engage with their clients (which assists in developing multicultural competence), and it also provides a capacity to articulate important numinous issues in a manner easily understood by their clients. Acquiring basic competencies in various theologies provides the foundation for pastoral counselors' ability to engage in pastoral reflection, the third component of being spiritually grounded. This is the process by which pastoral counselors examine the essential numinous space of their clients to assess how these intrinsic motivations are operating, the ultimate meaning clients have created for organizing their own life journeys, and the personal archetypes they use to characterize their identity. Oft times these issues are themselves couched in the language of the wisdom traditions endorsed by the clients. Regardless of the level of religiousness of a particular client, numinous qualities are human universals. Pastoral counselors ought to have the ability to engage clients in a discussion of these numinous dynamics in a language that will make sense to the clients. The pastoral reflection process has the aim of helping clients construct a meta-perspective on themselves that contrasts their ultimate sense of being with the difficulties they are experiencing. This critical reflection process calls clients to examine how their own self-understandings and their problems may be mutually reinforcing of one another. Pastoral reflection helps to identify conflicts and inconsistencies among the numinous motivations and to promote more adaptive ways of managing these essential drives.

The fourth quality, which is uniquely characteristic of pastoral counselors, is their usage of spiritual/theological models as foundational resources both for developing psychosocial theories that expand the social sciences' understanding of intra-psychic functioning and for developing new ways of intervening that access these new qualities in ways that promote healing and growth. Pastoral counselors are ultimately focused on how individuals create meaning and definition for their lives. While this understanding can be organized and understood within the language of various wisdom traditions, it is the pastoral counselor's understanding of the psychological mechanisms by which these archetypes are expressed that form the basis for intervening. Pastoral counselors are ultimately oriented towards expanding clients' sense of meaning that will include a sense of the transcendent.

Implicit from this final quality is another defining characteristic of the pastoral counselor: the understanding of R/S variables as intrinsic motivational features of the individual and not only as cultural constructs. The social sciences most commonly understand R/S constructs as being cultural variables: dimensions that speak to the lifestyles of clients. Religious beliefs inform many aspects of functioning from dress and cuisine, to styles and patterns of interpersonal relationships, to a particular type of world view. Thus, most social science counselors use a religious assessment as a way of orienting themselves to clients and their way of being. The goal of this process is to facilitate the development of a therapeutic rapport by creating a context for treatment with which clients can feel comfortable. While there is great value to this, pastoral counselors recognize that R/S constructs are more than just a lifestyle orientation and carry with them important insights into the existential motivations of clients. R/S practices may provide a structure and direction for expressing and gratifying these underlying needs, but ultimately these needs themselves require examination and engagement as part of the treatment process. Having a psychological ontology for spirituality provides the grounding for how social science counselors can accomplish this spiritual engagement in a manner that fits comfortably within their training and scope of practice.

What Does the Pastoral Counselor Do?

From a treatment perspective, we propose that pastoral counselors orient themselves towards their clients from four axes. This multi-axial system represents the *Comprehensive Psycho-Social Clinical Intake* (CPSCI), and it serves as an initial assessment for all clients (this will be presented in more detail in Chapter 7). The following provides a general overview.

The first axis is "the presentation." Who is the person sitting in front of the therapist? Basic information about cognitive style, alertness, and relevant history (e.g., previous psychological treatments, factors that may facilitate treatment, factors that may hinder treatment). These qualities convey a basic sense of personal status and cultural perspective. The second axis is "the presenting problem." As social scientists, we know clients come seeking alleviation of their psychosocial difficulties. This axis is concerned with identifying the sources of distress and suffering, the duration of the problem, and the extent of impairment. The third axis is "the person." Here the pastoral counselor evaluates the basic personality motivations of the individual. This assessment includes an analysis of both the positive and negative qualities of clients along dimensions that are relevant to the counseling process (e.g., levels of negative affect, insight, cognitive distortion, coping ability). This information can be helpful for selecting potential treatments and anticipating possible issues in treatment.

The fourth axis is "the predicament." This concerns the larger context of meaning clients have for understanding the form and course of their lives. It also includes appreciating the personal philosophies clients use for engaging in their worlds as well as a consideration of any religious involvements they may have. It is in this aspect of understanding that pastoral counselors carry out the pastoral reflection process with their clients. What are the larger pastoral themes that appear to dominate clients' ultimate sense of self? What aspects of clients' current presenting problem can be used to access larger existential archetypes that may address essential existential aspects of meaning? There is a two-way process occurring here: understanding how clients create their ultimate meaning and identifying archetypal themes emerging from their presenting problems (e.g., suffering, guilt, worthiness, redemption) that can be used to expand clients' ultimate meaning.

The CPSCI provides a structure for understanding and dialoguing with clients. It insures that the numinous dimension is assessed for all clients. Regardless of whether a client is religious or not, or has an identified spirituality or not, everyone has a numinous dimension, and it needs to be considered as part of the Pastoral Counseling process. While R/S information is collected as part of the assessment process, it is important to stress that the goal of this is to help clients better manage their essential existential issues. Aspects of finitude, meaning, and worthiness are the key dynamics at the heart of our humanity. It is in this psychological space that pastoral counselors want to engage with their clients. The wisdom traditions provide a ready and available language for discussing these themes in ways that are familiar to clients and with which they may be very comfortable. However, pastoral counselors need to be mindful that while using the language and concepts of a particular theology, the aim of treatment is not to work out their metaphysical consequences. Rather, the goal is to use this language as a venue for promoting an enhanced level of self-understanding that promotes coherence and well-being in clients. The multi-axial structure of the CPSCI reminds pastoral counselors that the examination of the predicament needs to be grounded in the reality of clients' presenting psychosocial problems, the need for symptom relief, and the attainment of wellness.

Concluding Comments

As defined here, PC represents the social scientific effort at understanding the ultimate, unique psychological dynamics that characterize the human experience and to therapeutically engage them in treatment. While the term "Pastoral Counseling" has a long, evolving history, its usage here is to highlight the focus on numinous motivations. However, it must be made clear that while PC may share a similar interest in human nature as theology and philosophy, it distinguishes itself from these other fields by its lack of involvement with metaphysical questions and outcomes. Such concerns are better served by referrals to appropriate professionals (e.g., spiritual director, chaplain, or clergy member). To help support the ongoing evolution of PC, it is important that increasing clarity for the psychological focus be constructed and a clear scope of practice obtained. Pastoral counselors today are a broad and varied group, consisting of a wide range of helping professionals representing varying amounts of theology and psychology. Such diversity makes it difficult for pastoral counselors to define and market themselves as a unified profession. This presentation aimed to address these issues by providing maximum clarity to one conceptualization of PC. By exclusively defining PC as a social science, it becomes obvious how to interpret our constructs of interest and the goals of our interventions. Adopting this definition will enhance the professional identity of pastoral counselors by situating them within a clearly defined discipline. With an established ontological model that defines the nature of our work, the utility of PC and the value it adds to the helping professions can be unequivocally demonstrated. Ultimately, new terms will need to be used to better capture the essential work of pastoral counselors, representing this new focus on one's numinous psychology.

References

The American Heritage Dictionary (5th ed.). (2019). Boston, MA: Houghton Mifflin Harcourt. Retrieved from https://ahdictionary.com/word/search. html?q=integration

Association for Spiritual, Ethical, and Religious Values in Counseling. (2009). Competencies for addressing spiritual and religious issues in counseling. Retrieved from www.aservic.org/resources/spiritual-competencies/

Aten, J. D., O'Grady, K. A., & Worthington, E. L., Jr. (Eds.). (2012). *The psychology of religion and spirituality for clinicians: Using research in your practice.* New York, NY: Routledge.

Bandura, A. (1977). *Social learning theory.* Englewood Cliffs, NJ: Prentice-Hall.

Bandura, A., & Walters, R. H. (1963). *Social learning and personality development.* New York, NY: Holt, Rinehart and Winston.

Bhikku, T. (2003). Making a cup of tea: Some aspects of spiritual direction within a living Buddhist tradition. In N. Vest (Ed.), *Tending the holy: Spiritual direction across traditions* (pp. 3–18). New York, NY: Morehouse.

Buss, D. M. (2002). Sex, marriage, and religion: What adaptive problems do religious phenomena solve? *Psychological Inquiry, 13,* 201–203.

Cheston, S. E. (2000). A new paradigm for teaching counseling therapy and practice. *Counselor Education & Supervision, 39,* 254–269.

Edinger, E. F. (1972). *Ego and archetype: Individuation and the religious function of the psyche.* New York, NY: G. P. Putnam and Sons.

Freud, S. (1913). *Totem and taboo.* New York, NY: Random House.

Funder, D.C. (2002). Why study religion? *Psychological Inquiry, 13,* 213–214.

Hathaway, W. L., & Ripley, J. (2009). Spirituality and ethics. In J. Aten & M. Leach (Eds.). *Spirituality and the therapeutic process* (pp. 25–52). Washington, DC: American Psychological Association.

Helminiak, D. A., Hoffman, L., & Dodson, E. (2012). A critique of the "theistic psychology" movement as exemplified in Bartz's (2009) "theistic existential psychotherapy." *The Humanistic Psychologist, 40,* 179–196. doi:10.1080/08873 267.2012.672351

James, L. (2004). *Theistic psychology: The scientific knowledge of God extracted from the correspondential sense of sacred scripture.* Retrieved from www.theisticpsychology. org/books/theistic/ch1.htm#basic

Kaplan, D. M., Tarvydas, V. M., & Gladding, S. T. (2014). 20/20: A vision for the future of counseling: The new consensus definition of counseling. *Journal of Counseling and Development, 92,* 366–372. doi:10.1002/j.1556-6676.2014.00164.x

Leech, K. (1977). *Soul friend.* San Francisco, CA: Harper & Row.

Lesser, E. (1999). *The new American spirituality: A seeker's guide.* New York, NY: Random House.

McMinn, M. (2009). Ethical considerations with spiritually oriented interventions. *Professional Psychology: Research and Practice, 40*, 393–395.

Nelson, J. M., & Thomason, C. (2012). Theistic psychology: A patristic perspective. *Research in the Social Scientific Study of Religion, 23*, 95–106. https://doi.org/10.1163/9789004229549_007

Pargament, K. I. (2007). *Spiritually integrated psychotherapy: Understanding and addressing the sacred.* New York, NY: The Guilford Press.

Piedmont, R. L. (2014). Looking back and finding our way forward: An editorial call to action. *Psychology of Religion and Spirituality, 6*, 265–267. doi:10.1037/rel10000014

Post, B. & Wade, N. (2009). Religion and spirituality in psychotherapy: A practice-friendly review of research. *Journal of Clinical Psychology, 65*, 131–146.

Richards, P. S., & Bergin, A. E. (1997). *A spiritual strategy for counseling and psychotherapy.* Washington, DC: American Psychological Association.

Rose, E. M., Westefeld, J. S., & Ansley, T. N. (2001). Spiritual issues in counseling: Clients' beliefs and preferences. *Journal of Counseling Psychology, 48*, 61–71.

Slife, B. D., Reber, J. S., & Lefevor, G. T. (2012). When God truly matters: A theistic approach to psychology. *Research in the Social Scientific Study of Religion, 23*, 213–238. https://doi.org/10.1163/9789004229549_014

Sloan, R. P., Bagiella, E., & Powell, T. (2001). Without a prayer: Methodological problems, ethical challenges, and misrepresentations in the study of religion, spirituality, and medicine. In T. G. Plante & A. C. Sherman (Eds.), *Faith and health: Psychological perspectives* (pp. 339–354). New York, NY: The Guilford Press.

Snodgrass, J. L. (2018). Why pastoral counseling? *American Association of Pastoral Counselors.* Retrieved from www.aapc.org/page/WhyPastoral

Snodgrass, J. L., McCreight, D., & McFee, M. R. (2014, December 3). To whom shall I refer? *Counseling Today, 57*(6), 54–59. Retrieved from https://ct.counseling.org/2014/12/to-whom-shall-i-refer/

Sperry, L. (2012). *Spirituality in clinical practice: Theory and practice of spiritually oriented psychotherapy* (2nd ed.). New York, NY: Taylor & Francis Group.

Substance Abuse and Mental Health Services Administration. (2016). *What health providers and organizations need to know about wellness.* Rockville, MD: Author. SMA16-4951

Townsend, L. (2009). *Introduction to pastoral counseling.* Nashville, TN: Abingdon.

Van Deusen Hunsinger, D. (1995). *Theology and pastoral counseling: A new interdisciplinary approach.* Grand Rapids, MI: William B. Eerdmans Publishing Co.

Van Wicklin, J. F. (1990). Conceiving and measuring ways of being religious. *The Journal of Psychology and Christianity, 9*, 27–40.

Weld, C., & Eriksen, K. (2007). Christian clients' preferences regarding prayer as a counseling intervention. *Journal of Psychology and Theology, 35*, 328–341.

4   An Epistemological Approach to Understanding Spirituality and the Numinous

There has been a tremendous amount of research conducted on religious and spiritual constructs in the last 25 years. The weight of this work provides solid support for R/S constructs as useful predictors of a wide array of outcomes. A number of compendia have appeared that attempt to outline and distill this vast literature in ways that are manageable. Volumes appeared to review work done in health (e.g., Koenig, McCullough, & Larson, 2001; Plante & Sherman, 2001), psychiatry (Huguelet & Koenig, 2009), clinical psychotherapy (e.g., Pargament, 2007; Shafranske, 1996; Worthington, Johnson, Hook, & Aten, 2013), and general handbooks that provided a broad spectrum of results across a variety of psychological specialty areas (e.g., Paloutzian & Park, 2013; Pargament, Exline, & Jones, 2013). The last decade has also seen the appearance of two new journals published by the American Psychological Association (APA) to help facilitate the dissemination of psychologically oriented research in this area (*Psychology of Religion and Spirituality* and *Spirituality in Clinical Practice*). However, despite such a large research literature, there still are numerous scientific issues that need to be addressed (Piedmont, 2014).

At the heart of all this work is measurement. It is interesting to note that while most therapists understand numinous issues as cultural-type variables, the presence of so many instruments/scales/inventories demonstrates that the larger applied fields understand the numinous from an organismic perspective. The existence of so many scales is both a curse and a blessing for the field. Gorsuch (1984) noted that the presence of so many instruments on spiritual and religious constructs was a "boon" to the field; it indicated the great interest and diversity of ideas that characterized that field. It was also a "bane" because many of these scales have no developed validity databases nor have researchers examined how these different scales all relate to one another. Without any type of organizing validity research (i.e., examining the overlap among scales and their relative incremental validity), little could be gleaned from this work. How do researchers combine findings across studies that use different scales? Thus, having so many unconnected scales pre-empts the field's ability to develop a cumulative body of knowledge.

There are a number of issues related to the development and testing of numinous scales (see Kapuscinski & Masters, 2010), and they need to be considered when evaluating any single instrument. A sampling of these issues is considered here. It is hoped that this overview will make readers intelligent consumers of test-related information. It is important that when choosing a numinous measure, one is careful to select a scale that reaches the necessary standards of quality demanded by the field (e.g., the APA's *Standards for Educational and Psychological Testing*, 2014). The following section outlines five of the more common measurement issues and can serve as a checklist for assessing the quality of any instrument.

Methodological Issues in the Assessment of R/S Constructs

Protestant Bias in Items

Most scales in the field represent a mainline Protestant approach to spiritual and religious content. While such a Christian bias may work well in the US, where most people ascribe to such beliefs, problems in generalizability are rife. For example, the Faith Maturity Scale (Benson, Donahue, & Erickson, 1993) contains the item, "My life is committed to Jesus Christ." While a Christian would not find much difficulty in responding to this item (although this scale may be biased against certain Christian faiths, like Catholics; see Slater, Hall, & Edwards, 2001), non-Christians would certainly be put off by this question. Frequently measures of R/S constructs contain language very much infused with specific theological content. In fact, for some, not including such material may render a scale as merely a secular measure of popular or New Age spirituality; only scales that contain specific God language are considered truly spiritual in nature (see Slater et al., 2001 and their review of the Spiritual Transcendence Scale [STS]). From a cultural perspective, such types of scales have value for understanding how individuals use their faith in creating a personal worldview and in influencing specific behaviors. However, from an organismic perspective, such scales have little practical utility. Their specificity makes them relevant to only select groups of people and does little to inform our understanding of the broader psychological dynamics that are operating.

Control for Acquiescence

Acquiescence is the tendency of respondents to answer "true" or "yes" to an answer. This is a real source of error in testing (see McCrae, Herbst, & Costa, 2001). Acquiescent responding artificially inflates scores on a scale, which in turn negatively impacts the reliability and validity of the scale. Ideally, scores indicate the extent to which some quality is present in a person. For acquiescent responders, their tendency to agree with items will give them higher scores when they may not have higher amounts of the quality. This is error in measurement and leads to errors in score interpretation. However, the problem with acquiescence is that it also impacts other features of the scale, most notably the ability of scale scores to correlate with other measures. In correlation, it is the extreme scores that drive the correlation coefficient (see Cohen & Cohen, 1983). When scores from a scale with acquiescence effects are entered into correlational-based analyses (e.g., factor analysis, correlation, regression, etc.), these high scores, which are confounded with a response style, will be creating artificial associations with other measures (these associations can be greatly inflated if all the scales being correlated contain this acquiescence effect).

To control for this bias, scale developers will differentially reflect the direction of items. In other words, to score high on the scale an individual will need to agree with positive items and disagree with negative items. Having both positively and negatively phrased items will place an acquiescing respondent's score in the middle of the distribution of scores rather than at the top. Moving such a person's score to the middle of the distribution protects one from making an incorrect interpretation (average scale scores carry with them no real prediction of standing on the quality, because such scores are usually interpreted as reflecting an individual who is merely "average, like most people") and statistically keeps these scores from creating spurious associations. Unfortunately, a large number of R/S measures do not control for acquiescent responding, which creates a serious problem for the quality of research done in this area. Any measure that does not control for acquiescence just should not be used.

Lack of Normative Data

One of the values of a psychological test is that it can provide users with a sense of how strong or weak some trait is within a person. This is done through the use of normative comparisons. Normative comparisons occur when an individual's scores on some scale is compared to the range and frequency of such scores in a representative sampling of the population. This is an important function of scales, because it helps individuals get a real sense of how much or how little of some quality they actually possess. The ability to examine magnitude is provided by the use of standardized measures of relative standing (e.g., z-scores or T-scores), which makes identifying truly high or low scores easy and interpretations straightforward.

Understanding magnitude is an important, and common, issue in assessment. From our own experiences in teaching assessment with graduate counseling students, often when they receive their scores on various instruments they are frequently surprised by the magnitude of their scores. Many do not appreciate or recognize just how "high" or "low" they truly are on a dimension. But understanding this feature of a test score is important and carries significant interpretive implications. Two people may score above the mean on some trait, but if one has a *T*-score of 55 and the other a *T*-score of 75 (*T*-scores have a mean of 50 and *SD* of 10), there are important clinical differences here that go beyond the fact that both score above average.

Another value of normative data is that they also allow one to control for relevant covariates that influence scores on the scale. For example, in terms of numinous constructs, it is not uncommon to find that women score higher than men or that younger individuals score lower than older people (e.g., the ASPIRES; see Piedmont, 2010; Brown, Chen, Gehlert, & Piedmont, 2013). Why these variables influence scores is not clearly known and may be a function of any number of factors (e.g., age or gender-linked response styles, bias in the item content). Nonetheless, the influence of these demographic characteristics on scores needs to be controlled for, in order to allow one to make useful comparisons across these categories. Norming data within these categories serves to remove their influence on scores and provides standardized metrics that can be readily compared across groups.

Because the use of normative data allows for the use of standardized scores, one is able to quickly determine whether or not one's current sample is representative of the population on the quality being assessed. For example, when using *T*-scores it is known that the average range is represented by values between 45 and 55. This is the center of the distribution. So, when collecting group data, as in a research study, having a mean score on a scale in this range provides confidence to the researcher that he or she has a representative sample. Scores higher, or lower, indicate that the sample is skewed. This has important implications for the internal validity of a study and for deriving inferences from the data.

While normative data seem to be an essential feature of any test, unfortunately the great majority of scales in this field do not have any normative data. To be clear, normative data are represented by the collection of scores from a large number of individuals who have been selected in some effort to be representative of the population. The essential feature of a norms group is that it attempts to document what the distribution of scores looks like in its most general form. While most development studies for numinous scales provide descriptive information on their samples, almost none provide any population data. Thus, most research relies simply on raw scores that are not adjusted for any potential confounds. This introduces a great amount of uncertainty in the data, because it is not clear why any observed relationships were obtained. Was it because the distribution of scores is skewed and thus relationships are being driven by these non-normal distributions, or was it because scores are being influenced by other confounding factors (e.g., gender, age)? Not knowing how representative the sample is on the measured construct, it will be unclear how generalizable the obtained findings will be. We have always stressed to our students that when conducting research, one uses at least one instrument that is normed so that some determination of sample representativeness can be made.

The Reliance on Self-Report Scores

The workhorse in numinous assessment has been the closed-ended, self-report questionnaire. There is an almost universal reliance on this single type of measurement (Gorsuch, 1984; Kapuscinski & Masters, 2010; Leach & Sato, 2013). Hill and Pargament (2003) have noted this and called for the development of other types of assessment strategies, such as the use of reaction times to stimuli. The use of multiple methods and measures is a sound research technique; it reduces the influence of method-specific error from contaminating the data. Two closed-ended questionnaires will correlate with each other to some degree because both share a common source of assessment. Whatever unique response styles are involved in such questionnaires, because these styles are common across instruments they will naturally correlate to some degree. Different types of measures (questionnaire vs. reaction time) each having different styles will help suppress such spurious associations. While such a recommendation is important, we assert that it does not go far enough. The problem with using different types of scale formats misses the larger issue that all these scales are self-report in nature. Thus, whatever unique styles of responding a person has will be infused in all the instruments he or she completes, regardless of their format. This is what is referred to as *common method error*: the reliance on a single source of information. As Campbell and Fiske (1959) have clearly demonstrated, overlapping method variance artificially inflates inter-scale associations. Thus, avoiding this confound entails more than just using different types of scales but employing different sources of information.

John and Soto (2007) noted that the field has identified four major sources for collecting psychological information. The first domain is denoted as *L* and refers to *life outcome data*. This is information that can be gleaned from an individual's life history and reflects the various events that occurred, such as whether or not someone is married, number of children, how many times they visited a physician, etc. The second domain is *O* and refers to *observer-rated data*. These can be ratings of specific (e.g., teacher's ratings of a student's class behavior) to broad level assessments (e.g., overall assessment of life satisfaction). The essential defining element here is that some knowledgeable informant or judge is providing information about the person of interest. The third domain is *T* and refers to *test data*. Test data is the acquisition of information from standardized instruments, usually psychophysical machines (e.g., EEGs, EKGs, EDRs, etc.) that capture specific information that the subject may not be aware of how he/she generates this information or how the information will be interpreted. For example, we may all know what an EKG measures and what the produced lines look like. However, what we do not know is what these lines are really representing and how they are interpreted. Finally, there is the *S* domain, which refers to *self-reports*. Self-report scales are the most commonly used scales because of their ease of administration and because they collect information directly from the person we wish to assess.

The value of these four information domains is that they capture different aspects of the individual from various perspectives. The very best assessment models are those that acquire data across all four sources. What is important to realize is that when it comes to acquiring information from others, there are no foolproof methods; there is no gold standard. Each of the four information domains has its own strengths and weaknesses. Yet, these sources of error will not correlate across the domains; thus, the weaknesses of any one approach can be compensated for by the strengths of another domain. For example, the strength of a self-report is that you are gathering information directly from the person. If anyone should know what is going on inside this person's mind, it should be him or her. However, there are also limitations to self-reports, such as the person not knowing the answers to the questions being asked, or the person may try to manipulate or manage the impression he or she gives on the scale, all of which represent sources of measurement error. When one relies on only self-report scores, then whatever distorting factors are operating in one scale, they are operating in all the scales. These common response biases will indeed correlate with each other when scores across the different scales are inter-related.

That is where the other sources come in. An observer rating has its own perspective on a person. Observers do see things about an individual that the individual may not be aware of, such as reputation. One's reputation is really in the hands of those around us. Others see us in ways very different from how we see ourselves, and this information has value in its own right. Mount, Barrick, and Strauss (1994) demonstrated that observer ratings were significant predictors of outcomes over and above self-reports. However, observer ratings do have their own sources of error as well, such as halo effects. What is important though, is that the sources of error contained in self-reports are not the same dynamics as those found in observer ratings. Observers do not have the same motivations to manipulate or influence how they present the target as the target does him or herself. Thus, when scores between a self-report and observer rating are correlated, one can be confident that this association is not artificially inflated by correlated error; the errors are different across the two methods! Therefore, *cross-observer convergence* becomes a very powerful method for demonstrating the substantive validity of a scale. Showing that what people say about themselves agrees with what knowledgeable others say about them has three important implications. First, it demonstrates that the scales are indeed capturing important qualities of the people, because consistent information is being gathered from different sources. Second, such convergence shows that the psychological qualities being assessed are important because they find expression in behaviors that can be perceived by others. Finally, that the specific behaviors represented in the measure can be recognized by different people as all reflecting the same underlying dispositions indicates that there is a consensual understanding of the qualities being assessed that is shared by all the raters. Everyone recognizes these behaviors as representing the underlying disposition because this underlying trait is one with social value. As McCrae (1994; p. 151) noted, "self-reports and observer ratings together may tell us more about personality than either could separately."

Establishing the *cross-observer validity* (COV) of numinous measures should be a high priority in the field. Unfortunately, very few scales in the field have a validated observer form (see the ASPIRES; Piedmont, 2010). Given that spirituality is a very personal, and private, aspect of the individual, COV becomes a vital tool for demonstrating that it does not represent a solipsistic aspect of functioning. If everyone has a different, and unique, definition of spirituality, then it would be impossible to define consensually what the construct is and how it is expressed, if it is expressed at all. Measurement in this scenario is essentially useless. If spirituality is just something that is "in the mind of the beholder," then it really does not carry sufficient value to be studied normatively. As such, COV is a critically important aspect of a numinous scale to be demonstrated. It shows that spirituality is more than a simple, self-reflective quality. Rather, it represents something that does find expression behaviorally, and these behaviors are recognized by the larger social world as being spiritual in nature. We believe that any scale that does not demonstrate COV has limited value for the field (see Piedmont, Ciarrocchi, Dy-Liacco, & Williams, 2009).

Univariate Paradigm

In their content analysis of articles published in *Psychology of Religion and Spirituality* (*PRS*), Leach and Sato (2013) noted that over 70% of the published studies relied on simple correlational designs. Such univariate methods characterize the field. Frequently, studies simply correlate their R/S measure with some outcome as evidence of convergent validity. Rarely is there any control for relevant covariates or potential mediators. Also lacking is any comparison of the relative value of different R/S measures (Piedmont, 2014). Such a methodologically limited approach unnecessarily restricts any assessment of the overall value and utility of numinous constructs for the larger field. While correlational designs are useful in exploratory studies for identifying potentially meaningful relationships between a scale and various outcomes, they are limited techniques for understanding the substantive value of constructs. Zero-order correlations are not sufficient for assessing the empirical *robustness* and *distinctiveness* of a construct.

Robustness refers to the interpretive and predictive range of convenience of a construct. For example, it is well known that measures of religious involvement are correlated with a variety of physical health-related outcomes (see Masters & Hooker, 2013 for a review of research in this area). People rating higher on religiousness are likely to experience less physical problems and, when ill, appear to recover faster than those who are less religious. Oft times such associations are interpreted causally, which is a common mistake made with such data. It would be unwise, and perhaps unethical, for practitioners to urge their clients and patients to become more involved in religious activities as a way to improve health (Sloan, Bagiella, & Powell, 2001). Correlation does not equal causality!

What are needed are multivariate models that attempt to examine the value of scales by controlling for other, related constructs that may also be relevant. While R/S constructs are associated with a wide variety of outcomes, they are influenced by a number of other qualities, such as age, gender, religious denomination, and sexual orientation. In order to understand the intrinsic predictiveness of these constructs, analyses must control for these other influential variables. Doing so will prevent spuriously high associations from being substantively interpreted.

Related to this idea is the need to demonstrate the distinctiveness of R/S constructs. Critics of the field have often raised the issue that R/S constructs are merely the *religification* of already existing psychological constructs (e.g., van Wicklin, 1990; see also Funder, 2002). In other words, the question is whether numinous constructs carry any unique predictiveness or are merely relabeled psychological variables? In a field that has so many scales, it seems essential that some determination of uniqueness be provided. For example, the Spiritual Well-Being Scale (Paloutzian & Ellison, 1982) is designed to measure both existential and religious well-being. The field has been assessing well-being for decades and much is known about the construct. So, does spiritual well-being tell us anything new about this dimension that is not already contained in existing scales? Does the term *spiritual* denote something new about well-being, or is it just a way of repackaging the concept in a numinous-friendly manner?

Sechrest (1963) introduced the term *incremental validity* to address this very issue. His argument was that for any new scale to be deemed useful to the field, it was important that there was some demonstration that the new index incorporated personological information not contained in already existing scales. This is a rigorous method for determining the value of any new construct. This is especially true in the psychology of religion and spirituality, where many scales implicitly take the organismic perspective and presuppose motivational aspects to their measured constructs. As relatively new constructs in the field, it is imperative to demonstrate that these scales reflect new aspects of the individual not contained by current measures. Failing to do this will result in what Funder (2002) referred to as the increasing Balkanization of the field. Relabeling constructs does not promote the scientific agenda.

Research has looked to explain the many identified relationships between religiousness and physical and mental health outcomes. The goal of these studies was to identify other psychological processes that may be driving these associations. For example, George, Ellison, and Larson (2002) reviewed the literature on this topic and identified several different psychological processes as potential mediators of the R/S-health linkage (e.g., health-related practices, social support, psychosocial resources like self-esteem and one's sense of meaning, and personal coherence). What these data suggest is that the R/S variables are serving as stand-ins or as representatives of other constructs, which are themselves the causal agents that impact the outcome of interest. Being religiously oriented may be linked with positive health benefits, but this relationship exists not because religious involvement offers something unique in predicting health. Rather, it is the fact that being in a religious context provides people with access to social support (i.e., they can reach out to others when in need or can rely on others to provide the support they require), and it is this social support that is the key predictor of better health and emotional well-being (e.g., Salsman, Brown, Brechting, & Carlson, 2005). The implication of these findings is that being part of any organization (e.g., bowling league, sewing club) can provide individuals with this type of benefit; there is nothing special about being a member of a religious group. While the empirical evidence on mediation is mixed, to the extent that these mediators are real undermines the independent value of R/S constructs to make a unique contribution to explaining and predicting behavior. It is imperative that R/S scales are developed that are not overlapping with other psychological constructs and have their own exclusive, predictive aspects. As such, methods need to be used to address this key issue.

We have long advocated that one approach to tackling this problem is by examining the incremental validity of numinous constructs within the framework of the Five Factor Model (FFM) of personality (Piedmont & Wilkins, 2013). As we noted in Chapter 2, the FFM is an empirically robust, universal model of personality traits traditionally involved in the social sciences. These five dimensions have been found to be genetically heritable, cross-culturally valid, and predictively useful (Haslam,

Whelan, & Bastian, 2009; Kern & Friedman, 2008; McCrae, 2010). Piedmont (1999a, 2001) has argued that the FFM can be used to develop numinous scales that are independent of the model and thus capture non-redundant personological qualities. Piedmont (1999a) has asserted that the numinous should be considered a sixth dimension of personality. Research, both domestic and international, is consistently providing empirical support for this assertion (e.g., Joshanloo, 2012; Piedmont et al., 2009; Rican & Janosova, 2010; Tomcsányi et al., 2012).

One way to demonstrate the incremental validity is through use of hierarchical multiple regression analyses. More on this is presented below, so only a brief overview is given here. From this approach, one selects a relevant variable as the outcome (e.g., well-being, mental health, etc.). Then, on Step 1 of the regression, measures of the FFM personality domains are entered as a block. In this manner, all the variance related to the outcome that has any overlap with established personality constructs is assigned to this step. On Step 2, the numinous constructs can be added (usually employing a forward entry method in order to control for any overlap among these constructs). An examination of the partial F-test for this step will readily determine whether or not the numinous constructs add any significant, additional explained variance in the criterion construct. We believe that any numinous construct that does not evidence incremental validity over the FFM should not be considered a valid measure of spirituality. Factor analysis can be another way of examining the independence of numinous constructs (e.g., MacDonald, 2000; Piedmont, Mapa, & Williams, 2006).

It is clear that basic, univariate methods for examining numinous constructs are insufficient for assessing their key empirical qualities. Multivariate tests and related analytic analyses are required, which can control for the presence of other relevant co-variates and potential mediators. Zero-order correlations between a numinous variable and some outcome is insufficient for advancing research in this area. Researchers need to develop and test multi-variable models, employing measures capturing different information sources, which embed numinous constructs as essential elements of larger psychosocial processes, and their unique predictiveness determined. Ultimately, the field will need to test the causal role of our constructs, the epitome of distinctiveness. While numinous constructs relate to a wide array of outcomes, it has yet to be determined whether the numinous has a causal impact on these variables or is merely an outcome from them.

Conclusions Regarding Methodological Issues

It is clear that there are several, serious issues that the field needs to grapple with in order to advance our understanding of the numinous and determining its ultimate value for the field. While the five issues overviewed above speak mostly to technical and methodological issues related to the assessment of numinous constructs, at the heart of these issues is the need for some conceptual model for understanding R/S constructs from which a coherent, empirically rigorous set of standards can be created for both developing and evaluating numinous constructs. Chapter 2's presentation of a psychological ontology for the numinous was a first step in this process. It outlined the evolutionary development of the numinous as a species-specific psychological characteristic. This model makes some basic assumptions about the nature and function of the numinous in the larger mental life of the person. However, a more specific, methodological framework is necessary that would be able to guide the development of numinous constructs in a manner that will rigorously establish their empirical pedigree. The following section will outline such an empirical model that can be used for developing, extending, and testing a numinous construct.

A Methodology for Developing Numinous Constructs

Assumptions of the Model

The purpose of this section is to provide a detailed overview of a methodology for developing R/S constructs and for evaluating their empirical value. While the scientific method is a very flexible process for finding data-driven answers to questions, one needs to consider what follows to be one such approach to creating robust and distinctive numinous constructs; there may be other approaches. However, we believe there is much to commend this model, and we hope that it will provide a point of departure for future discussions on methodological strategies in the field. There are three issues that need to be discussed: a) the perspective, b) the assumptions, and c) the specific procedures. All of these issues are related and emerge from both the ontology presented earlier and the psychological perspective held by these authors.

The perspective being taken here is that R/S constructs represent organismic aspects of the individual. In other words, spirituality is understood to be an intrinsic, psychological construct that motivates behavior. There is something inside of us which makes concepts such as the sacred, God, religion, and metaphysical ultimacy important stimuli for us. We seek out these topics because we are hardwired to address these types of issues (Newberg, D'Aquili, & Rause, 2001). These underlying qualities, which are genetically embedded in our genome (Waller, Kojetin, Bouchard, Lykken, & Tellegen, 1994), are what we refer to as the numinous. The numinous is that domain of psychological qualities that motivate us to seek out a transcendent sense of self; to find ultimate meaning within our own totality of being that confers on us a sense of personal durability to our strivings, ultimate purpose and meaning to our lives, and an overarching source of acceptance and worthiness for our place in life. The numinous is what makes religion and spirituality important to us.

Given this perspective, there are nine basic assumptions that characterize this approach, which are listed in Table 4.1. The **first assumption** is that the numinous is a *psychological* quality that drives, directs, and selects behaviors that center on a personal sense of ultimacy. The numinous is an intrinsic, species-defining quality of our nature, and as such it is genetically based and expressed within the physicality of our being. The numinous is not a product of, nor defined by, any specific religion, philosophy, or worldview; it is something that precedes these things. The **second assumption** about the numinous is that it represents a *universal* quality, something that all people share in common to some degree. It is an individual-differences variable, in that people vary on how much of this quality they possess. This variability does have implications for behavior. While involvement in religious and spiritual activities may be one manner in which these motivations most commonly are expressed, as a universal drive it can and does find expression in other types of outcomes as well (e.g., Piedmont, Wilkins, & Hollwitz, 2013).

The **third assumption** is that as a universal, motivational quality, the numinous is a material construct that can be measured and tested *empirically*. The numinous represents a variety of trait-like constructs that operate in ways similar to traditionally defined personality characteristics. As such, scores on numinous constructs should be stable over time, especially in adulthood. They should evidence consistency across situations, in that those high in standing on these variables will seek to find gratification for these motives across many different life settings.

Table 4.1 List of Assumptions Underlying an FFM-based Model for Developing Numinous Constructs

Empirical Assumptions
1   The numinous represents a class of psychological motivations.
2   The numinous is a universal psychological quality.
3   Numinous constructs can be empirically developed and tested.
4   Numinous qualities represent non-redundant aspects of personality as defined by the FFM.
5   The numinous dimension is sufficiently broad as to contain multiple facets.
6   To be valid, a numinous scale must evidence incremental predictive validity over the FFM.
7   Numinous constructs evidence significant cross-observer convergence.
8   Numinous constructs generalize well across religious and cultural groups.
9   Numinous constructs have a causal impact on the quality of one's mental life.

The numinous represents an intrinsic, adaptive quality of the individual that allows people to create and establish a lifestyle that supports and encourages personal growth and self-enhancement. Like other personality dimensions, the numinous creates a trajectory through time for an individual. The numinous is a genotypic characteristic whose expression can and does morph over time, but it always represents a consistent quality that can be identified as such by oneself and others. In short, how numinous constructs express themselves does vary over the lifespan. A teenager scoring high on the numinous dimension may become very much involved in his/her religion, go on retreats, and engage in simple acts of kindness. As an adult, this same individual may be invested in different kinds of activities, such as types of volunteer work, deployment of financial assets, and vocational choices. While the behaviors associated with the numinous are different at different life stages, the underlying motivation is the same.

These assumptions portray the numinous as a personality-type construct. As such, it should be subsumable under other, larger models of personality. Ultimately, the numinous needs to be folded into comprehensive models of personality. We believe that as a trait-like dimension, numinous qualities can be understood within and defined by the FFM. While the elements of this model were presented above, the FFM can serve as an important empirical scaffolding for developing and understanding numinous constructs (e.g., Saroglou, 2010). It is a comprehensive taxonomy of personality traits (John, 1990). As such, one can understand the FFM as a map that can be useful for understanding the personological qualities of any construct (Ozer & Benet-Martínez, 2006). Maps are important to cartographers because they situate all land and sea locations within an organized set of parameters: the grid of lines that are known as latitude and longitude. These lines enable location of any place on the globe and help one to determine if some observed land mass represents a new discovery or a known place. Latitude and longitude can tell one how close two points are to one another, can demonstrate whether the points share come common climatic features, or can locate one specifically in space on the globe.

The FFM can also serve a similar role for evaluating personality constructs. The FFM provides a set of independent dimensions that contain very specific personological content. By correlating one's construct with these domains, one can discern the kinds of motivations being reflected in the measure. For example, a scale that correlates with Neuroticism (N) will reflect aspects of emotional distress and correlate with outcomes associated with poor emotional adaptation, stress experience, and coping ability. The pattern of correlates a scale has with the FFM domains represents what we refer to as its *personological fingerprint*: the unique combination of traits reflected in a test score. The extent that two scales share similar patterns of correlation with the FFM domains would indicate the extent to which the two scales are redundant. Different patterns of correlation would indicate that the two scales are unrelated to each other. Thus, the FFM provides an empirically useful venue for identifying uniqueness and redundancy across measures. In reviewing a special issue on Religion and Spirituality in the *Journal of Personality*, McCrae (1999; p. 1213) urged, "researchers owe readers the courtesy of mentioning how their variables relate (if at all) to the FFM . . . we will make more rapid progress in understanding such topics . . . if we build on what is already known."

Piedmont (1999b) identified four ways that the FFM could be useful for understanding R/S constructs. One recommendation was to correlate such scales with the FFM domains to "illuminate the larger motivations and anticipated outcomes of [such] scales" (p. 344). Collating data from three different studies (involving over 1,250 individuals), Piedmont presented correlations between the FFM domains and 12 spirituality and religiousness scales. Many associations were found, although most were less than $r = .35$. All five personality factors correlated with these scales. Saroglou (2010) conducted a meta-analysis linking the FFM domains to measures of religiousness and spirituality in more than 70 studies. This international sample of more than 21,000 subjects noted the role of A and C as central correlates of spiritual and religious constructs. The linkage with Agreeableness (A) and Conscientiousness (C) helps to put into context many observed findings using religious constructs, such as the effects of religiousness on physical and mental health (outcomes also linked to C) and relations with social support and prosocial behavior (correlates of A).

There are two points of interest from these findings. The first is that to the extent numinous constructs do have any substantive association with the FFM, then interpretations of the personological implications of the R/S constructs are possible. While the findings indicate small to no associations between the two sets of constructs, there are some reliable patterns identified by Saroglou (2010). It is clear that Openness (O), A, and C are the major correlates with R/S constructs. Specifically, spiritual-related variables associate with O and C while religiousness associates primarily with A and C. The linkage with C supports those who see a very strong commonality between religiousness and spirituality (e.g., Hill et al., 2000 who believe both constructs share a focus on the search for the sacred). Both types of constructs include aspects of personal discipline and dutifulness. Whether one is committed to performing religious rituals or is dutiful in maintaining a strong, satisfying relationship with a transcendent reality, being conscientious is important for maintaining long-term commitments to these endeavors. For spirituality, the correlation with O makes sense, because one needs to have a willingness to encounter and explore new and different experiences (e.g., cognitive, sensory, emotional). A lack of a defensive and rigid personal style is essential for this intimate encounter with the divine. For religiousness,

A seems a key ingredient behind efforts at social justice, volunteerism, and acting in a caring and supportive role towards others.

Based on these associations, it is also clear why R/S constructs correlate with positive health outcomes (high levels of C lead to better compliance with medical regimens and better levels of personal control over impulses) and higher levels of social support (individuals scoring high on A enjoy being with others and acting in ways that support and encourage them). The association with O explains why many spirituality measures correlate with scores on psychological maturity measures and with attitudes associated with sexuality and abortion. Further, the common association with C also helps to explain why the two types of scales are so strongly interrelated (Piedmont et al., 2009 indicated that the latent, disattenuated correlation between religiousness and spirituality was 0.71).

The second point of interest is based on an observation made by Piedmont (1999b) concerning these data: The magnitude of associations between the R/S constructs and the FFM domains were small to modest. Intercorrelations rarely passed the $r = 0.30$ level. Given that these data were all based on self-report scores, the question arose whether these observed associations were substantive or merely the product of correlated method error. Piedmont (1999a) demonstrated that when observer ratings of spirituality were correlated to self-rated scores on the FFM, most significant correlations were lost, and the magnitude of those remaining significant associations did not exceed $r = 0.20$. From these data Piedmont concluded,

> Scores on these religious scales contain much information about people that is not accounted for by the FFM . . . it is ultimately what religious constructs do *not* have in common with the FFM that is of the most importance.
>
> (1999b, p. 346; emphasis in original)

What is exciting about these findings is that numinous constructs appear to capture aspects of personality not yet catalogued by the FFM. This leads to our **fourth assumption** about numinous variables: They are not redundant with currently existing personality dimensions. Numinous constructs are not the "religification" (van Wicklin, 1990) of already existing constructs but rather represent a new domain of functioning. As a consequence, the numinous holds the potential to expand our understanding of personality into new dimensions, such as identifying novel intervention techniques that target these qualities or developing more comprehensive predictive models that enhance our understanding of important psychological processes such as pathology and resilience. As a map of the personality landscape, the FFM outlines clearly those traits that it has identified as well as demarcating areas of characterological functioning that are not contained by the model. It is in this space that the FFM provides the greatest support for developing numinous constructs: It can guide one in identifying personological content that is non-redundant with established personality constructs.

This leads to the **fifth assumption** of this approach: that the numinous does not represent a single variable or construct. Rather, it represents a *domain* of variables: The Numinous dimension contains a similar level of conceptual breadth as the other FFM dimensions. This is demonstrated by the identification of multiple, correlated facet scales that all cohere on a single dimension (hence the numinous is a unidimensional, multifaceted construct) but that each element contains sufficient unique, reliable, variance to warrant individual interpretation. Thus, like the other FFM domains, the Numinous is a single, multifaceted dimension that organizes diverse constructs related to qualities like transcendence, mysticism, faith maturity, and spiritual well-being, among others, under a single umbrella concept. What ties them together is that all of these primary constructs are independent of the FFM and are correlated with each other.

Our **sixth assumption** is that this domain should evidence incremental predictive validity over the FFM. Incremental validity is a critical quality to attach to numinous-based scale scores (Sechrest, 1963). Too often scale developers suffice it to show simple convergent validity for their measures (rarely is discriminant validity examined). A much more rigorous approach is needed that can determine the unique interpretive and predictive value of potential numinous constructs, and the incremental validity paradigm is an excellent method to employ. There are two reasons for this. The first is that the value of a numinous scale's scores is being tied to its ability to predict an outcome over already existing, meaningful constructs. While any number of scales can be created to capture a specific quality, like spirituality, not all of them will evidence an ability to tell us something new about an outcome. Doing so removes questions of redundancy about numinous constructs; they are not merely the repackaging of already existing scales but instead represent something new and different (e.g., van Wicklin, 1990).

The second value to the approach we are advocating here is that this test of incremental validity is being performed using the dimensions of the FFM as the standard. Each domain is well defined both conceptually and empirically, and scores from these scales have been shown to link up with a wide array of outcomes. Thus, the FFM is a substantive standard against which individual-difference constructs can be compared and evaluated. The FFM provides a high bar to pass for demonstrating incremental validity because these domains have been shown to contain the majority of variance held by constructs traditionally thought to be personality (see Piedmont, 1998 for an overview of the comprehensiveness of the FFM). If a numinous construct can add significant predictive variance over and above the explanatory power of the FFM, then we believe that a strong case has been made for the uniqueness and value of the construct.

The **seventh assumption** is that the numinous does not represent a solipsistic quality of the individual that does not express itself in behavior; rather it captures consensually validated qualities that do find expression in behavior. Thus, scores on numinous scales should evidence convergence across the four different information sources (e.g., life outcome, observer rating, self-report, and test data). Specifically, scores on self-report measures of the numinous should converge significantly with scores obtained in numinous measures generated by knowledgeable observers. Cross-observer validity should be an essential element of the validation process for numinous constructs. Such evidence demonstrates that spirituality is not "in the eye of the beholder," but instead represents an important psychological quality that impacts behavior in ways that can be detected by others and identified by them as representing a spiritual dynamic. As noted earlier in this chapter, there are very few validated observer-rated versions of numinous constructs.

A validated observer-rating scale is one that has its own normative sample for evaluating individual scores. It is clear that the distribution of observer ratings is different from the distribution of scores obtained from self-reports (see, for example, the NEO PI-3: McCrae & Costa, 2010; or the ASPIRES: Piedmont, 2010). These differences need to be considered when evaluating the magnitude of individual scores. Normative data based on an observer form can also control for the influence of extraneous variables, such as age and gender. When raw scores are then transformed into T-scores based on these normative values, one then has an index that can be directly compared to T-scores obtained from self-report scores. This is a very important quality of a normed test: The use of standardized scores removes the influence of extraneous factors associated with the magnitudes of scores in a particular distribution and allows for a more accurate determination of a score's relative standing, which is an index that can be directly compared to other measures of relative standing.

For example, the ASPIRES is currently the only numinous measure that has a validated observer-rating form. For self-reports, the mean total score on Spiritual Transcendence (ST) for adults over age 45 is 79.74. For observer ratings, the comparable mean score is 89.57. How is this difference to be interpreted? Do raters see older individuals as being more spiritual than they see themselves? Are ratings biased, in that observers overestimate ST in people? The bottom line here is that these two numbers cannot be directly compared because they emerge from different distributions, both having different mean levels. Why do these different mean levels exist, what causes them? It could be due to any number of factors, the most likely of which may relate to the response styles of the different rater types: Items are interpreted differently from the perspective of a self-evaluation than from the perspective of an observation.

It is clear that these two sets of ratings come from different distributions having different parameters. The only way to directly compare these two scores is to put them into a common metric that moves beyond simple mean level and considers the relative standing of these scores. This is the value of an index such as the *T*-score, which transforms raw scores into a distribution where the mean is 50 and the standard deviation is 10. By applying the *T*-score, scores from distributions having different means and standard deviations can be put into a common metric that will allow for direct comparisons. So for the ASPIRES, the *T*-scores for the two mean values presented above are the same, i.e., $T = 50$; both values are located at the mean of their respective distributions. Therefore, a simple reliance on raw scores will introduce a source of distortion into the interpretation of a scale score.

Once scores are standardized on their respective normative distributions, correlating scores across the two information sources ought to evidence a significant level of association [for the ASPIRES total score on ST, cross-observer convergence was found to be quite strong in the normative groups: $r(979) = .57$, $p < .001$]. Levels of cross-observer convergence should be similar to levels found with the FFM domains, which range typically from .30 to .48 (Funder, Kolar, & Blackman, 1995; McCrae & Costa, 1987; Piedmont, 1994). What cross-observer validity indicates is that numinous motivations can and do find expression in behavior in ways that are easily and accurately identified by others as being numinous in nature.

The **eighth assumption** works clearly out of the previous ones: As a robust, universal, psychological motivation, it is a quality that all individuals possess regardless of their faith status (e.g., believer versus non-believer), denominational commitment (e.g., Christian, Jewish, Muslim, Hindu, etc.), and cultural perspective (e.g., collectivistic versus individualistic). While some may score high on the numinous and others low, scores should carry significant personological implications for all people. Support for this assumption can only be found by cross-cultural, cross-faith, and cross-belief research, endeavors not frequently encountered in the psychology of religion and spirituality research literature. More of this type of work is necessary to advance the field (Piedmont, 2014).

Perhaps the most controversial aspect of this assumption is that the numinous would be a relevant descriptive and predictive construct for use with non-believers (e.g., atheists and agnostics). For some in the field, it is a commonly held belief that spirituality is only for religiously committed people because spirituality evolves out of religion (e.g., Hill et al., 2000; Pargament, 1999). After all, why assess one's commitment to an eternal, transcendent Being or reality if one does not believe in such a figure or place? The point to keep in mind is that the numinous does not reflect any type of theological orientation or basis. Rather, it is a psychological construct that exists independent of any religious values or social commitments. We argue that religion evolves out of our numinous motivations. It is also myopic to think that atheists do not have any spirituality. As Comte-Sponville (2007) has asserted, "Atheists have as much spirit as everyone else; why would they be less interested in spiritual life?" (p. xi). For the atheist, spirituality becomes a commitment to and fidelity towards larger values that give meaning and depth to life, values so important that one would be willing to die for them. As Comte-Sponville (2007, p.18) has noted, "the sacred is that which would justify, if necessary, the sacrifice of our lives . . . but [this] requires neither a particular metaphysics nor, properly speaking, a religious faith!"

What this assumption implies is that the numinous is a central part of our species' psychological make-up, which provides a broad perspective on our lives and our understanding of the role of our personhood in the process of living. It calls us to commit to higher goals and values that, ideally, enable us to fully engage in life with passion, purpose, and a sense of worthiness. This capacity, as we have argued earlier, represents those psychological qualities that define us as human beings. The Numinous dimension is not just a given in all people's lives, it is the core sense of being that comes, to one degree or another, to help define the course and texture of the lives we are leading. While all religions employ spirituality to some extent, spirituality itself is not religious in nature. This distinction is important because it highlights the psychological nature of the numinous and its importance in the mental life of people. Therefore, while mean level scores on measures of the numinous may vary between believers and non-believers, the reliability and validity of numinous scores should be evident in both groups. This is what makes the study of spirituality psychological in nature.

Finally, the **ninth assumption** relates to the ultimate causal role that numinous variables play in the mental life of people. While it is clear that numinous constructs relate to a wide array of outcomes, the question that has yet to be answered is "why these associations?" There are two possible answers. The first answer, which is the least interesting, is that numinous variables represent outcomes from existing psychological processes. For example, an individual may have a negative view of God, believing that God is punishing him or her, or that God is just not interested in the person. Such a negative view may be a consequence of the person being depressed. A depressed person has a rather dark view of the world: The glass is just "half empty," and the person feels worthless and of little value. The negative image of God fits cleanly into this larger dysphoric pattern. After receiving treatment for the depression, the person feels better emotionally, has a more upbeat attitude towards life, and also now sees God in a more positive manner. Obviously, how the person perceived God was a consequence of their internal emotional state. As an outcome, numinous variables hold little value or interest for psychology. After all, the field is ultimately interested in identifying the antecedents of behavior. Outcomes may be catalogued but only for their potential diagnostic value.

The second answer to this question is of greater importance: Numinous variables serve as *inputs* into our psychological system. In this scenario, our spirituality and religiousness are core motivations that directly impact our engagement with the world. Our relationship to a transcendent reality has direct consequences for our psychological status. In a longitudinal study examining psychotherapeutic outcome among outpatient clients, Cheston, Piedmont, Eanes, and Lavin (2003) demonstrated that changes in clients' images of God were associated with counselor ratings of symptom experience. While very few studies attempt to address this most important of questions, extant data do support the assumption that the quality of one's relationship to God has important implications for symptom experience. As Cheston et al. (2003, p. 104) concluded,

> Disturbances in one's relationship with God may exacerbate or even create psychological symptoms. Thus, interventions that do not focus on an individual's spirituality may not be as successful in alleviating the symptoms as treatment that focuses on spirituality because the client will not be reconciled with the higher power object that is central to the presenting problems.

Addressing the issue of causality has major consequences for the role and value of the numinous in the psychological area. This is a question that will need to be addressed, the sooner the better, and studies will need to employ more sophisticated methodologies (e.g., experimental designs, structural equation modeling, cross-lagged panel designs, longitudinal studies) in order to provide the needed answers. Nonetheless, what data that are available (see also Dy-Liacco, Kennedy, Parker, & Piedmont, 2005) seem to support this assumption and raise some exciting possibilities about research with numinous constructs. It may be possible to identify a whole new class of interventions that are designed to access numinous processes. The negative aspects of the numinous may be implicated in the development of various pathologies (e.g., personality disorders: Piedmont et al., 2007). Perhaps there may exist new types of disorders that center around dysfunctions in the numinous motivations, like moral injury or body-image/eating disorders. If the numinous plays a role as a cause in healthy and unhealthy functioning, then the potential exists for a radical change in the current social science paradigm: Current theories and understandings will need to be significantly re-aligned in order to accommodate this new insight into human functioning. This new understanding will need to appreciate the unique role of the numinous as an exclusively human trait.

Conclusions about the Assumptions of the Numinous Model

The nine assumptions presented here play a pivotal role in the development of processes for creating, testing, and employing numinous constructs in diverse applications. The numinous is seen in a very unique role within our mental lives, and special techniques and procedures will need to be employed that are capable of testing these assumptions. It will require more sophisticated theories and analytic techniques to accomplish this goal. The "nuts and bolts" of such an empirical process will be presented in more detail below, but suffice it for now to note that the assumptions presented here can serve as a checklist for evaluating the utility of any numinous measure. Showing independence from the FFM domains is a first place to start in this examination process. Failure to demonstrate uniqueness coupled with an inability to demonstrate incremental validity would be sufficient evidence, we believe, to dismiss a scale from further consideration. These assumptions should also serve as a blueprint to follow for anyone interested in developing a new numinous measure. Every effort would need to be made to ensure that a scale meets the outcomes expected from the various assumptions. Complying with the expectations of this model will result in a scale that has empirically demonstrated its conceptual and empirical value, providing confidence that the instrument has its unique role to play within larger assessment models (Chapter 5 will present an actual example of the empirical process in detail).

Methodologies for Testing Numinous Constructs

The purpose of this section is to provide specific methodological procedures and techniques to be used in the construction, development, and validation of numinous constructs. In following these guidelines, there are two issues to keep in mind. First, at the heart of this process is the FFM. These basic personality dimensions are empirically clear domains of functioning that carry with them very specific interpretations. Becoming familiar with this model and its structure is essential for developing relevant numinous items. Ideally, one would want to construct items that do not overlap with any of the content of these five factors. This is difficult to do, especially at the initial item development phase. When thinking about numinous functioning, it is easy to merge into FFM content. Aspects of coping (N, Extraversion (E), and C domains), happiness and well-being (N, E and A domains), commitment (O and C domains), receptiveness to new experiences (O domain), compassion (A domain), to name a few, all have very strong presences on the FFM domains. The more familiar one is with the FFM, the more precision can be directed towards the generation of novel item content.

The second issue concerns the focus of the scale development process. The most common approach for scale development takes a convergent validity approach. Specifically, a set of items that are related to specific outcome criteria is developed. The approach being advocated here is more of a discriminant approach: The search is for identifying items that do not correlate with the FFM domains. The goal is to identify items that are orthogonal to these domains. Only in this manner can a separate dimension be identified and validated. As noted above, it is not what the numinous has in common with the FFM that is important; rather, it is what is unique from these factors that is relevant.

Item Development Phase

Constructing appropriate items for a numinous scale can be a difficult process. Finding an item that represents something distinct from the FFM can be challenging. Items that include content relating to physical or mental well-being will find associations with the domains of N and E (e.g., "My relation with God contributes to my sense of well-being" from the Spiritual Well-Being Questionnaire [Moberg, 1984]). Further complicating item development are cultural beliefs and values that surround our understandings of spiritual and religious people. Culturally, we view spiritual individuals as peaceful, caring, compassionate, loving, faithful people, who are open to the "Spirit" and have extra-ordinary experiences where they feel a connection to a transcendent reality. Images of Mother Teresa, Gandhi, and Martin Luther King, all generate such images of humility, gentleness, inclusiveness, and commitments to faith. While these descriptions may drive current mores surrounding the "spiritual" person, a direct examination of major biblical figures shows the limitations of these images. Consider, for example, the prophet Jonah and his trenchant bigotry surrounding the Ninevites; or King David and his fateful actions around Bathsheba; or Moses, who presented God's laws that contained such harsh punishments for those who disbelieved. Despite lower presumed levels of O, A, and C, these characters certainly are spiritual because they had a direct relationship with God. The Bible grounds spirituality within the reality of our own humanity, imperfect as it is. As we have argued, there is no FFM profile for the spiritual/religious person because our spirituality is grounded in its own personality dimension, which is orthogonal to the FFM domains (Piedmont & Wilkins, 2013).

Thus, care needs to be exercised in framing items that minimize reliance on FFM-based descriptors and maximize content based on definitions of the new construct. To accomplish this requires that some measure of the FFM be included in this process. The first step is to give the list of potential new items along with a measure of the FFM and validated measure(s) of the numinous. We suggest that the *Assessment of Spirituality and Religious Sentiments* (ASPIRES) scale be used (Piedmont, 2010). This measure, whose development is presented in detail in Chapter 5, has met all the above nine assumptions of the presented model.

In beginning this research process, it is imperative that an adequate number of subjects be acquired. The usual rule of thumb is 10 subjects for each variable. However, this rule can become onerous, especially when dozens of proto-items have been written for the new numinous scale. Nonetheless, large samples are required, and we recommend that between 300 to 500 subjects be recruited for this initial stage of development. With the availability of research sites such as MTurk, it can be quite easy to obtain such large samples; however, be aware of potential biases inherent to these subject communities (see Burnham, Le, & Piedmont, 2018).

Creating useful items can be a challenge, and it may take several iterations of item development, testing, and further modification before an adequate set of items is obtained. In our experience, item writing is very difficult because the numinous, when defined as something not contained as part of the FFM, can be very hard to articulate. There are very few single adjectives that define the numinous (e.g., Ashton, Lee, & Goldberg, 2004), suggesting that the concept of the numinous is complex and requires more than just single terms to capture it. Even constructing simple sentences can be a challenging endeavor to economically capture such complex issues. Perhaps an even more difficult challenge is to identify negatively phrased items (i.e., declarative statements that reflect the negative pole of the numinous). While there is much clarity as to what spirituality is, there is much less agreement on what it is not. Positive items are easy to write (e.g., "I am a spiritual person," or "I believe that this life is only one stage in a larger, eternal process"), but what exactly does the negative side look like? In our experiences over the years, creating negatively reflected items has been a great challenge for us. This is because it is hard to define what a lack of spirituality is. We have examined different concepts here (e.g., materialism or secularism), but with little success (one successful negatively phrased item is "When I die, everything that I am will cease to exist": Piedmont, 2017). In order to create a balanced scale, the most efficient process for doing so was to create a positively oriented item and then add the word "not" to it (e.g., "Spirituality is **not** a central part of my life": Piedmont, 2010). While not an ideal way to create negative items, given what is currently known about the numinous, this may be the best method currently available.

Once the data have been collected, a planned series of analyses is conducted. First, the pattern of correlations for each item with the FFM domains and the numinous scales needs to be examined. Ideally, the numinous items should evidence moderate to strong correlations with the numinous scales and nonsignificant associations (e.g., $r < 0.30$) with the FFM domains. Practically, often one finds items that have some correlation with the FFM domains while having larger associations with the numinous scale. At this stage of development, our strategy has been to select items whose level of association with the numinous criterion is *at least* two orders of magnitude higher than the item's highest association with an FFM domain. For example, a potential item correlates at $r = 0.65$ with overall Spiritual Transcendence from the ASPIRES. To be useful, that item should not correlate any higher than $r = 0.45$ with any of the FFM domains. While a correlation of $r = 0.45$ seems rather robust, at this stage of development this is not problematic, although it is a good rule to delete any item that correlates greater than $r = 0.45$ with the FFM regardless of how strong its association is with the numinous criterion.

After this first empirical pass is completed, one is left with a subset of potentially good items. The next step will be to submit these remaining items, along with scores for the FFM domains and the numinous criterion scale(s), to a joint principal components analysis. In this analysis, the FFM domain scores are being used as marker scales for defining variance associated with the traditional personality domains, and the numinous criterion scale will define the numinous variance. Three factors should be extracted from this analysis. Typically, what is found is that one factor will contain loadings for all of the FFM domains, another factor will contain loadings for all of the numinous criterion scales, and the final factor will contain all other extraneous variance, items that seem to be independent of both personality and the numinous. Any item whose highest loading is on the "personality" factor needs to be deleted from further consideration. This analysis is then repeated with the reduced item set and their factors re-examined. This process should continue until there are no items having their primary loading on the factor containing the FFM scales. Please note that items whose primary loadings are on either the numinous or independent factors must be larger *by at least* an order of magnitude of two or more than any secondary loading on the personality factor. Items loading on the factor not containing the personality or numinous scales are kept at this stage because they may represent aspects of the numinous not yet defined and may contribute to broadening the empirical definition of the numinous.

Once a subset of items that do not have a primary loading on the personality factor has been identified, these items alone are then subjected to their own principal components analysis and their internal structure identified. It is suggested that oblique rotations be used at this step (either orthogonal or oblique can be used in the above series of analyses) because all of these items should be correlated with one another, and such overlap needs to be appreciated during the analysis. The goal of these analyses will be twofold: to obtain simple structure and to arrive at an interpretable set of factors (keep in mind that one needs *at least* three items to define a useful factor). This process may require several analyses where items that do not load on any factor or inadequate factors are deleted and the process repeated. The end result of this process will be the identification of several, correlated factors. Items load primarily on one factor, and all items load significantly (i.e., > .30) on one factor.

We label this final factor structure as the *initial normative factor structure* (INFS) for the new scale. We will come back to this result later in the validation process.

Item Analysis and Scale Evaluation

With a final factor structure obtained, some evaluation of the basic psychometric properties of the identified subscales needs to be undertaken. Much of this information is available through many computer-based data analysis programs (e.g., SPSS) through their "reliability analysis" routines. We will be assuming a familiarity with SPSS, although other programs are equally valid but may produce different output (see Tabachnick & Fidell, 2007).

Items from each of the factors obtained from the previous analysis are identified and are used to define the different scales. In running the "RELIABILITY" routine in SPSS, select item statistics and item-total correlations for output. For each of the new scales, several issues need to be examined. First, the means and standard deviations for each item are examined. Assuming that a standard, 5-point Likert-type scale is being employed, ideally, means should center around 3 for each item. Scores higher or lower than this indicate that most people are either agreeing or disagreeing with the item. While this does not automatically indicate an item should be deleted, further examination of the item would be necessary. Standard deviations should be around 1.0. Again, items with larger or smaller values would need further examination (e.g., IRT analyses that examine difficulty and discrimination levels would be a place to start).

The next issue to examine is inter-item correlations. Perhaps the most commonly used measure of reliability is Cronbach's alpha, an easy to compute and use measure of internal consistency. Alpha is based on the amount of overlapping variance among the scale items. The more they are related, the higher alpha will be. The question that arises is how high should alpha be? While alpha over .60 is considered to be acceptable for a scale, usually the higher the value, the more sound the scale is perceived to be. However, care needs to be taken here. On the one hand, we develop a scale to assess some construct at a particular level of functioning. Psychological constructs, like personality dimensions, have a wide range of applicability. For example, we can measure the trait of anxiety. But at what level? We can measure it as a normal range construct or as an abnormal range construct, depending on the reason for which we wish to use the instrument. Do we want to diagnose a psychiatric disorder or are we interested in examining how anxiety influences normal behavior? The answer to this question determines the level of analysis or the range of predictive convenience for the scale. Normal anxiety may be assessed by an item such as, "At times I feel nervous and apprehensive," while an abnormal item may be, "I frequently suffer from panic attacks." The intensity levels are very different, but the underlying construct is the same: anxiety.

The goal in scale development is to assess the construct of interest as completely as possible in its intended range. The multiple items on a scale are designed to provide a diversity of questions that capture the construct at the level of interest from different perspectives. We gain confidence in the scale items as representing a similar level of analysis when they all overlap with each other. Thus, a high alpha reflects internal coherence among scores across the different items. However, as alpha gets higher, the items overlap so much that we may need to question whether we have adequately sampled the construct at our level of interest. We may have too narrow an assessment. Having a lower alpha may indicate that the items are providing the level of coverage that is necessary to provide a total score that has useful predictive and interpretative value (see John & Soto, 2007 for an overview of these issues). Values of alpha .70 or above are ideal, although when the alpha goes over .90 questions about the range of predictiveness will arise. Such a high value may indicate too much redundancy among the items.

One way to examine this is to consider the inter-item correlations. It is ideal when the average inter-item correlation is between 0.20 and 0.40. Items that correlate higher than 0.60 may start becoming overly redundant with each other, leading to scores with a more limited range of predictive utility. Values below .10 indicate a more complex scale that may contain multiple dimensions. Such items should be discarded. When inter-item correlations are in the ideal range, in general, this will lead to an overall acceptable alpha for the scale (e.g., alpha > .70). Longer scales can tolerate lower overall inter-item associations while shorter scales may require higher redundancy to reach adequate levels.

Item analysis provides another view of the item content and their utility as part of a larger scale. Items with very skewed response distributions are candidates for removal as are pairs of items that seem overly redundant with each other. Finally, items that do not seem relevant to the overall score are also potential candidates for removal. Note, when items are deleted from the scale on the basis of these analyses, then another principal components analysis will need to be conducted to examine the final factor structure of the items. This new, reduced item set now becomes the working version of the scale, and the results of its principal components analysis serve as the official INFS.

Demonstrating Structural Validity

Once the final structure of the new numinous measure has been determined, it is time to collect a second sample to evaluate the robustness and generalizability of the factor structure and to provide evidence of convergent and discriminant validity. Again, a large, representative sample is required for obtaining the best results (e.g., $N > 300$). The value of this second sample is to replicate the factor structure in a new sample. Given that correlational techniques, like factor analysis, capitalize on sample-specific features, it is important to demonstrate that the obtained structure generalizes across samples. Thus, a confirmatory approach is taken.

It has been long argued that *structural equation modeling* (SEM) is not an ideal method for determining factor replicability for personality type data, both in general (e.g., Church & Burke, 1994) and with FFM and numinous data in particular (e.g., McCrae, Zonderman, Costa, Bond, & Paunonen, 1996; Piedmont, Werdel, & Fernando, 2009). One reason for the diminished value of SEM is that it requires factor loadings to be either 0 or 1 and that, ideally, all the variance is explained. While the FFM personality and spirituality domains are understood to be orthogonal, there are complex relationships among various elements of these dimensions that makes recovery of this simple structure difficult to obtain. Frequently, the amount of explained variance in these models ranges from 50% to 75% of the total variance, too little to enable the model chi-squares to reach non-significance. As such, McCrae et al. (1996) proposed a more efficacious process for determining comparability across factor structures. Their method involved performing a conventional principal components analysis of an obtained data set and then submitting the results to an orthogonal Procrustes rotation (Schönemann, 1966) that used normative factor loadings as the target matrix. Then, congruence coefficients (Gorsuch, 1983) would be calculated to assess the degree of fit. Significance levels can be readily obtained through Monte Carlo analyses that fit random data to the normative values. This process has been shown to be useful for assessing factor comparability across personality instruments and samples (see Hopwood & Donnellan, 2010 for a comparison of EFA versus CFA techniques).

To accomplish this, the item data from this second sample are submitted to a principal components analysis and the appropriate number of factors extracted using an oblique rotation (the number of factors to extract is the same as that identified in the original study). Then, the pattern loadings from this analysis are included in another analysis that will compare these loadings to the values identified in the INFS. Appendix A at the end of this chapter provides the SPSS syntax for conducting this analysis. What this analysis does is to recognize that the results of a factor analysis are always influenced by the specific statistical features of the sample upon which it is based. Thus, when one uses the scale a second time and then factor analyzes it, the second set of pattern loadings will not exactly match the original loadings. There are two reasons for this. First, the scale may operate differently in the new sample: The different loadings indicate that respondents understand the items in a psychologically different manner than the original subjects. Second, sample specific error may be influencing the scores. The Procrustean analysis examines this issue directly.

What the Procrustean analysis does is take the pattern loadings from the second sample and then rotates those data using the original normative pattern loadings as the target: How close can the data from the second sample get to the loadings of the original data? The results of the Procrustean analysis will be a new set of factor loadings (not pattern loadings because this analysis uses an orthogonal rotation). Congruence coefficients (CCs) will determine the extent to which these new loadings are identical, in terms of both pattern and magnitude, to the normative loadings.

Because CCs do not have a known sampling distribution, the significance of each value is evaluated by determining whether the observed CCs exceed the critical values that are obtained from a Monte Carlo sampling distribution of randomly generated congruence coefficients. This sampling distribution is obtained by creating 10,000 random factor loading matrices and fitting each to the normative factor structure. CCs from each analysis are kept and comprise the null distribution of CCs. The 95th, 99th, and 99.9th percentiles in this distribution serve as the critical values for the .05, .01, and .001 alpha levels. See McCrae et al. (1996) for an overview and example of this process using FFM data. These null distributions are essential for establishing confidence that the convergence of two sets of loadings is not due to sampling error. Appendix B contains the SPSS syntax for running this analysis. CCs are calculated for each factor and item (and an overall fit CC is also obtained). The CCs will determine: a) the extent to which the items on the scale have the same loadings across each factor as found with the normative data; b) the extent to which the item loadings within each factor are the same as the normative data; and, c) the extent to which the overall set of loadings obtained in the second sample are identical to those found with the normative group. Demonstrating that the factor CCs and the overall CC are significant provides support for the generalizability of the factor structure across samples. Keep in mind that rarely will the CCs for all the items be significant; there are always issues with regard to how different subjects interpret various items. Nonetheless, finding that at least 60% of the items show significant convergence will give support to the hypothesis that individual items are being understood in a similar manner across samples.

We believe that these procedures should be followed anytime the numinous scale is given to a new sample and structural invariance is tested. This is especially true when applying the scale with individuals from different cultures or different religious backgrounds. This method is excellent for discerning whether any observed discrepancies in factor loadings are due to sample-specific issues or are a consequence of the scale being differentially understood by the new sample (see Piedmont et al., 2009).

Demonstrating Convergent and Discriminant Validity

The next step in the development process is to demonstrate how the new numinous measure relates to constructs it should be related to and how it is independent of constructs to which it should not be related. Correlating scale scores with appropriate outcome criteria (e.g., other numinous measures, FFM domain scores, relevant outcomes such as emotional maturity, interpersonal style, well-being, etc.) is the first step in this process. Convergent validity is most simply demonstrated by correlating the new scale with other, relevant numinous measures. Ideally, these other measures would be ones already shown to have independence from the FFM, but given the current paucity of such scales the use of available instruments would need to suffice. Then, correlating the new instrument with important psychosocial outcomes is next. Such outcomes would include behavioral indices of involvement in spiritual/religious activities, such as prayer frequency and church attendance. Depending on the hypothesized nomological net established for this new scale, correlations with various psychosocial criteria would outline the breadth of association the scale has. These psychosocial constructs should contain a wide range of activities, such as emotional well-being, psychological maturity, and interpersonal styles. Larger constructs would include broader domains of functioning such as vocational interests, socio-political attitudes, and lifestyle preferences (e.g., spending and savings habits, hobbies, health risks, and occupational choices). Finding associations with these types of operant outcomes demonstrates the larger psychological value for numinous constructs and affirms their underlying motivational status. Finally, linking the numinous construct to important outcomes like response to psychotherapy, health consequences, and coping abilities outlines the potential, practical, clinical implications of the numinous construct.

Discriminant validity is frequently the overlooked aspect of numinous construct development. This is a consequence of current thinking about R/S constructs, where energy is given to defining what the construct is, but little is said about what it is not. This second aspect helps to clearly define, both theoretically and empirically, the limits and boundaries of the construct. The numinous, while a key organizing construct of our mental world, does not explain everything about who we are. It is important that the concept of the numinous is not "over packed" with expectations. The first step in demonstrating discriminant validity is to correlate the new scale with measures of the FFM. Ideally, the extent of overlap should be limited, reflecting only small associations that are a consequence of mostly common method variance (i.e., the reliance on just self-report data). Correlations between the numinous measure and the FFM domains should be less than $r = 0.30$. Such small correlations would prove the success of the initial development process, where items were selected on the basis of their orthogonality with the FFM domains. Larger correlations with the FFM would indicate a lack of precision in the numinous items as they are merging non-relevant material into their content. This may require a re-examination of the items and further redaction.

Incremental Validity

This is a very important step in supporting the validity of the new numinous measure. At a minimum, this process involves showing that the new scale evidences significant predictive power over the FFM domains. Such findings reinforce both the independence of the numinous construct from the FFM dimensions as well as the practical empirical value of the scale: its ability to improve predictive fit for any model.

Accomplishing incremental validity is very straightforward and requires the use of hierarchical multiple regression methods. The most basic regression model to be tested involves the use of some psychosocial measure (e.g., well-being, emotional maturity, attitudes, etc.) as the outcome criterion. The analysis would proceed with step 1 of the regression entering in all the FFM scales simultaneously. What this does is to associate all personality-related variance in the outcome with the FFM scales. Once this variance is partialed out of the outcome, what is left is only that uniquely reliable variance in the criterion that has nothing to do with personality, as defined by the FFM. Then on step 2, the numinous scale(s) is entered into the equation. If there are multiple facet scales, then they should be entered using the forward entry option. This is done to manage the natural overlap that exists among the subscales.

Multiple regression's value is that it allows one to link together several predictors to a single outcome to determine their unique predictive ability, controlling for any redundancy among the predictors. While such partialing out of redundant variance gives regression its value, it can lead to some paradoxical outcomes. Specifically, while a set of variables may explain a significant amount of variance in the outcome, an examination of each predictor's contribution to the outcome variance may indicate that none of the predictors makes a significant individual contribution. The overall model R^2 may be significant, but the beta weights attached to each predictor may be nonsignificant. This unintuitive result occurs because the overlapping variance among the predictors (which is correlated to the criterion) is not being assigned to any specific predictor in the equation. This is a problem for using multiple numinous scales, which should all have some level of overlap. In order to avoid this paradox from occurring, the numinous scales should be entered using a forward entry process. In this manner, the scale with the largest overlapping variance is entered first and thus will be assigned all the overlapping variance with the other numinous subscales. On each successive entry point, the incoming predictor will only contribute predictive variance that is unique to itself. In this manner, the useful overlapping variance is assigned to one of the predictors, thus enabling one to determine which of the numinous aspects is relevant to predicting the outcome.

Once the numinous scales have been entered into the regression, a partial *F*-test is conducted to determine whether the predictive variance uniquely associated with these scales is significant. A significant effect indicates that the numinous scales bring added value to understanding the criterion. The ultimate goal of this type of research is to demonstrate that any predictive psychological model will need to include measures of the numinous if it wishes to be considered comprehensive.

The incremental validity approach can also be extended to determine whether some new measure of the numinous is itself useful and not merely redundant with already existing numinous constructs. The value of the approach to testing the numinous being advocated here is that it is essentially an open-ended model. There are no a priori assumptions about how many different facet scales there are within the Numinous domain; this is left as a completely empirical issue. Aspects to the numinous are added as the data determine. Gorsuch (1984) asserted that before developing a new R/S measure, one would need to argue for the value of the new construct and what it adds to the field over and above already existing measures. Such an argument can be made here by extending the incremental validity paradigm to include these other, baseline numinous measures. So, on step 1 of the regression equation the FFM domains are added, as usual. On step 2, currently existing measures are entered, using simultaneous entry. Then, on step 3, the new numinous construct is entered (using forward entry if there are multiple subscales) and the partial *F*-test conducted. If the new scale does not add significant explained variance, then it ought not be considered a useful construct (Piedmont, 2017 provides an example of this process). In this manner, the field can move systematically forward in developing new constructs by empirically examining their predictive value over existing scales. We believe that incremental validity analyses ought to be considered an indispensable aspect of the scale development process for every numinous scale. Again, we believe that any numinous scale that fails to evidence incremental validity over personality ought not be considered a valid measure of the numinous.

Causal Influence

While SEM may not be an ideal method for examining the structural validity and invariance of a numinous scale, the technique does have value for determining the causal role of the scale, viz. some outcome. As noted earlier in this chapter, ultimately numinous scales need to demonstrate their value as actual causal indicators of important psychosocial processes. Without such documentation, then numinous constructs become of limited interest and value to the social sciences. The value that SEM offers is the ability to test the causal assumptions underlying multivariable models as well as the capacity to examine the relative value of multiple models (see Kline, 2005 for an introduction to SEM). SEM does not require any special type of data (e.g., experimental, multi-group, etc.) to conduct its analyses. It relies on simple correlational data. While the dictum, "correlation does not mean causality" is certainly a truism, it must be remembered that SEM is not evaluating causality based on the simple intercorrelation matrix of variables. Rather, the focus in SEM is testing the underlying assumptions of causality that are implied in the tested model. Further, it enables the comparison of multiple, competing models to determine which of them better "fits" with the data.

Figure 4.1 presents three different models that postulate different causal roles for the numinous and overviews the types of comparison models one should use in evaluating numinous constructs. The hypothetical outcome here is a measure of mental health. Model A is the preferred model because both personality and the numinous constructs are seen as independent causal predictors of the outcome, mental health. The assumption of this model is that the personality variable (in reality, the personality construct would consist of five, independent constructs, one for each of the FFM domains. Only one is used here for simplicity and didactic purposes) is independent of the numinous variable. Model B represents both mental health and the numinous as outcomes (characteristic adaptations) of personality. Finally, Model C views the numinous as a consequence of both personality and mental health, with the numinous in this instance representing an outcome of psychological functioning. A typical SEM analysis would examine all three models and determine which one fitted the data the best (see Piedmont et al., 2009 for an example of this type of analysis).

In assessing fit for each model, there are a few issues that need to be considered. First, in SEM there is only one statistic: the overall chi square. This statistic examines how well the model as a whole explains the data. As noted above, when using personality-type data the underlying assumptions to this statistic are too restrictive, resulting in significant chi square values (a significant chi square means that the model does not fit the data well). As a consequence, researchers have developed a menu of indices to examine fit from different perspectives (the difference between a statistic and an index is that the former has a known null distribution while the latter does not). Because fit indices do not have known null distributions, it is not always clear what level of fit is represented by the index's value. Thus, one needs to consider multiple fit indices to better understand the adequacy of a particular model.

For our purposes, there are several measures that should be examined (Kline, 2005 provides descriptions of all the indices covered here). The first is the ratio of chi square divided by the degrees of freedom for the

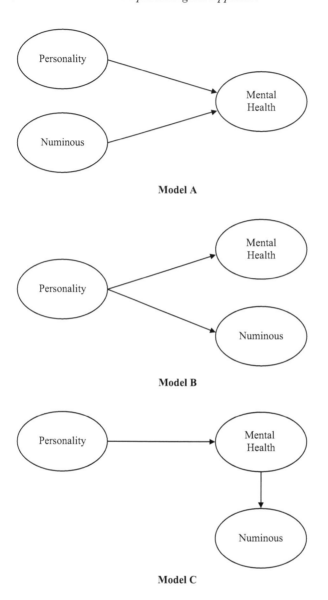

Model A

Model B

Model C

Figure 4.1 SEM Models Testing the Causal Influence of a Numinous Scale on
       Mental Health

model. This is a crude index of model fit given the number of postu-
lated constructs in the model. Values of 3.5 or less indicate a parsimonious
model that fits the data reasonably well. The next two indices, Root Mean
Square Error of Approximation (RMSEA) and Standardized Root
Mean Square Residual (SRMSR), are very strong measures of fit because

they both examine the residuals (i.e., the differences between the anticipated correlations based on the model and the actual level of association found in the data). They are both directly based on observed data. While there is no strict cut-off for determining levels of fit, values less than .10 are considered adequate fit; values .08 and below are good fit; values of .05 and below denote excellent fit. A final measure of fit is the Akaike Information Criterion (AIC). The AIC is a predictive fit index that assesses how well the model would fit in hypothetical replication samples of similar size. An important component to this index is the complexity of the model. Models with many observed variables are more likely to explain more of the variance in the data than models with fewer observables. Yet, the latter is to be preferred given science's preference for parsimony. The AIC yields smaller values for parsimonious models and larger values for more complex ones. While the actual value of AIC is of little concern, its importance is found when compared to AIC values obtained in other, non-nested models. This ability to compare AIC values across models makes it indispensable for work with the numinous. In comparing the fit of the different models presented in Figure 4.1, it is hoped that Model A will generate the *lowest* AIC value. This would indicate that Model A is the best fitting and most parsimonious of the three tested. These indices should serve as the core set of fit metrics in addition to any others that may be preferred by the researcher.

Very little research has been done examining the causal impact of the numinous (see Piedmont et al., 2009), yet it is an indispensable program of research that needs to be done. Causal analysis will determine the ultimate value of the numinous and identify those constructs that are potentially useful as well as those with less value. Testing causal models may also help to identify conditions that promote or inhibit the influence of numinous constructs on behavior. It can also provide another window into the redundancy issue as well as identifying potential mediators and moderators.

Conclusions

This chapter overviewed some of the key methodological issues involved in research with numinous constructs. A new model of the numinous is presented along with its basic assumptions. The aim of the model is to test the ultimate psychological value of numinous constructs. It is hoped that the methodology outlined here will help to focus and direct future research in this area by providing professionals with a key set of techniques that are designed to answer important questions about our constructs. Ultimately, the use of the FFM as an organizing empirical scaffold for developing and testing numinous variables will eventually create a set of empirically sustainable definitions of the numinous that can serve as an organizing praxis for understanding what is, and is not, numinous. This would lead to the development of a truly cumulative research database, which in turn would provide greater focus, consensus, and precision to both clinical and research endeavors.

Chapter 5 will overview the development and validation of the ASPIRES, a truly singular measure of the numinous in the field today. This review will highlight the application of the research methods outlined here and provide examples of the form and interpretation of the kinds of data that emerge from the analyses overviewed here.

References

American Psychological Association. (2014). *Standards for educational and psychological testing*. Washington, DC: Author.

Ashton, M. C., Lee, K., & Goldberg, L. R. (2004). A hierarchical analysis of 1,710 English personality-descriptive adjectives. *Journal of Personality and Social Psychology, 87,* 707–721.

Benson, P. L., Donahue, M. J., & Erickson, J. A. (1993). The Faith Maturity Scale: Conceptualization, measurement, and empirical validation. *Research in the Social Scientific Study of Religion, 5,* 1–26.

Brown, I. T., Chen, T., Gehlert, N. C., & Piedmont, R. L. (2013). Age and gender effects on the Assessment of Spirituality and Religious Sentiments (ASPIRES) scale: A cross-sectional analysis. *Psychology of Religion and Spirituality, 5,* 90–98.

Burnham, M. J., Le, Y. K., & Piedmont, R. L. (2018). Who is MTurk? Personal characteristics and sample consistency of these online workers. *Mental Health, Religion & Culture.* https://doi.org/10.1080/13674676.2018.1486394

Campbell, D. T., & Fiske, D. W. (1959). Convergent and discriminant validation by the multitrait-multimethod matrix. *Psychological Bulletin, 56,* 81–105.

Cheston, S. E., Piedmont, R. L., Eanes, B., & Lavin, L. P. (2003). Changes in clients' images of God over the course of outpatient therapy. *Counseling and Values, 47,* 96–108.

Church, A. T., & Burke, P. J. (1994). Exploratory and confirmatory tests of the Big Five and Tellegen's three- and four-dimensional models. *Journal of Personality and Social Psychology, 66,* 93–114.

Cohen, J., & Cohen, P. (1983). *Applied multiple regression/correlation analysis for the behavioural sciences* (2nd ed.). Hillsdale, NJ: Lawrence Erlbaum Associates.

Comte-Sponville, A. (2007). *The little book of atheist spirituality.* New York, NY: Penguin Press.

Dy-Liacco, G. S., Kennedy, M. C., Parker, D. J., & Piedmont, R. L. (2005). Spiritual Transcendence as an unmediated causal predictor of psychological growth and worldview among Filipinos. *Research in the Social Scientific Study of Religion, 16,* 261–286.

Funder, D.C. (2002). Why study religion? *Psychological Inquiry, 13,* 213–214.

Funder, D. C., Kolar, D. C., & Blackman, M. C. (1995). Agreement among judges of personality: Interpersonal relations, similarity, and acquaintanceship. *Journal of Personality and Social Psychology, 69,* 656–672.

George, L. K., Ellison, C. G., & Larson, D. B. (2002). Explaining the relationships between religious involvement and health. *Psychological Inquiry, 13,* 190–200.

Gorsuch, R. L. (1983). *Factor analysis* (2nd ed.). Hillsdale, NJ: Lawrence Erlbaum.

Gorsuch, R. L. (1984). Measurement: The boon and bane of investigating religion. *American Psychologist, 39*, 228–236.

Haslam, N., Whelan, J., & Bastian, B. (2009). Big Five traits mediate associations between values and subjective well-being. *Personality and Individual Differences, 46*, 40–42.

Hill, P. C., & Pargament, K. I. (2003). Advances in the conceptualization and measurement of religion and spirituality: Implications for physical and mental health research. *American Psychologist, 58*, 64–74.

Hill, P. C., Pargament, K. I., Hood, R. W., Jr., McCullough, M. E., Swyers, J. P., Larson, D. B., & Zinnbauer, B. J. (2000). Conceptualizing religion and spirituality: Points of commonality, points of departure. *Journal for the Theory of Social Behavior, 30*, 51–77.

Hopwood, C. J., & Donnellan, M. B. (2010). How should the internal structure of personality inventories be evaluated? *Personality and Social Psychology Review, 14*, 332–346.

Huguelet, P. & Koenig, H. G. (2009). *Religion and spirituality in psychiatry*. New York, NY: Cambridge University Press.

John, O. P. (1990). The "Big Five" factor taxonomy: Dimensions of personality in the natural language and in questionnaires. In L. A. Pervin (Ed.), *Handbook of personality: Theory and research* (pp. 66–100). New York, NY: The Guilford Press.

John, O. P., & Soto, C. J. (2007). The importance of being valid: Reliability and the process of construct validation. In R. W. Robbins, R. C. Fraley, & R. F. Kreuger (Eds.), *Handbook of research methods in personality psychology* (pp. 461–494). New York, NY: The Guilford Press.

Joshanloo, M. (2012). Investigation of the factor structure of spirituality and religiosity in Iranian Shiite university students. *International Journal of Psychology, 47*, 211–221. doi:10.1080/00207594.2011.617372

Kapuscinski, A. N., & Masters, K. S. (2010). The current status of measures of spirituality: A critical review of scale development. *Psychology of Religion and Spirituality, 2*, 191–205. http://dx.doi.org/10.1037/a0020498

Kern, M. L., & Friedman, H. S. (2008). Do conscientious individuals live longer? A quantitative review. *Health Psychology, 27*, 505–512.

Kline, R. B. (2005). *Principles and practice of structural equation modeling* (2nd ed.). New York, NY: Guilford Press.

Koenig, H. G., McCullough, M. E., & Larson, D. B. (2001). *Handbook of religion and health*. New York, NY: Oxford University Press.

Leach, M. M., & Sato, T. (2013). A content analysis of the *Psychology of Religion and Spirituality* journal: The initial four years. *Psychology of Religion and Spirituality, 5*, 61–68.

MacDonald, T. A. (2000). Spirituality: Description, measurement, and relation to the Five Factor Model of Personality. *Journal of Personality, 68*, 153–197.

Masters, K. S., & Hooker, S. A. (2013). Religion, spirituality, and health (pp. 519–539). In R. F. Paloutzian & C. L. Park (Eds.), *Handbook of the psychology of religion and spirituality* (2nd ed.). New York, NY: The Guilford Press

McCrae, R. R. (1994). The counterpoint of personality assessment: Self-reports and observer ratings. *Assessment, 1*, 151–164.

McCrae, R. R. (1999). Mainstream personality psychology and the study of religion. *Journal of Personality, 67*, 1209–1218.

McCrae, R. R. (2010). The place of the FFM in personality research. *Psychological Inquiry, 21*, 57–64.

McCrae, R. R., & Costa, P. T., Jr. (1987). Validation of the five-factor model of personality across instruments and observers. *Journal of Personality and Social Psychology, 52*, 231–252.

McCrae, R. R., & Costa, P. T., Jr. (2010). *NEO Inventories: Professional manual.* Odessa, FL: Psychological Assessment Resources.

McCrae, R. R., Herbst, J. H., & Costa, P. T., Jr. (2001). Effects of acquiescence on personality factor structures. In R. Riemann, F. M. Spinath, & F. Ostendorf (Eds.), *Personality and temperament: Genetics, evolution, and structure* (pp. 217–231). Berlin, Germany: Pabst Science Publishers.

McCrae, R. R., Zonderman, A. B., Costa, P. T., Jr., Bond, M. H., & Paunonen, S. V. (1996). Evaluating replicability of factors in the Revised NEO Personality Inventory: Confirmatory factor analysis versus Procrustes rotation. *Journal of Personality and Social Psychology, 70*, 552–566.

Moberg, D. O. (1984). Subjective measures of spiritual well-being. *Review of Religious Research, 25*, 351–359.

Mount, M. K., Barrick, M. R., & Strauss, J. P. (1994). Validity of observer ratings of the Big Five personality factors. *Journal of Applied Psychology, 79*, 272–280.

Newberg, A., D'Aquili, E., & Rause, V. (2001). *Why God won't go away.* New York, NY: Ballantine Publishing Group.

Ozer, D. J., & Martínez, V. (2006). Personality and the prediction of consequential outcomes. *Annual Review of Psychology, 57*, 401–421.

Paloutzian, R. F., & Ellison, C. W. (1982). Loneliness, spiritual well-being and quality of life. In L. A. Peplau & D. Perlman (Eds.), *Loneliness: A sourcebook of current theory, research and therapy* (pp. 224–237). New York, NY: Wiley Interscience.

Paloutzian, R. F. & Park, C. L. (Eds.). (2013). *Handbook of the psychology of religion and spirituality* (2nd ed.). New York, NY: The Guilford Press.

Pargament, K. I. (1999). The psychology of religion *and* spirituality? Yes and no. *The International Journal for the Psychology of Religion, 9*, 3–16.

Pargament, K. I. (2007). *Spiritually integrated psychotherapy: Understanding and addressing the sacred.* New York, NY: The Guilford Press.

Pargament, K. I., Exline, J. J., & Jones, J. W. (Eds.). (2013). *APA handbook of psychology, religion, and spirituality* (Vol. 1). Washington, DC: American Psychological Association.

Piedmont, R. L. (1994). Validation of the NEO PI-R observer form for college students: Toward a paradigm for studying personality development. *Assessment, 1*, 259–268.

Piedmont, R. L. (1998). *The Revised NEO Personality Inventory: Clinical and research applications.* New York, NY: Plenum.

Piedmont, R. L. (1999a). Does spirituality represent the sixth factor of personality? Spiritual transcendence and the five-factor model. *Journal of Personality, 67*, 985–1013.

Piedmont, R. L. (1999b) Strategies for using the five-factor model of personality in religious research. *Journal of Psychology and Theology, 27*, 338–350.

Piedmont, R. L. (2001). Spiritual Transcendence and the scientific study of spirituality. *Journal of Rehabilitation, 67*(1), 4–14.

Piedmont, R. L. (2010). *Assessment of Spirituality and Religious Sentiments, technical manual* (2nd ed.). Baltimore, MD: Author.

Piedmont, R. L. (2014). Looking back and finding our way forward: An editorial call to action. *Psychology of Religion and Spirituality, 6,* 265–267. doi:10.1037/rel10000014

Piedmont, R. L. (2017). *Numinous Motivation Inventory: Preliminary technical manual.* Timonium, MD: Author.

Piedmont, R. L., Ciarrocchi, J. W., Dy-Liacco, G. S., & Williams, J. E. G. (2009). The empirical and conceptual value of the Spiritual Transcendence and Religious Involvement Scales for personality research. *Psychology of Religion and Spirituality, 1,* 162–179.

Piedmont, R. L., Hassinger, C. J., Rhorer, J., Sherman, M. F., Sherman, N. C., & Williams, J. E. G. (2007). The relations among spirituality and religiosity and Axis II functioning in two college samples. *Research in the Social Scientific Study of Religion, 18,* 53–73.

Piedmont, R. L., Mapa, A. T., & Williams, J. E. G. (2006). A factor analysis of the Fetzer/NIA Brief Multidimensional Measure of Religiousness/Spirituality (MMRS). *Research in the Social Scientific Study of Religion, 17,* 177–196.

Piedmont, R. L., Werdel, M. B., & Fernando, M. (2009). The utility of the Assessment of Spirituality and Religious Sentiments (ASPIRES) scale with Christians and Buddhists in Sri Lanka. *Research in the Social Scientific Study of Religion, 20,* 131–146.

Piedmont, R. L., & Wilkins, T. A. (2013). Spirituality, religiousness, and personality: Theoretical foundations and empirical applications. In K. I. Pargament, J. J. Exline, & J. W. Jones (Eds.), *APA handbook of psychology, religion, and spirituality* (Vol. 1; pp. 173–186). Washington, DC: American Psychological Association.

Piedmont, R. L., Wilkins, T. A., & Hollwitz, J. (2013) The relevance of spiritual transcendence in a consumer economy: The dollars and sense of it. *Journal of Social Research and Policy, 4,* 59–77.

Plante, T. G., & Sherman, A. C. (2001). *Faith and health.* New York, NY: The Guilford Press.

Rican, P., & Janosova, P. (2010). Spirituality as a basic aspect of personality: A cross-cultural verification of Piedmont's model. *The International Journal for the Psychology of Religion, 20,* 2–13.

Salsman, J. M., Brown, T. L., Brechting, E. H., & Carlson, C. R. (2005). The link between religion and spirituality and psychological adjustment: The mediating role of optimism and social support. *Personality and Social Psychology Bulletin, 31,* 522–535.

Saroglou, V. (2010). Religiousness as a cultural adaptation of basic traits: A five-factor model perspective. *Personality and Social Psychology Review, 14,* 108–125.

Schönemann, P. H. (1966). A generalized solution of the orthogonal Procrustes problem. *Psychometrica, 31,* 1–10.

Sechrest, L. (1963). Incremental validity: A recommendation. *Educational and Psychological Measurement, 23,* 153–158.

Shafranske, E. P. (1996). *Religion and the clinical practice of psychology.* Washington, DC: American Psychological Association.

Slater, W., Hall, T. W., & Edwards K. J. (2001). Measuring religion and spirituality: Where are we and where are we going? *Journal of Psychology and Theology, 29,* 4–31.

Sloan, R. P., Bagiella, E., & Powell, T. (2001). Without a prayer: Methodological problems, ethical challenges, and misrepresentations in the study of religion, spirituality, and medicine. In T. G. Plante & A. C. Sherman (Eds.), *Faith and health: Psychological perspectives* (pp. 339–354). New York, NY: The Guilford Press.

Tabachnick, B. G., & Fidell, L. S. (2007). *Using multivariate statistics* (5th ed.). Boston, MA: Allyn and Bacon.

Tomcsányi, T., Martos, T., Ittzés, A., Horváth-Szabó, Szabó, T, & Nagy, J. (2012). Spiritual Transcendence and mental health of psychotherapists and religious professional in a Hungarian adult sample. *The International Journal for the Psychology of Religion, 23,* 1–10.

Van Wicklin, J. F. (1990). Conceiving and measuring ways of being religious. *The Journal of Psychology and Christianity, 9,* 27–40.

Waller, N. Kojetin, B., Bouchard, T., Jr., Lykken, D., & Tellegen, A. (1994). Genetic and environmental influences on religious interest, attitudes, and values: A study of twins reared apart and together. *Psychological Science, 1,* 138–142.

Worthington, E. L., Jr., Johnson, E. L., Hook, J. N., & Aten, J. D. (2013). *Evidence-based practices for Christian counseling and psychotherapy.* Downers Grove, IL: InterVarsity Press.

Appendix 4.A
SPSS Syntax for Conducting a Procrustean Factor Analysis for a Numinous Scale

```
matrix.

comment put in loadings from the principal components analysis
in scale order.

compute loadings={

}.

Comment the above will be a row^i by column^j matrix with each row
representing a variable and the columns are the pattern loadings
for each item across all factors.

compute norms={

}.

comment Insert here the INFS results this table should be the same
row^i by column^j as above.

compute s=t(loadings)*norms.

compute w1=s*t(s).

compute v1=t(s)*s.

call eigen(w1,w,evalw1).

call eigen(v1,v,evalv1).

compute o=t(w)*s*v.

compute q1=o &/abs(o).

compute k1=diag(q1).

compute k=mdiag(k1).
```

(continued)

(continued)

```
compute ww=w*k.

compute tl=ww*t(v).

compute procrust=loadings*tl.

compute cm1m2=t(procrust)*norms.

compute ca=diag(cm1m2).

compute csum2m1=cssq(procrust).

compute csum2m2=cssq(norms).

compute csqrtl1=sqrt(csum2m1).

compute csqrtl2=sqrt(csum2m2).

compute cb=t(csqrtl1)*csqrtl2.

compute cc=diag(cb).

compute cd=ca&/cc.

compute faccongc=t(cd).

compute rm1m2=procrust*t(norms).

compute ra=diag(rm1m2).

compute rsum2m1=rssq(procrust).

compute rsum2m2=rssq(norms).   ·

compute rsqrtl1=sqrt(rsum2m1).

compute rsqrtl2=sqrt(rsum2m2).

compute rb=rsqrtl1*t(rsqrtl2).

compute rc=diag(rb).

compute faccongr=ra&/rc.

comment the following commands calculate the overall congru-
ence coefficients

for the data set.

compute top={ca;ra}.

compute bot={cc;rc}.

compute ctop=csum(top).

compute cbot=csum(bot).

compute total=ctop/cbot.
```

comment the following commands merge the above matrices into one overall matrix that will be printed out.

compute procrust={procrust,faccongr;faccongc,total}.

COMMENT for the purposes of this example, we assume a scale with 22 items and three factors.

printprocrust/title="FACTORCONGRUENCECOEFFICIENTS"/ format f5.2

/clabels= "FACTOR 1" "FACTOR 2" "FACTOR 3" "ITEMCONG"

/RLABELS= "item 1" "item 2" "item 3" "item 4" "item 5" "item 6" "item 7" "item 8"

"item 9" "item 10" "item 11" "item 12" "item 13" "item 14" "item 15" "item 16"

"item 17" "item 18" "item 19" "item 20" "item 21" "item 22" "FACTCONG"

/space=newpage.

END MATRIX.

Appendix 4.B

SPSS Syntax for Conducting a Monte Carlo Analysis to Develop Null Distributions for Congruence Coefficients for a Numinous Scale

```
set mxloops=10000.

matrix.

loop #I=1 to 10000.

COMMENT THIS EXAMPLE ASSUMES THE SCALE BEING
EVALUATED HAS 23 ITEMS AND 3 FACTORS.

compute loading1=uniform(23,3).

compute loading2=uniform(23,3).

compute loadings=loading1 - loading2.

COMMENT THESE ARE EXAMPLE DATA ONLY INTENDED TO
DEMONSTRATE WHAT THE MATRIX SHOULD LOOK LIKE.

compute norms={

.73 , .02 , -.05;

.61 , .33 , -.05;

.78 , -.09 , .02;

.81 , .02 , .10;

.76 , .13 , -.05;

.86 , -.01 , .07;

.86 , .00 , .04;

.81 , .08 , .04;

.83 , .03 , .10;
```

.73 , .17 , .07;

.26 , .66 , -.12;

.07 , .75 , -.01;

.25 , .59 , -.04;

-.18, .69 , .14;

.12 , .66 , -.09;

.13 , .57 , -.02;

.25 , .62 , .00;

-.02 , -.07 , .00;

.15 , -.21 , .82;

.15 , .06 , .75;

-.08, .33 , .57 ;

.09, .32 , .34;

-.07 , .46 , .31}.

```
compute s=t(loadings)*norms.
compute w1=s*t(s).
compute v1=t(s)*s.
call eigen(w1,w,evalw1).
call eigen(v1,v,evalv1).
compute o=t(w)*s*v.
compute x1=diag(o).
compute q1=x1 &/abs(x1).
compute k=mdiag(q1).
compute ww=w*k.
compute t1=ww*t(v).
compute procrust=loadings*t1.
compute cm1m2=t(procrust)*norms.
compute ca=diag(cm1m2).
compute csum2m1=cssq(procrust).
```

(continued)

(continued)

```
compute csum2m2=cssq(norms).

compute csqrtl1=sqrt(csum2m1).

compute csqrtl2=sqrt(csum2m2).

compute cb=t(csqrtl1)*csqrtl2.

compute cc=diag(cb).

compute cd=ca&/cc.

compute faccongc=t(cd).

compute rm1m2=procrust*t(norms).

compute ra=diag(rm1m2).

compute rsum2m1=rssq(procrust).

compute rsum2m2=rssq(norms).

compute rsqrtl1=sqrt(rsum2m1).

compute rsqrtl2=sqrt(rsum2m2).

compute rb=rsqrtl1*t(rsqrtl2).

compute rc=diag(rb).

compute faccongr=ra&/rc.

compute top={ca;ra}.

compute bot={cc;rc}.

compute ctop=csum(top).

compute cbot=csum(bot).

compute total=ctop/cbot.

compute procrust={procrust,faccongr;faccongc,total}.

compute finaldat={faccongc,t(faccongr),total}.

save finaldat /outfile="ENTER THE NAME OF A SCALE HERE"

/variables=FACTOR1,FACTOR2,FACTOR3,FAC
TOR1_ITEM1 to FACTOR1_ITEM10,FACTRO2_ITEM1 to FACTOR2_
ITEM7,FACTOR3_ITEM1 to FACTOR3_ITEM6, total.

end loop.

END MATRIX.
```

```
comment FREQUENCIES

VARIABLES= FACTOR1,FACTOR2,FACTOR3,FACTOR1_ITEM1
to FACTOR1_ITEM10,FACTRO2_ITEM1 to FACTOR2_
ITEM7,FACTOR3_ITEM1 to FACTOR3_ITEM6, total /
FORMAT=NOTABLE

/PERCENTILES= 95 99 99.9

/STATISTICS=MEAN MEDIAN .
```

This appendix contains material that is in the public domain.

5 Overview of the Only FFM-Based Measure of the Numinous

The *Assessment of Spirituality and Religious Sentiments* (ASPIRES) Scale

As a personality psychologist trained by Drs. Costa and McCrae (RLP), it was not much of a stretch to approach the study of religiousness/ spirituality (R/S) phenomena from the perspective of the Five-Factor Model (FFM) of personality. This empirically developed taxonomy has been shown to represent a robust structure capable of serving as a meaningful paradigm for understanding character-based individual difference constructs (McCrae, 2010; Piedmont, 1998; Piedmont, McCrae, & Costa, 1991). As noted in Chapter 4, McCrae (1999) has argued that any examination of a trait-based construct would benefit from evaluating it within this framework. Embedding a construct within the FFM would accomplish two things: a) to demonstrate the empirical pedigree of the construct and to provide acknowledgment of its psychological relevance; and, b) to facilitate the integration of the construct into larger models of psychosocial functioning.

When the effort to develop a trait-based measure of spirituality began in the mid-1990s, there were no other such inventories (see Hill & Hood, 1999), making this type of scale a novel contribution. Further, the implied assumptions of such a trait scale would help to clarify some of the basic ontological questions associated with measures of this type. The result of this effort was the *Assessment of Spirituality and Religious Sentiments* (ASPIRES) scale. We believe it is a unique instrument in the field for several reasons. First, it is the only trait-based measure of the numinous. Second, it is the only such scale to have a validated observer-rating form. Third, it has normative data that provide insights into the magnitude of responses and control for naturally occurring age and gender effects. Fourth, it has a very large and expanding validity literature that demonstrates the utility of scores from this scale for not only predicting a wide array of psychosocial outcomes (e.g., Piedmont, 2012) but also has been shown to generalize well cross-culturally (e.g., Rican & Janosova, 2010) and cross-religiously (e.g., Piedmont & Leach, 2002). The ASPIRES provides empirically sustainable definitions of spiritual and religious functioning that is couched within a psychologically clear model of personality.

The purpose of this chapter is to provide an overview of the development of the ASPIRES and how the previous assumptions and empirical criteria for creating a trait-based measure of the numinous were applied. The chapter will provide examples of the data acquired in the development and application process. The goal is to give potential users guidelines for the development of their own measures. Those interested in more details on the ASPIRES are referred to available documents in the literature from Buros (Bernt, 2014; Schoenrade, 2014), extended chapters (e.g., Piedmont, 2012), and from the manual itself (Piedmont, 2010). The ASPIRES is a copyright protected instrument, so any unauthorized usage or reproduction of its content, in any form, is expressly forbidden without permission. Questions and requests for information (e.g., specimen sets) can be directed to the first author at: ralphpiedmont01@gmail.com

Finding the Universal Aspects of Spirituality

When starting this program of research over 25 years ago, we did not have a developed psychological ontology for understanding spirituality. As such, we needed to collect and bootstrap information that would be considered to have good face and ecological validity. In other words, while our intention was to create a trait-based construct, it was important to demonstrate that the information upon which this scale was based had a clear pedigree grounded in various theological and spiritual models. To this end, we began by conducting a qualitative research study involving experts from diverse religious traditions. Termed the "Interfaith Forum on Transcendence," a panel of eight individuals included: a Hindu Swami, Jesuit priest, Lutheran minister, Baptist minister, Quaker, orthodox Jewish Rabbi, Shamanic minister, and a member of our Pastoral Counseling Department who was both a psychologist and former Catholic priest. Also included was myself (RLP), who led the panel discussion, and several graduate students who served as note takers.

The panel convened for a 5-hour session that was based on a series of 14 questions that were prepared for this event. Questions were presented to the group and all were free to respond to and discuss. The 14 questions addressed a range of issues, including: What is spiritual transcendence from your faith perspective? What are the faith indicators of those in your faith tradition who are high on transcendence? Can someone outside of your faith community have transcendence? If yes, how, and if no, why not? Where does transcendence come from? What is the opposite of transcendence? What is the downside of transcendence? What are some of the dimensions that comprise transcendence? As the discussion proceeded, areas of agreement and difference clearly emerged across the diverse faith traditions. The focus of interest to this process was to develop areas of overlap across denominations. Once a consensus was reached, the group was tasked with articulating specific qualities that characterize and/or identify someone who would be considered transcendent across these different groups. It was interesting to note the presence of so many areas of agreement.

The group identified a number of qualities that reflected this more universal aspect of transcendence. Qualities such as: gratitude, compassion, ability to live with paradox, ability to deal with dualities and accept ambiguities, attachment to one's public image (a quality identified as the opposite of transcendence), desire to get more from God, and self-absorption (another negative quality) were among those the group consensually identified. The final step in this quorum was for these individuals to write specific items that they believed reflected these qualities. These items were later examined, and redundant items as well as those that were clearly personality related were deleted (e.g., I hate myself), others were modified to fit into a trait orientation, and finally items that were not clear were also deleted (e.g., I want to learn; I believe that all phenomena are the product of shifting causes and conditions). This process resulted in an overall set of 65 items that were selected for further testing and development. Both positive (e.g., I feel that my gifts/talents come from a higher source) and negative (e.g., I worry about attaining material success) phrased items were included.

Initial Development

This item set was then given to a sample of 277 women and 102 men, ages 17 to 40 years of age (Mean = 18.5), who were enrolled as part of an Introductory Psychology course at a Midwestern university. Subjects completed a number of questionnaires including the BiPolar Adjective Rating Scale (Piedmont, 1995; a measure of the FFM personality dimensions); the Faith Maturity Scale (Benson, Donahue, & Erickson, 1993), the only other measure of spirituality that had shown incremental predictive validity over the FFM (Piedmont & Nelson, 2001); the Social Support Scale (Insel & Roth, 1985), a measure of the extent to which a person receives or obtains social and psychological support from community activities, friends, and relatives; Prosocial Behavior Inventory (De Conciliis, 1993/1994), an act-frequency measure that provides an actuarial index of performing prosocial behaviors over a 6-month period; vulnerability to Stress Scale (Miller & Smith, 1987), which evaluates one's proneness to experience stressful events; Type A Behavior Scale (Baron, 1985), a brief measure to quickly assess one's type orientation; Internal Health Locus of Control Scale (Wallston, Wallston, & DeVellis, 1978), which assesses the degree to which people believe that they feel personal control over their health; Attitudes Towards Abortion Scale (Parsons, Richards, & Kanter, 1990), which determines whether someone is pro-life or prochoice; a Likert-type rating scale of one's attitude towards abortion was also completed (scores ranged from 1 *prolife* to 9 *prochoice*); and the Interpersonal Orientation Scale (Swap & Rubin, 1983), which looks at the degree to which one is interested in and responsive to other people. A demographic questionnaire was also completed that asked individuals to rate the frequency with which they engaged in various religious rituals and practices, as well as their perceived relationship to a transcendent being. This wide range of measures was given to assess the predictive breadth of the newly identified construct.

The first step involved correlating responses to each of the 65 Transcendence items with scores on the five personality dimensions and the Faith Maturity Scale total score. Items that correlated significantly with only the personality scales were deleted. Items that were more strongly related to the personality variables relative to the spirituality scales were deleted. As noted in Chapter 4, if an item correlated with both the FMS and the FFM, there would need to be *at least* two orders of magnitude difference between the two correlations, and no item that correlated $r > 0.45$ with any of the FFM domains would be retained. Table 5.1 presents a sampling of associations for both items selected and not selected.

The top half of Table 5.1 presents items that were retained for further analysis. As can be seen, all of these items have very strong correlations with the FMS total score and small to nonexistent associations with the FFM domains. In cases where an item has a significant correlation with an FFM domain, that value was much smaller than the corresponding association found with the FMS. The second and fourth items are examples of such findings. The bottom half of Table 5.1 contains four items that were discarded following this initial pass through the data. The reasons for deletion should be obvious. While each item did have a significant association with the FMS scale, these items also had associations of similar magnitude with scores from the FFM. What is particularly noteworthy of these correlations is that the item content for each seems very appropriate for a measure of spirituality. For example, the item, "I have had the experience of transcending this world and experiencing a larger reality" seems, on its face, to be very relevant and appropriate, yet it also correlates with Openness (O), the FFM dimension that addresses the ability of an individual to seek out and be receptive to new and different experiences that may enhance one's sensory experience of the external world.

The important point to note here is that face validity is a very superficial method for establishing the usefulness of an item. An item may have all the right phraseology and the best terminology yet still bring in other aspects of personality not related to spirituality, like the item noted above. Therefore, the only satisfactory method for determining the validity of an item is empirical. This is why the FFM is such an important component to developing numinous measures: It helps one

Table 5.1 Sample of Spirituality Items' Correlations with the Faith Maturity Scale and FFM Domain Scores.

Items	Criterion Scales					
	FMS	N	E	O	A	C
Retained Items						
I find inner strength and/or peace from my prayers or meditations	.64***	−.04	−.06	.02	.00	.03
Sometimes I find the details of my life to be a distraction from my prayers and/or meditations (R)	.44**	.11*	−.06	−.07	.01	.02
I have experienced deep fulfillment and bliss through my prayers and/or meditations	.58***	−.02	.06	.10	.03	.02
I have had a spiritual experience where I lost track of where I was or the passage of time	.31**	−.02	.02	.18**	−.01	−.02
Discarded Items						
I am able to experience the world in ways beyond my five senses	.22**	−.09	.01	.16**	−.01	.03
I have found a centering in my life that external events cannot disturb	.25**	−.22**	.11*	.10	.10	.08
I have had the experience of transcending this world and experiencing a larger reality	.18**	.03	.08	.11*	−.07	−.01
I have sacrificed something of myself for another	.23**	−.00	.21**	.21**	.09	.12*

Note: FMS = Faith Maturity Scale, total score; N = Neuroticism; E = Extraversion; O = Openness; A = Agreeableness; C = Conscientiousness. $N = 373$.
* $p < .05$. ** $p < .01$. *** $p < .001$, two-tailed.

to discern the extent to which an item reflects its anticipated content. Removing FFM-related content is absolutely essential, because doing so will serve to minimize the impact of confounding factors, like contamination with the criterion. Contamination with the criterion refers to the situation when items in a scale are similar or identical to items in the criterion measure being assessed. Koenig (2008) indicated that many measures of spirituality capture superficial aspects of the construct that are aimed at assessing factors of well-being, happiness, and positive adjustment. As such, these "spirituality" scales (Koenig put the term in quotes) contain items that assess these more general constructs. Thus, it is not surprising to find that these spiritual measures correlate with these outcomes because both scales share the same item content. Partialing out FFM-related variance from measures of the numinous is one way to address this issue. Once the FFM material is removed from the spiritual scale, any associations with well-being, happiness, and/or positive adjustment cannot be attributed to overlap with those personality dimensions underlying these outcomes (e.g., N, E, and C). Rather, they represent the numinous' own unique associations with these outcomes.

Leaving in FFM material also creates interpretive errors. While there may be something numinous in these items, there are also other qualities that compromise the purity of the score, rendering interpretation tenuous at best. For example, consider the item, "I have found a centering in my life that external events cannot disturb." Is this spiritual person undisturbed by the events of the external world because his/her relationship to the Transcendent provides him/her with the reassurances and emotional support needed in order to face life on its terms? Or, is it because this individual already has a strong sense of emotional stability, resilience, and coping ability that enables him/her to manage very well the stressors of life, leading to better focus on the faith connection? Correlations with FFM-related material represents confounds that need to be removed from numinous scales so that scores will reflect one, and only one, aspect of character to be operating (see Hall, Meador, & Koenig, 2008).

The Search for Structure

Once items overlapping with the FFM were removed, a series of principal components analyses (PCA) were done with the remaining items. The first series of analyses combined the remaining items along with scores on the FFM domains and the FMS scale, creating a joint analysis. This technique helps to sort out variance that is clearly associated with personality and variance that is clearly associated with spirituality. Items loading on both these dimensions represent unclear operationalizations of the numinous and would need to be deleted, as would any item that loaded primarily on the FFM factors. This is going to be an iterative process of examining items, removing those not meeting criteria, redoing the analysis, and re-examining structure until arriving at a final set of items.

The first PCA should extract from three to six factors. The logic for this is that ideally, the final joint PCAs should use three-factor solutions. The three factors that ought to emerge should consist of one factor for the personality dimensions; because only single scale scores are being used for each domain, there is not enough variance for any one factor to emerge independently from the others. A second factor ought to be the scales from the numinous scale (in this case the FMS total score), and the final factor ought to include items that do not load on either of the other factors. These items represent potentially useful numinous items that capture aspects of this domain that are not related to the FMS scale. Obviously, an inspection of item content will be necessary to determine whether these items represent a coherent numinous quality.

Initially, though, many factors may emerge as having an eigenvalue greater than 1, but it is easier to restrict the number to six. Six is selected to represent the five personality domains plus the spirituality scale. It is possible that the content of some of the new items may represent only personality, and their presence in the analysis may help to bolster the presence of some or all of the personality domains. Allow six factors to be extracted on the first PCA and then evaluate the scree plot and the content of the extracted components to determine if fewer factors can be used. In the current data set, when six factors were extracted, we found one factor where the FMS scales loaded, and three factors were various combinations of the FFM domains (e.g., one factor had a combination of N and C, another combined E and O, and the third had loadings for A and C). The remaining three components contained no loadings for either the personality or spirituality measures. Based on these results, we deleted all of the items that loaded with the personality domains, and the analysis repeated again extracting six factors.

Inspection of these data resulted in deleting more items that loaded primarily on the FFM domains as well as items with no significant loadings at all. The PCA was repeated, this time only extracting three factors. Inappropriately loading items were deleted. The reason for so many analyses is that when items are deleted, the entire inter-correlation matrix will change, and new patterns of interrelationships will emerge. Once a three-factor solution was performed that resulted in no items loading with the personality scales, this set of 24 items was submitted to its own PCA, without including the personality or spirituality measures. The goal here was to determine the factor structure of just these remaining items. A three-factor solution was found to be most appropriate, with the components being labeled Prayer Fulfillment, Universality, and Connectedness.

This was a surprising finding because none of the dimensions identified by the Interfaith Group had survived the analytic process. The qualities they noted, like self-absorption, compassion, and ability to live with paradox, all fell out clearly on various combinations of the FFM personality domains (e.g., high N and O, high A, and high O, respectively). We viewed these findings as demonstrating how imprecise definitions of spirituality really are, even when used by theological experts. The relationship of these putative spiritual qualities with personality underscores the need to better articulate the truly defining qualities of the numinous. People who are high on spirituality do indeed have a complete personality profile across all five domains. It may be possible that some of these FFM qualities may also co-occur with spirituality. People who are compassionate, caring, and empathetic certainly see the world in ways different from those who are hardheaded, uncaring, and unresponsive to others' needs. Clearly, the former are more likely to appear spiritual than the latter. For us, what is clear, is that the transcendent perspective is not part of these other personality features. The question we are trying to answer is whether once these other ancillary qualities are removed, is there is anything left that uniquely defines the numinous?

This process left 24 items that defined a single dimension that was independent of the FFM domains and would serve as our starting point for defining a new dimension. These items formed a single dimension, which was labeled *Spiritual Transcendence* (ST). ST was defined as the capacity of individuals to stand outside of their immediate sense of time and place and to view life from a larger, more detached perspective. This transcendent perspective is one in which a person sees a fundamental unity underlying the diverse strivings of nature and finds a bonding with others that cannot be severed, even by death. On this broader, more holistic, and interconnected perspective, individuals recognize a larger organization to life and sense of commitment to others. This single dimension was broken into three, correlated facet scales. The three subscales were defined as: *Prayer Fulfillment*, an experienced feeling of joy and contentment that results from prayer. Prayer provides a sense of personal strength. Prayer is consuming and orients one to another state of being (sample item: I meditate and/or pray so that I can reach a higher spiritual plane of consciousness); *Universality*, a belief in the unity and purpose of life, a feeling that all life is interconnected and a sense of a shared responsibility of one creature for another (sample item: All life is interconnected); and *Connectedness*, a sense of personal responsibility to others that is both vertical, cross generational commitments and horizontal commitments to others in one's community (sample item: I still have strong emotional ties with someone who has died). Alpha reliabilities for scores on these scales were adequate: alpha = .85, .85, .65, respectively.

Construct and Incremental Validity

Scores on these three scales were correlated with a series of questions related to one's religious involvement/activities, the FMS scales, and scores on the FFM domain scales. It was expected that the numinous items would correlate significantly with the religious involvement items and FMS scales but would be mostly independent of the FFM domains. Table 5.2 presents the results of these analyses. As can be seen, all of the numinous scales correlated significantly, with moderate to strong effect sizes, with the religious behaviors and spirituality scales. These findings provide support for the conclusion that the items contained in the new scale capture aspects of religious and spiritual functioning. Correlations with the FFM domain scores are much smaller; only 3 of the 15 correlations are statistically significant, with no correlation being larger than $r > .19$. This is evidence of discriminant validity; content on the new scale remains mostly orthogonal to the FFM domains. It is interesting to note

Table 5.2 Correlations of the Newly Identified Numinous Scales with Measures of Religious Involvement, Spirituality, and FFM Personality Domains.

Criterion Variable	Transcendence Scale		
	Prayer Fulfillment	*Universality*	*Connectedness*
Frequency Read the Bible	.50***	.18***	.01
Frequency Read Religious Texts	.46***	.17***	.09
Frequency of Prayer	.54***	.25***	.16**
Union with God	.67***	.39***	.19***
Relationship with God	.57***	.31***	.19***
Frequency Attend Services	.35***	.11*	.09
FMS Vertical Scale[a]	.68***	.45***	.27***
FMS Horizontal Scale	.41***	.31***	.29***
Neuroticism	−.01	.02	−.06
Extraversion	-.01	.04	.13*
Openness	.10	.19***	.10
Agreeableness	.01	.03	.07
Conscientiousness	.03	.03	.16**

$N = 478$. * $p < .05$. ** $p < .01$. *** $p < .001$, two-tailed.

[a] Faith Maturity Scale, Vertical and Horizontal Subscales.

that despite the numerous PCAs that were done in an effort to remove items with any substantive association with personality, in the end some of this content does remain in the new items. It is also possible that these non-zero correlations represent correlated method error; all scales are based only on self-reports.

The next step was to evaluate the degree to which these scales predicted psychosocially relevant outcomes over and above the predictiveness of the FFM. Table 5.3 presents the results of a series of hierarchical multiple regression analyses. As outlined in Chapter 4, these analyses entered the FFM domains on the first step of the equation simultaneously. On step 2, the new numinous subscales were entered using a forward entry method. As can be seen, with the exception of Type A Personality style, the numinous scales significantly improved predictiveness over and above the FFM personality domains. Prayer Fulfillment was the most robust predictor for this set of criterion variables, although Connectedness had a more limited predictive role. Universality appeared to have no unique predictive linkage with these outcomes.

In comparing the Transcendence scales' predictive power to that of the FFM domains, they do hold up very well. Concerning Attitudes Towards Abortion, the numinous scales were far superior predictors than the FFM scales. Thus, the numinous may play a more pivotal role in predicting values, beliefs, and attitudes than personality. When

Table 5.3 Incremental Validity of the Transcendence Subscales over the Five-Factor Model Scales in Predicting Various Life Outcomes.

Criterion Variable	FFM R^2	Transcendence ΔR^2	Subscale	Partial F
Attitudes Towards Abortion	.01	.07	Pray Fulfil.	8.89***
Pro Abortion	.01	.11	Pray Fulfil.	13.28***
Pro Life Likert Scale	.01	.07	Pray Fulfil.	25.41***
Internal Health Locus of Control	.06	.03	Pray Fulfil.	11.11***
Vulnerability to Stress	.12	.03	Pray Fulfil.	6.47**
Perceived Social Support	.14	.08	Pray Ful/Con.	6.98***
Interpersonal Orientation	.12	.06	Pray Fulfil.	13.31***
Type A Personality	.23	.00	NONE	
Prosocial Behavior	.11	.08	Pray Ful/Con.	10.45***

FFM: Five-Factor Model Scales. Pray Fulfil.: Prayer Fulfillment; Con.: Connectedness; UNIV: Universality. * $p < .05$. ** $p < .01$. *** $p < .001$. Table republished with permission of the *Journal of Personality* by Duke University et al. and Blackwell Publishing, Inc. from *Does spirituality represent the sixth factor of personality? Spiritual transcendence and the five-factor model*, 67(6), 1999 by R. L. Piedmont; permission conveyed through Copyright Clearance Center.

considering the numinous' prediction of the more trait-type constructs, the predictive power of select facets of this single dimension contributed from 25% (Vulnerability to Stress) to 73% (Pro Social Behavior) of the entire FFM's explained variance.

In conducting incremental validity analyses, it is not uncommon to find that the numinous scales account for very small amounts of additional variance (e.g., 1–3%). On the surface, this may seem like a minimal unique contribution of dubious practical significance. However, it ought to be kept in mind that these statistics are partial coefficients and represent what each numinous variable had to offer once the predictive effects of the five personality dimensions, and other predictors, were removed. Thus, these incremental predictive variances are low because there was little reliable variance left to explain in the criteria. Nunnally and Bernstein (1994) have observed that increases in R^2 are generally very small by the time a third substantive predictor is added to a regression equation. As more predictors are entered, their incremental contributions will be increasingly smaller. Hunsley and Meyer (2003) suggested that an R^2 increase of between .02 and .04 would indicate a reasonable contribution for a variable entered on the third step. Given that the numinous variables in the present study were being added into the regression equations on the *6th step* (the five FFM variables constitute the first five steps), the 3–8% additional variance represents a quite robust contribution.

These new numinous items have demonstrated some important qualities. First, they were found to be independent of the FFM personality domains. Second, they evidenced significant incremental validity over the FFM in predicting an array of salient psychosocial constructs. These are the fundamental data needed to justify the value of a numinous construct (for more information about this version of the scale, readers are referred to Piedmont, 1999, 2001). However, after some use, four important issues emerged regarding this scale. The first issue concerned the reading level and vocabulary of the items. Included in the scale were some very sophisticated terms, such as bliss, peak experience, and consciousness. A number of individuals noted difficulties in understanding these terms, so a Glossary was added to the scale that provided definitions. The presence of some complex terms raised a second issue: cross-cultural translations of the items became challenging. Oft times the target language would not have a comparable term (e.g., peak experience), so a more complex phraseology would be required to capture the idiomatic concept. A third issue was the fact that all the items were positively phrased; there was no control for acquiescent responding, a major weakness for the scale (McCrae, Herbst, & Costa, 2001). A final issue concerned the comprehensiveness of the scale.

While the Spiritual Transcendent dimension was clearly obtained and was shown to capture a distinct, motivational quality, the question arose as to whether there could be other types of numinous functioning that could also be included. In examining the literature, two topic areas were identified. The first concerned the role of religiousness. There is much discussion over the usage of the terms "spiritual" and "religious" (e.g., Zinnbauer et al., 1997) which has generated much controversy. Zinnbauer et al. (1997) noted that people tend to use the terms somewhat differently, with most individuals in their study considering themselves spiritual but not religious. From a lay perspective, people see differences between these two concepts. However, Musick, Traphagan, Koenig, and Larson (2000) noted in their sample of adults that these two terms were highly related to one another. Hill and Pargament (2003) saw the two terms as being highly overlapping in that both involve a search for the sacred. There are those, however, who do emphasize the distinctiveness between these two concepts (e.g., Piedmont, 2001; Piedmont & Leach, 2002; Rayburn, 1996). In a factor analysis of the Fetzer/NIA Brief Multidimensional Measure of Religiousness/Spirituality (MMRS; John E. Fetzer Institute, 1999) by Piedmont, Mapa, and Williams (2006), items capturing individuals' involvement in religious practices and rituals emerged as a correlated, separate factor from spirituality, and they were also found independent of personality. Some measure of such practices and involvements ought to be examined.

The second topic area concerned the area of spiritual struggles (Exline & Rose, 2005). This aspect of numinous functioning appears very interesting because it captures individuals' feelings of rejection, conflict, crisis, and emotional negativity in relation to the transcendent. Spiritual crisis erupts when individuals feel that God has let them down or injured them in some manner (e.g., allowed a loved one to die, permitted one to suffer). Conflict can also arise when individuals feel unwelcomed or unaccepted by their faith community. In the factor analysis of the MMRS noted above (Piedmont et al., 2006), a religious crisis factor emerged that was independent of personality, spirituality, and religiousness. This was intriguing because this factor represented a dimension of emotional distress and angst that was clearly independent of personality in general and N in particular. It raised the question, "Is there another pathway to emotional distress independent of neuroticism?" This finding opens the possibility that psychopathology may have more than one characterological cause. Consequently, the aim was to develop and include an index to capture this quality.

The next step was to create an expanded instrument that contained a more efficient measure of spirituality (i.e., more readable, easier to translate) as well as additional scales that assessed other aspects of the numinous domain. The results of this was the development of the *Assessment of Spirituality and Religious Sentiments* (ASPIRES) scale. More than just an inventory, it also represents a specific conceptual model for understanding these various elements of the numinous.

The ASPIRES Model and Scale

The late 1990s and early 2000s saw efforts in the field to find some type of consensus on what constituted the R/S domain. Much of this effort began with literature reviews aimed at categorizing various published definitions of the terms. McGinn (1993) identified over 35 different R/S definitions; Scott (cited in Hill et al., 2000) identified 31 different definitions for religiousness and over 40 for spirituality. This type of research continues now, with the quest for consensus still remaining out of reach and elusive (e.g., Harris, Howell, & Spurgeon, 2018). Still others took more empirical approaches to finding consensus. One method, which is the focus of this book, was to examine R/S constructs within the context of the FFM. MacDonald (2000) attempted to empirically isolate the R/S domain by identifying 11 constructs that would relate to this area either directly (e.g., spiritual orientation, spiritual experience, and mystical experience), or indirectly (e.g., peak experiences, paranormal beliefs, transpersonal orientation to learning). He identified five dimensions independent of the FFM.

Another approach to this issue was undertaken by the Fetzer Institute and the National Institute on Aging (NIA), who assembled a working group of professionals to examine the current state of assessment. The aim of this group was to identify key R/S elements and their related assessment instruments. The underlying question was, "What kinds of measures assessing which types of constructs are being employed in the field?" There was the recognition that given the diversity of measures, any attempt to organize this field would need to appreciate this variety by recognizing the multidimensionality of R/S content (John E. Fetzer Institute, 1999). As a consequence, this working group acknowledged that it would be impossible for any single scale to effectively capture this type of content on its own. Rather, any measure that pretended to be comprehensive would need to include this multiplicity of constructs.

The Fetzer/NIA Working Group identified 12 different constructs as key categories for characterizing R/S qualities, and items from each of these domains were selected and compiled into a single scale called the MMRS. Some of these items were selected from specific instruments, while others captured spiritual or religious themes found in the literature. From these item sets, from one to six items were selected to represent the 12 foundational constructs identified by the Working Group. Although they acknowledged that this brief assessment instrument did not represent all domains of R/S functioning, they asserted that it does serve as a useful starting point for researchers who are interested in examining the role of spirituality in health situations. The MMRS contains items that represent a putatively wide range of salient R/S constructs. While an interesting effort, essentially the MMRS is a product of a shotgun marriage of a number of constructs. Each of these constructs, however, is only a short-form variant of their larger measures. The use of such short forms raises a number of significant technical questions that the developers did not address (see Smith, McCarthy, & Anderson, 2000 for an overview of the kinds of problems inherent to short forms). Another issue was that the presence of so few items per construct pre-empted an ability to create real scales that would reflect specific content. The original document provides no normative information regarding scores on each construct; rather, only item-level information is given. Thus, the MMRS represents more of numinous screener than a real measure.

An additional concern was that no effort was made to identify the underlying structure of the instrument, although others have. Masters et al. (2009) analyzed the internal structure of the MMRS and identified seven factors, although three of these factors were simple doublets. Nonetheless, the compelling point here was that while 12 different constructs were identified as important components of the R/S domain, not all 12 emerged in the data, suggesting substantive overlap among these 12 dimensions. Further, no effort was made in this study to validate whether all of these 12 scales contained content that reflected the numinous. However, we found this scale to provide an interesting opportunity to determine exactly how much of the scale's content can be considered exclusively numinous in nature, what may be overlapping with personality, and the number of unique numinous dimensions that may be present.

Piedmont et al. (2006) jointly factored the items of the MMRS with marker scales from both the FFM and the three facet scales from the STS, overviewed above. This study proved to be foundational to developing our empirical understanding of the numinous and for guiding our work in developing the ASPIRES. Employing over 450 undergraduate students who completed these measures, the MMRS items and the marker scales were submitted to a principal components analysis, and four factors were found that accounted for 45% of the total variance. The first factor represented what we considered to be "spirituality" and included items such as "feel God's love for me" and "my life is part of a spiritual force." Also loading on this factor were the three facet scales from the ST scale. Factor 2 was labeled "religiousness" and included items such as "frequency of reading Bible and other religious literature" and "frequency of attending religious services." These two factors correlated $r = 0.41$ (all other inter-factor correlates were less than $r = .05$). Factor 3 was labeled "personality" because four of the five FFM marker scales loaded on this factor (E did not load on any factor) along with the items, "I have forgiven myself" and "I have forgiven those who hurt me." This finding suggested that personal forgiveness, while frequently associated with a spiritual or religious orientation, is not a numinous quality but rather a function of established personality dynamics (see also Walker & Gorsuch, 2002). Factor 4 contained items that were independent of the other three domains and was labeled "religious crisis" and contained items like, "God has abandoned me" and "God is punishing me for my sins."

We found these findings informative and reinforcing. First, it was clear that spirituality and religiousness cannot be considered isomorphic constructs. While significantly overlapping, they each have sufficient amounts of unique variance to support them being understood as two distinct constructs. The second point was something that we already believed, that not all content that we may assume to be spiritual or assume to be a characteristic of the spiritual person, is actually spiritual. This is the case of forgiveness, which is commonly thought to reflect a spiritual orientation. As found in this study, forgiveness is more about low N, high O, high A, and high C than it is about anything numinous. This again reinforces our belief that the development of numinous scales must be empirically established. Third, while spirituality and religiousness are frequently assumed to be multidimensional in nature (e.g., Hill et al., 2000), this may not necessarily be the case. Rather, it may be more beneficial, both empirically and interpretively, to view the construct to be *multifaceted*. A multifaceted scale is one that is unidimensional but contains a variety of facet scales that, while significantly correlated, do have sufficient unique variance to warrant their separate interpretation (see McCrae & Costa, 1989 for an example of an empirical process for managing such data with the FFM). Whereas research has noted a number of qualities associated with spirituality, these aspects are not mutually exclusive but rather all share a common core nature. There seems to be a unity underlining numinous functioning: a persuasive level of parsimony that can bring focus and cohesiveness to this domain. Finally, the finding that items associated with religious crisis emerged as their own factor, independent of personality, religiousness, and spirituality was a surprise that was believed to hold much potential promise for significantly expanding our understanding of emotional distress and psychological impairment.

These four conclusions provided the foundation for the revisions to be made to the ST scale. It was important that new qualities be added in order for the instrument to become a more comprehensive tool. Unlike the MMRS, this new scale would possess only those constructs with empirical support as representing something unique from the established FFM personality domains. Having a constellation of such constructs would be valuable to the field in several ways. First, the numinous dimension becomes an additional element to the FFM taxonomy (now considered a six-factor model), expanding the range of motivations now catalogued by the field. Second, this domain can serve as its own empirical reference point for future research that aims to further develop and extend this construct. Finally, having an empirically robust measure of the numinous can help the field to better identify those personological qualities that define the dimension, both from a convergent and discriminant perspective.

The Conceptual Foundation to the ASPIRES

In designing the new scale, there were three specific constructs that were selected for inclusion: Spiritual Transcendence (ST), Religious Involvement (RI), and Religious Crisis (RC). ST has already been discussed in detail above. RI consisted of eight items that examined aspects of one's involvement in, and commitment to, religious practices. Six of these items asked the frequency with which one reads religious literature, prays, attends services, and has a relationship with God. Two items examined the importance of one's beliefs and whether or not levels of involvement have changed over the past 12 months. These two items addressed issues of perceived importance of one's involvements (e.g., is it merely a perfunctory, socially commanded involvement or is it a personally valued endeavor?), and if there have been any significant conversion or deconversion events in the recent past. The RC scale contained four items that query about personal feelings that God is punishing or rejecting and feelings of acceptance by one's faith group. These two scales comprised a larger dimension referred to as *Religious Sentiments* (RS).

In examining these two constructs of ST and RS, it was evident that they do not represent similar qualities. ST was defined as an operant motivational construct: a force that drives, directs, and selects behavior. ST was an inherited quality that acts on many aspects of behavior. While certainly relevant for predicting some specific outcomes (e.g., life satisfaction, psychological maturity), it also influences the direction and tempo of one's life. Operant motivations orient individuals to take a specific pathway in the more global aspects of functioning. For example, Piedmont, Wilkins, and Hollwitz (2013) examined ST as a predictor of broad life outcomes, such as vocational choice and economic perspectives. They found that those working in Public Service (e.g., health care, education, non-profits) and Skilled Non-Professional (e.g., customer service, restaurant/food services) industries scored significantly higher on the ST scales than those in the Professional Services (e.g., accounting, banking, insurance) and Skilled Professional (e.g., engineering, manufacturing) industries. Further, they noted that those high on ST indicated spending habits different from those lower on ST. Specifically, the high ST individuals were much more likely to donate money to charity while those lower on ST were more likely to use their money to travel or to put into savings.

The RS scales seemed to capture a different aspect of the numinous: attitudinal values concerning the importance of individuals' specific beliefs. While still a motivating construct, it appeared that these values were less innate and more situationally acquired as a function of upbringing and cultural background. While substantially related to ST, RS does evidence some different patterns of correlates than ST. For example, Piedmont (2010) noted in the technical manual for the ASPIRES that the RS scales correlated more strongly with attitudinal constructs, such as attitudes towards abortion and sexuality, than did the ST scale (or personality for that matter). Another interesting pattern noted by Piedmont (2010) was that ST positively correlated with positive affect, but RI was independent of this outcome. Further, RI was found to be negatively correlated with negative affect, but ST was independent. This intriguing pattern was interpreted to show that spirituality is a quality that provides an inherent sense of joy to life, over and above any sense of well-being described by personality. However, being spiritual does not protect one from emotional pain. RI, on the other hand, is not related to positive feelings in life. Rather, involvement in religious ritual and practice can help reduce the amount of negative affect one may experience. Perhaps the repetitive aspects of ritual may help to reduce anxiety and worry by concentrating one's focus on specific, circumscribed actions. Thus, ST and RS may be mediated by different psychological systems, underscoring the need for both constructs in any predictive model. As a consequence of these findings, RS was labeled as a *sentiment*.

Sentiments and motives represent very different types of psychological qualities. Piedmont (2010) pointed out that the RS scales capture religious involvements and experiences, as well as the importance attributed to those beliefs. As such, they represent an aspect of functioning very different from the qualities assessed by the ST scale. Rather than an intrinsic, inherited quality of the individual, these items reflect instead personal sentiments. The term *sentiments* is an old term in psychology and reflects emotional tendencies that develop out of social traditions and educational experiences (Ruckmick, 1920; Woodworth, 1940). Sentiments can be very powerful motivators for people and have very direct effects on behavior. However, sentiments, like love, gratitude, and patriotism, do not represent innate, genotypic qualities like spirituality. That is why the expression of sentiments can and does vary across cultures and time periods. Sentiments may also be more amenable to change and modification.

The ASPIRES model makes an important distinction between spirituality and religiousness. The two, although very much related, reflect different sets of psychological variables. This model postulates that one's religious sentiments develop out of one's spiritual motivations, a clear departure from the more traditional, mainstream view that considered spirituality as an outgrowth from one's religious roots (e.g., Sheldrake, 1992; Wulff, 1997). Therefore, spiritually motivated individuals may, or may not, choose to develop religious sentiments. In fact, spirituality may underlie a number of different types of sentiments (e.g., patriotism, love, social activism), which are frequently embedded in spiritual qualities (e.g., Mahoney, 2013). Conversely, an individual low on spirituality but reared in an environment that is heavily committed to religious values may develop a strong sense of religious sentimentality. However, he/she will lack a transcendent orientation (e.g., a belief in the unitive nature of life). The religious background may shape specific values, beliefs, and attitudes but may have less of an influence on larger life outcomes, like vocational choice. Therefore, the two constructs are related but are understood by the ASPIRES model as capturing different psychological dynamics.

A final assumption of the ASPIRES model relates to the RC dimension. The underlying perspective assessed by the RC scale is that an individual has lost an ultimate sense of value and worthiness. This is seen as a catastrophic situation where a person perceives a sense of inadequacy and unacceptance coming from the very fabric of the universe. What is so tragic about these feelings is that they leave the person bereft of any avenue for reconciliation. In short, when God finds you lacking and of little value, to whom does one turn to find support? What court of appeal is there to remediate this situation and to find expiation? The consequence of this perspective is a potentially inconsolable sense of negative emotionality that is independent of any other psychological qualities (i.e., neuroticism). Frankl (1997) referred to this situation as nöological distress: a massive breakdown in meaning and purpose. Maslow (1971) spoke of *meta-pathologies* where self-actualized individuals are deprived of key elements of their ultimate self, such as their uniqueness, meaningfulness, and goodness. The resulting motivational pathologies from such deficiencies include despair, feelings of being unneeded, selfishness, and hatred. Maslow noted that these core negative feelings may be at the heart of psychological diseases not yet observed or classified. The ASPIRES model agrees with these perspectives and, as will be shown below, argues that RC represents a new pathway for creating psychopathological problems for individuals that conventional therapies do not address. Difficulties in the realm of the transcendent will carry pervasive implications for the core and ultimate psychosocial stability of the individual. More than just negative affect, religious crisis creates a sense of profound emptiness and emotional pain about which a person may not perceive any avenue of escape.

The Empirical Structure of the ASPIRES

In revising the ST scale, 45 new items were written. These items were constructed to better represent the basic qualities signified by the three facet scales with attention paid to simplicity of phraseology and clarity in exposition. Empirical attention was paid to items that helped to reinforce the internal structure of the scale. This was especially true for the Connectedness scale, which had a relatively lower alpha, a complex factor structure, and contained language that was potentially objectionable to certain religious groups. For example, the item, "Although dead, images of some of my relatives continue to influence my current life" was seen by some conservative Christian faiths as representing a belief in ghosts and spirits that interact with living people. A new item was written that conveyed the sense that an individual maintains personal feelings of connectedness to someone who has passed on: "Although dead, memories and thoughts of some of my relatives continue to influence my current life."

Two other concerns figured into this revision. The first was that there was no validated observer form for the scale. Consequently, efforts were made to collect a sample that contained ratings on these items (each item was changed to the third person, e.g., "He/she does not have any strong emotional ties to someone who has died"). The second concern was that there was no short form. Although the original ST scale was only 24 items long, in some applications it may be deemed too burdensome (e.g., use with elderly). As such, in selecting new items special consideration was given to those items that improved internal consistency and buttressed the clarity of the three-factor, correlated structure. Three items from each scale were selected for inclusion into the short form. These items needed to demonstrate a reasonable alpha and to be recoverable in any principal components analysis.

Items for the RI scale were selected from a set of those that had been used in earlier research studies to validate the original ST scale scores as representing qualities that are tied to religious activities (see Table 5.2 above). Eight items were identified and tested for inclusion in the new scale. Finally, items for the RC scale were created to capture aspects of crisis across personal and social areas (e.g., "I feel abandoned by God" and "I feel isolated from others in my faith group").

As a result of these concerns, a new list of 38 items was created and given along with the ST to a sample of 466 undergraduate students. Using correlational and factor analytic analyses, a new set of ST items was identified, and these items constitute the Spiritual Transcendence Scale (STS) now contained in the ASPIRES. The revised STS consists of 23 items, 10 original items and 13 new items. The alpha reliabilities for the scales were: .95 for Prayer Fulfillment, .82 for Universality, .68 for Connectedness, and .89 for the Total Score. The new STS facet scales evidenced good convergent and discriminant validity as well as demonstrating incremental validity in predicting psychosocial criteria over and above personality. The original and revised ST scales correlated substantially (rs = .83, .89, .55, and .87 for Prayer Fulfillment, Universality, Connectedness, and total score, respectively), indicating that the two instruments share much in common.

The items for the new ST scale are all quite readable, and no glossary of terms is necessary. The alpha for the Connectedness form was slightly higher than originally found but not much more. It may be that Connectedness represents a more complex construct than the other two facet scales (see Piedmont, 2004 for an explanation). Also created were short-form versions for both self and observer ratings. This version of the ASPIRES was then distributed to over 2,900 individuals from samples obtained from across the US. In addition, we obtained 968 individuals who provided observer ratings. These data comprise the current normative sample for the ASPIRES, and information about psychometrics and structure can be found in the manual (Piedmont, 2010). The ASPIRES is a copyright protected instrument that can be purchased directly from the first author. Also available is a technical/interpretive manual that presents normative information and guidelines for using and interpreting the scale, as well as an Excel program that will score the long form of self-report scores and will generate a four-page interpretive report. A copy of an actual report (the identity of the respondent has been protected) is presented in Appendix 5.A (this will be discussed in more detail below). The ASPIRES is one of only a few numinous measures that has been abstracted in Buros Mental Measurement Yearbook (Carlson, Geisinger, & Jonson, 2014).

In using the ASPIRES in research, there are two key issues that need to be addressed: factor structure recovery and generalizability. Both of these issues are interrelated because the determination of whether or not scores from the scale are appropriate across different types of samples (e.g., believers versus non-believers) is based on the extent to which the putative factor structure can be recovered in these new samples. In Chapter 4, techniques and procedures for factor analyzing the STS scale of the ASPIRES were given. Factor analysis is a useful tool for accomplishing this, but there are some issues to consider.

When a scale is factor analyzed, the result is a factor-loading (or pattern-loading) matrix where each item has a weight associated with each of the extracted factors. These weights are interpreted as representing which dimension(s) an item best loads on. Then, for each factor, the weights from each item are examined to determine the underlying construct that is represented in that factor. These loadings can also be seen as the manner in which the subjects psychologically understand the relationships among the items; the weights reflect the varying emphases respondents place on each item as they interpret it as signifying some perceived quality. An item with a high loading on a factor is seen as being indicative that respondents saw this item as clearly representing some quality, one they believed is shared in common with the other items that similarly load strongly on the same factor. Items having moderate to low weights on a factor are representing qualities that respondents believe have less relevance to the underlying dimension reflected by that factor. Therefore, factor loadings represent two aspects of a scale: the relative salience of items defining each factor, as well as the relative importance of each item as a perceived exemplar of the underlying measured construct.

It is possible that items of a scale can be factored in two independent samples and the observed factor loadings in each sample would correctly identify items on their intended factors. While one may claim that the factor structure has been replicated, if the primary loadings themselves are significantly different (e.g., in the first sample the defining items have weights between .75 and .95 but the same items in the second sample have loadings between .45 and .65), then the issue arises as to whether the subjects in the two samples understand the items in a similar manner. One group can identify the patterns among the items much easier than the other group. Depending on who comprises each group (i.e., are they demographically similar or not?), these diverse patterns of factor loadings may begin to take on more interpretive significance for the generalizability of the scale, with the different groups having very different perspectives on the items.

Another potential confound in conducting factor analysis is that it is a correlationally based technique that capitalizes on sample-specific error. Each data set, even when demographically similar individuals are employed, has its own unique features, some of which may be related to idiosyncratic aspects of this sample and some of which may be due to the normal vagaries of sampling error. These natural sources of error will impact the magnitude and pattern of the observed factor loadings. Even if the same scale is given twice to the same sample, it would not be surprising to find different factor loadings across the two analyses. Thus, it becomes important to find ways to control for these natural sources of error; one needs to determine whether the different loadings represent normal variation or something more substantive. That is where the use of an orthogonal Procrustean rotation of the factor data becomes important (Schönemann, 1966). As discussed in Chapter 4, the Procrustean rotation will examine how well the new data can be fitted to the original factor structure. Once this rotation is completed, then congruence coefficients (CCs) are calculated to determine how closely the Procrustean solution matches, in terms of both pattern and magnitude, the values of the target matrix.

Chapter 4 provided SPSS programs for conducting a Procrustean rotation of a new set of factor loadings to the normative values and for conducting the Monte Carlo study to identify critical values for the observed CCs. An example of their use will be covered here. Using a sample of 478 undergraduate students who completed the ASPIRES as part of a larger study examining personality disorders, the factor structure of the ST scale was examined to determine whether these individuals understood Spiritual Transcendence in a manner similar to those in the normative sample (more information about this sample can be found in Piedmont, Sherman, Sherman, Dy-Liacco, & Williams, 2009). Scores on the ST scale from the ASPIRES were submitted to a principal components analysis, and three, correlated factors were extracted and rotated. The resulting pattern-loading matrix was then entered into the SPSS syntax file presented in Chapter 4, and the Procrustean rotation was performed. The output from this analysis is presented in Figure 5.1, which reflects what this program produces.

There are four points of interest in Figure 5.1. First, the values in the heart of the table represent factor loadings from the Procrustean rotation. These values are different from those originally entered in the program because those values were subjected to another rotation that attempted to fit the data as closely as possible to the target matrix. So, these loadings represent the new coordinates for the items relative to these new axes. Often, these values will indicate better simple structure than the original loadings. The second point of interest regards the last column, which is labeled "ITEMCONG," and the numbers in this column are CCs that are comparing the factor loadings of each item with the comparable ones found in the normative factor structure. CCs range in value from 0 to 1. In order to evaluate the degree of fit represented by these CCs, one needs to refer to the null distribution determined from a Monte Carlo analysis that used the normative factor structure as the target (see Chapter 4 for details on conducting this analysis). For the ASPIRES, Table 5.4 presents the

FACTOR CONGRUENCE COEFFICIENTS

ITEM	FULFILL	UNIVER	CONNECT	ITEMCONG
F1	.57	.15	-.12	.96
F2	.60	.28	-.18	.98
F3	.79	-.04	.11	.99
F4	.78	.05	.11	1.00
F5	.76	.05	-.02	.99
F6	.87	.00	.08	1.00
F7	.87	-.07	.13	.99
F8	.83	.06	.04	1.00
F9	.85	.04	.11	1.00
F10	.75	.13	.08	1.00
U1	.21	.61	-.15	1.00
U2	.03	.64	.05	1.00
U3	.20	.48	-.12	.98
U4	-.18	.44	.10	.99
U5	.06	.63	-.10	1.00
U6	.27	.29	.15	.81
U7	.30	.51	06	.99
C1	-.10	-.01	.07	.29
C2	.17	-.01	.78	.97
C3	.20	-.06	.84	.99
C4	.00	.10	.69	.92
C5	.07	.39	.20	.94
C6	-.17	.51	.19	.96
FACTCONG	.99	.96	.96	.98

------ END MATRIX -----

Figure 5.1 Actual SPSS Output from Orthogonal Procrustean Rotation Program of the Spiritual Transcendence Items of the ASPIRES.

critical values for determining whether or not a CC is significant at the alpha = .05, .01, and .001 levels. In comparing the values in the last column against the critical values in Table 5.4, all of the ST items, except three (UN6, CN1, and CN4) show significant fit. This indicates that the factor loadings for these items across the three factors are identical (i.e., are not significantly different) from the corresponding normative factor loadings.

The third point of interest is the "overall" coefficients that are presented in the last row of Table 5.4. The first three values are examining the extent to which the factor loadings for the 23 items are the same on each factor as found in the normative sample. Comparing the observed CCs with the critical values shows that each factor's CC is statistically significant at the alpha = .001 level. This indicates that the item loadings on each factor are identical to those found normatively. Finally, there is an "overall" fit coefficient, which is the value in the fourth column of the last row (i.e., .98). This coefficient compares the entire matrix, both columns and rows, to their corresponding normative values. This value evaluates

Table 5.4 Normative Significance Values for Congruence Coefficients Based on a Procrustean Rotation for Spiritual Transcendence Scale.

Spiritual Transcendence Scale Items	.05	.01	.001
Prayer Fulfillment	.538	.624	.706
Universality	.535	.628	.715
Connectedness	.518	.604	.704
PF1	.950	.991	.999
PF2	.949	.987	.999
PF3	.949	.991	.999
PF4	.952	.990	.999
PF5	.946	.990	.999
PF6	.955	.991	.999
PF7	.954	.990	.999
PF8	.951	.991	.999
PF9	.957	.992	.999
PF10	.947	.990	.999
UN1	.956	.990	.999
UN2	.957	.991	.999
UN3	.950	.989	.999
UN4	.959	.991	.999
UN5	.955	.989	.999
UN6	.947	.987	.999
UN7	.948	.990	.999
CN1	.911	.983	.999
CN2	.972	.993	.999
CN3	.967	.994	1.00
CN4	.959	.992	1.00
CN5	.945	.990	.999
CN6	.950	.991	.999
OVERALL	.438	.498	.549

N = 10,000. *Note:* PF = Prayer Fulfillment, UN = Universality, CN = Connectedness.

the extent to which the entire matrix of loadings is similar to the original values. Comparing this value to the critical values indicates that this coefficient is significant beyond the alpha = .001 level. Together these findings specify that the underlying putative factor structure of the ST scale of the ASPIRES can be recovered in this general sample of undergraduate students and that these respondents understand the numinous constructs represented in these scales in a manner identical to the more representative normative sample.

A similar analysis was performed using the items from the two Religious Sentiment scales, and the results are presented in Figure 5.2. The factor structure of these items is essentially identical to that found in the normative data. These data demonstrate that the underlying factor structure of the ASPIRES can be recovered in this undergraduate sample and that these individuals understand the items in the same terms as the normative respondents. It is recommended that any time ASPIRES data are being factor analyzed, that a Procrustean rotation be performed and CCs obtained. In this manner, the generalizability of the scale to the new sample can be determined. An examination of the overall factor CCs can also show whether or not subjects in the new sample understand the items as originally conceived. These findings are very clear and supportive, which is not really a surprise given that respondents are US undergraduates, a community well represented in the normative sample. Frequently, however, the item CCs may not all emerge as being significantly replicated. There are many reasons for this, especially when evaluating cross-cultural data. It is acceptable if at least 60% of the items show significant convergence. Most important, though, are the overall factor CCs that indicate whether or not the entire factor is replicated. These are the most vital values to consider.

Generalizability of the ASPIRES Scale

One of the major assumptions behind the ASPIRES scales is that they capture a universal aspect of human psychological functioning. Spirituality and religiosity are uniquely human qualities that find expression in

```
Run MATRIX procedure:

FACTOR CONGRUENCE COEFFICIENTS
               Rel Inv     Rel Crisis    ITEMCONG
RI1             .79          .17          1.00
RI2             .66          .14           .99
RI3             .78          .03          1.00
RI4             .79          .03          1.00
RI5             .81         -.09          1.00
RI6             .80         -.09           .99
RI7             .67         -.01          1.00
RI8             .36         -.06          1.00
RC1             .01          .84          1.00
RC2            -.11          .85          1.00
RC3             .10          .85          1.00
RC4            -.28          .63           .97
FACTCONG       1.00          .99          1.00

------ END MATRIX -----
```

Figure 5.2 Actual SPSS output from Orthogonal Procrustean Rotation Program of the Religious Sentiments Items of the ASPIRES.

Note: RI = Religious Involvement, RC = Religious Crisis, FACTCONG = overall factor congruence coefficients, ITEMCONG = Item level CCs all cultures across every era. As such, the dimensions contained in the ASPIRES should be found reliable and valid across faith traditions and cultures. The ASPIRES has been increasingly used world-wide, both in its English version and in approved foreign language formats. Consistently the accruing evidence supports this position.

Goodman (2002) gave the ST scales to a sample of conservative, reformed, and orthodox Jews. She found the ST scales to be reliable in all three samples and to significantly predict outcomes. Piedmont and Leach (2002) gave the ST scales and elements of the Religiosity scale (in English) to an Indian sample of Hindus, Muslims, and Christians. The ST scales evidenced alpha reliabilities comparable to those found in the US, although the alpha for Connectedness scores was found to be quite low. Further, the ST scales were found to evidence significant incremental validity over the FFM personality domains in predicting emotional well-being and psychological maturity.

Cho (2004) translated the ST items into Korean and distributed the form to middle-aged married couples. The sample was comprised of evangelical Christians. The ST scales were found to significantly predict fear of intimacy. Bourdeau, Hinojosa, Perez, and Chu (2004) translated the ST scales into Spanish for use with gay Latino men. Alpha reliabilities were lower than those found in American samples, especially for Connectedness. However, the scales were found to capture native Meso-American religious themes that are not found with the more Christian-based spirituality measures.

Wilson (2004) gave the ST scales in English to a sample of aboriginal Canadians who were receiving inpatient treatment for alcoholism. The ST scales were found to be quite reliable (overall alpha for total ST scale was .90), and the overall score correlated significantly with other measures of spirituality and ethnic identity.

Piedmont (2007) translated the ST scales into Tagalog, a native language of the Philippines. This translation was given to a large adult sample across several different island locations. This sample was overwhelmingly Catholic (as is the population of the Philippines). Alpha reliabilities were comparable with American samples, save Connectedness which was much lower in both the self- and observer-rating versions. However, test-retest reliabilities were found to be very high for all scales (the 7-day-retest coefficient for Connectedness was .77). Thus, the lower alpha reliabilities for scores on the Connectedness scale appear to reflect the scale to be rather complex rather than unreliable. Piedmont found the expected three correlated factor structure in both the self and observer versions. Also, he found significant self-other convergence. The ST scales were also found to evidence significant incremental validity over the FFM personality domains. Perhaps most interesting, a comparison of the English and Tagalog versions of the scales showed the translation to be metrically equivalent to the original English version. Thus, the concepts of spirituality inherent in the English language can be found in a language that does not share a common lexical or cultural heritage with English. This finding is evidence that the STS represents a universal quality of humans.

Piedmont, Werdel, and Fernando (2009) gave the ASPIRES to a sample of Buddhists and Christians in Sri Lanka. The scales were completed in English. No mean level differences were found between the two groups except for the Religious Involvement scale, where Christians scored significantly higher. Scores on all scales, save Connectedness, evidenced adequate levels of internal consistency. Factor analyses recovered the putative structure of the Religious Sentiments and ST scales. However, the Connectedness facet scale was the least well recovered in this sample. In general, Connectedness contains some sophisticated concepts, making it a challenge to translate into other languages. Frequently, this scale may not be recoverable via factor analysis, and often scores on the scale yield a low alpha. However, the scale remains part of the ASPIRES because despite such psychometric infelicities, the scale does predict relevant outcomes and adds to the explanatory value of the instrument.

Rican and Janosova (2010) translated the ASPIRES into Czech and gave it along with other measures of spirituality and the NEO PI-R, a measure of the FFM. What is interesting in this study is that the Czech Republic is, according to these authors, "perhaps the least religious country in the world" (p. 3). An important question was whether a measure of spirituality would be relevant to understanding the mental world of highly secularized individuals. The results indicated that scores on the ASPIRES scales were indeed reliable and converged in expected ways with another measure of spirituality. Most importantly, the domains of the ASPIRES were shown to be independent of the FFM, supporting the contention that spirituality is an independent dimension of personality that is universal in its relevance. Being religious is not essential for developing a spiritual orientation. An important feature of this study is that the authors created their own measure of spirituality that they believed was most appropriate for this secular audience. This emically developed scale correlated significantly and of moderate to strong effect, with the ASPIRES' ST scale. This convergence between an etic and emic scale provides very strong evidence for the robustness of spirituality as a universal motivation.

The ASPIRES has also been translated into several languages in countries both secular and religious (e.g., Hungary: Tomcsányi et al., 2011; Iran: Joshanloo, 2012; Argentina: Simkin, 2017 and Lemos & Oñate, 2018; Mainland China: Chen, 2011; Hong Kong: Lau et al., 2016; Greece: Katsogianni & Kleftaras, 2015; India: Braganza & Piedmont, 2015; Australia: Akyalcin, Greenway, & Milne, 2008; Poland: Piotrowski, Żemojtel-Piotrowska, Piedmont, & Baran, 2018). Additional translations of the ASPIRES are available in French, Spanish, Saudi Arabian,

Indonesian, Vietnamese, and Russian. Taken as a whole, the research data provide clear support for considering the STS as a broad-based motivational construct. It is relevant for understanding behavior across diverse faith traditions, languages, and cultural backgrounds.

In performing a translation, there are guidelines to be followed in order to ensure that the translated version represents a useful and accurate form of the original English version. Essential to this endeavor is an iterative process of translating the scale into the new language and then having at least two different individuals back-translate it into English. This version is then examined for comparability in terminology and content. By using two back translators, it becomes possible to disentangle whether any discrepancies are a function of the translation itself or a by-product of the translator. The technical manual provides more detailed information on the translation process.

The Dark Side to the Numinous: Religious Crisis and Psychopathology

As noted above, when factoring the MMRS the dimension of Religious Crisis (RC) emerged as a separate factor from both personality and the R/S dimensions. This caught our attention because it suggested that there may be aspects of the numinous that are dysfunctional in nature that may operate as a new pathway for causing emotional distress. While the personality dimension of N has been clearly demonstrated to be the major predictor of many aspects of emotional distress and psychopathology (e.g., Bienvenu et al., 2001; Costa & McCrae, 1992), finding another personality dimension that also uniquely links to psychological impairment would be exciting and important. It would open the door for a more complete understanding of dysfunctional dynamics and hold out the possibility that a whole new class of potential interventions may lie in wait.

To examine this issue more clearly, Piedmont et al. (2007) examined how RC related to aspects of personality dysfunction. Regression analyses and structural equation modeling (SEM) were employed to determine what aspects of the numinous (spirituality vs. religiousness) were related to scores on two measures of personality dysfunction (the *Schedule of Nonadaptive and Adaptive Personality*, Clark, 1993; and a self-report version of the *Structured Clinical Interview for DSM-IV Personality Disorders Questionnaire*, First, Gibbon, Spitzer, Williams, & Benjamin, 1997). While various aspects of the ST scale would correlate with these outcome scores, the most consistent predictor was RC. SEM analyses were conducted that examined various models (see Figure 4.1 in Chapter 4) testing the causal role of both ST and RC in conjunction with FFM domain scores. These analyses indicated that the STS did not make any significant contribution to predicting personality disorder scores on both instruments, but models that posited RC as an independent contributor were found to be the best-fitting models.

In the data set outlined above in this chapter, subjects completed the *External Validators Scale* (EVS: Trull, Vergés, Wood, Jahng, & Sher, 2012), a measure designed to assess experiences with mental health issues across three domains: a) lifetime Axis I and Axis II diagnoses; b) lifetime treatment experiences for a mental health issue, and c) suicidal thoughts and behaviors in the past year. All items were dichotomous (yes/no). Hierarchical analyses were conducted where the FFM personality domains were entered on the first step and the ASPIRES scales on the second step using a forward entry technique. The results of this analysis are presented in Table 5.5.

As can be seen, the ASPIRES scales were related to all but one item (lifetime Axis II diagnosis). The RC scale was a significant predictor for all but two of the items ("any suicidal thoughts in the past year" and "in the last year, any suicide attempts"). What these data do indicate is that RC is an important predictor of actual, clinically salient behaviors, independent of any FFM personality domain scores. In this data set, RC correlated with N significantly, but with a small effect size [$r(476) = .24$, $p < .05$]. While there is a small overlap (perhaps due to the common focus on emotional pain implicit in the RC scale), it is clear that once this overlap is removed, RC continues to have additional, significant explanatory power. Future research needs to more fully examine this

Table 5.5 Hierarchical Regression Results of ASPIRES Scales Predicting Scores on the External Validators Index.

EVS Item	FFM R^2	ASPIRES R^2	Subscale	Partial F
1 Lifetime Axis 1 diagnosis?	.11	.14	RC	26.19***
2 Seen Therapist for mental health problem (MHP)	.10	.07	RC/UN/RI/PF	10.43***
3 Prescribed meds for MHP	.09	.06	RC/RI/UN	11.94***
4 Gone to ER for MHP	.05	.02	RC	11.58***
5 Received inpatient treatment for MHP	.04	.02	RC	10.67***
6 Last year any suicidal thoughts?	.20	.02	PF/UN	5.59**
7 Last year, any suicide attempts?	.03	.02	CN	11.48***
8 Last year, felt like you wanted to die?	.20	.02	RC	15.76***
9 Last year, thought about death?	.14	.02	RC/PF	6.17**
10 Lifetime Axis II diagnosis?	.03	.00	—	—

Note: RC = Religious Crisis, RI = Religious Involvement, PF = Prayer Fulfillment, UN = Universality, CN = Connectedness. ** $p < .01$, *** $p < .001$, $N = 478$.

construct and its potential role in psychopathology. Cheston, Piedmont, Eanes, and Lavin (2003) have noted that negative images of God (i.e., perceiving God as hostile, angry, uncaring) were associated with higher levels of psychological distress, after controlling for personality. Thus, difficulties in one's relationship with the Transcendent appear to carry implications for the stability of one's mental world.

RI was consistently negatively related to difficulties, suggesting that those who are not involved in religious activities are also more likely to experience problems. The role of the STS was a bit more complex. In some instances, positive associations between the STS scales and problems were found (e.g., PF and UN were positively related to "seen a therapist for MH problems") and in other instances negative associations were found (e.g., PF was negatively related to both "last year any suicide attempts" and "last year thought about death"). What is of value to these data is that rather than correlating two sets of scale scores together, the EVS is an indicator of actual behaviors expressed by a client. Such moderately strong associations with single-item behavioral indices should underscore the value of the numinous for influencing actual psychologically salient behaviors. More research is needed to fully develop and assess the contribution of numinous constructs for predisposing one to experience mental difficulties. The potential exists for the presence of disorders not yet catalogued that are related to these qualities. The role of the numinous in already existing disorders also needs to be explored, especially when dealing with issues surrounding moral injury, eating disorders, substance abuse, and suicide.

Interpreting ASPIRES Protocols

The ASPIRES has an Excel scoring program available for use with the long-form, self-report version. Users enter the raw data for each item, and the program will convert scores to *T*-scores based on normative data, which controls for age and gender. A four-page interpretive report is then generated. Appendix 5.A contains an actual report for a 42-year-old, male substance abuser (this information is being shared with the permission of the subject). The first page provides general demographic information. The second page presents scores graphically, and the final two pages provide a written interpretation of each score. These interpretations are based on research findings for each scale. This section will guide the reader through this profile and outline some of the key elements of its content.

The first page contains general demographic information: name, age, gender, denomination, and race. Aside from age and gender, the normative data make no adjustments based on religious affiliation and race. While our research has indicated that differences between religious groups do exist (e.g., Piedmont & Leach, 2002), we decided not to adjust for these differences normatively. We thought that individuals wishing to study the cultural effects of religious affiliation would benefit by examining these mean level differences and drawing inferences from them. Race differences have been more difficult to pursue because Caucasians make up such a large percentage of our samples. It was not uncommon to have Caucasians representing over 70% of the sample. Usually African-Americans would comprise between 12% and 20%, with the other racial groups comprising less than 5% of the sample. This low level of representation made it difficult to test for inter-group differences. While an inherent weakness in our sample recruitments, it was again believed that leaving such differences unadjusted would help foster research aimed at studying racial diversity.

The second page is a graphic representation of scores. It is clear to see where an individual may score high or low. This pictorial view can help frame the more salient numinous issues being experienced by the respondent. For the current client, inspection of the graph indicates someone who does not have many strong numinous motivations. Low on RI, this person does not engage in any religious practices or rituals. Examination of the ST facet scales shows rather low overall levels of spiritual transcendence. Scores on PF and UN are similarly in the low range. This person takes more of a concrete approach to existence, taking events as they come without much consideration for the broader possibilities in life. Interestingly, this person scores average on CN. Usually, substance abusers, especially those in the early phases of treatment, tend to score low on this dimension (see Piedmont, 2004). Low scores on the CN scale can indicate a more narcissistic, self-orientation to life. There is little appreciation for one's connections to family, friends, and society in general. This average level score may suggest that this person is in treatment, perhaps a 12-step program, and is beginning to see, and appreciate, larger interpersonal networks with which he is connected.

What is most striking about this profile is the very high score on RC, especially because the respondent scores low on RI and ST. At first glance, this pattern may seem contradictory given that the person avoids involvement in religious and spiritual issues, yet he feels he is being punished and rejected by the God of his understanding and faith community. Two points of interest here: First, the person feels a strong sense of personal unworthiness. He may believe that nature itself rejects him as being inadequate and useless. This creates a deep emotional hole that can bring feelings of despair and anger that can consume his inner life. Finding a sense of personal adequacy and acceptance would be a key thrust for any therapeutic intervention. The second issue is that such a high RC score in conjunction with such low scores on the other facets may indicate that this person may have felt himself to have been injured by God. Perhaps at some earlier time in life, he felt that God let him down at a moment that was perceived as personally important and crucial. When one thinks that God failed to come through in a time of crisis, one may feel completely rejected by God, and a natural response is to reject God. After all, if God does not want to help the person, the person may feel that he does not wish to help or accept God. Examining internal cognitions in this area would be very helpful. Pulling back from God forces the person to withdraw into himself and to rely only on his own efforts. This strategy will fail because there is the underlying feeling of overwhelming inadequacy. The person relies on himself, but he also feels that he is not worthy or adequate for the task. Hence, the substance abuse may be a way of finding external soothing for these powerfully conflicting and negative feelings.

The third page begins the interpretations for each scale. The report begins with the "Interpretive Context" section. Information presented here is based directly on responses given to items 7 and 8. Item 8 asks whether, over the past 12 months, the individual has encountered any change in his/her religious involvements. This item will identify individuals who have either had a conversion or a deconversion experience. Indications of these types of changes are important to know when considering scores. Clearly, when changes are occurring, either positive or negative, it is important that a therapist be aware of these extra-ordinary experiences and examine their details and impacts on the person.

Item 7 queries the person about the importance of his/her religious beliefs. This question can be very helpful in understanding a person's religious sentiments. Of particular interest are those who acknowledge that their beliefs are not very important, yet they are heavily involved in many religious practices. Such individuals may be very conventional in nature. They are involved in religious activities perhaps because it is an essential part of belonging to their community. It may be important for this person to fit in socially, and to do so he/she may need to be involved in these socially important activities, even though he/she may not find them important or relevant to his/her life. At the other end of this spectrum are people who find their religious interests very important, but they score low on overall RI. Such individuals may have their own unique religious practices and involvements and/or may not be members of more traditional faith groups. In this instance, the individual embraces faith practices, but the ASPIRES may not be picking up what those practices are. It would be important to explore how these clients give form and shape to their beliefs. Keep in mind that the purpose of assessment is not necessarily finding answers to personological questions, although this is certainly possible. Rather, the goal is the generation of hypotheses concerning the numinous stance of the person that will need to find confirmation in the ongoing therapeutic dialogue. Scores on the ASPIRES can help set the direction for this conversation in treatment. The items on the ASPIRES may raise questions and/or concerns in the respondent that he/she may wish to address in counseling. The results of the assessment can be used by the therapist to identify some key issues for discussion and to provide a platform for understanding the client and directing the course of treatment.

The current client's scores indicate that his R/S feelings have been consistent in this manner for a time. The individual has removed himself from involvement with religious activities and is comfortable with this position. In conjunction with his low RI scale, this man may have a strong amount of apathy towards religion, perhaps because he feels rejected by his faith group and his understanding of God. This lack of acceptance may be motivating him to avoid these types of endeavors.

The next section assesses the religious sentiments of the client. The first box evaluates overall RI while the second box examines RC. While it was clear this person does not have any interest in religious activities, and feels very rejected by God, the interpretive text here tries to provide more depth to this client's possible feelings. In developing this scale, research was conducted that performed a conceptual analysis of test scores. Gough (1965) proposed this process as an additional step to the usual construct validation process. The goal of the conceptual analysis is to specify "the characterological and personological dispositions of individuals who obtain scores defined by the measure itself as diagnostically significant" (p. 297). In the current context, a conceptual analysis would ask the question, "What kind of person scores high (or low) on the numinous?" One way to assess this is to describe the kind of social impressions such a person would make. In other words, if you were to meet someone high on the STS, what kind of interpersonal reactions would this person generate in you? This can be accomplished by obtaining observer ratings of the person's traits and styles (the Adjective Check List [ACL], Gough & Heilbrun, 1983 is a good instrument to use in this manner) and find which descriptions link up with his/her scores on the scale.

This was done for the ASPIRES scales; ratings on the ACL were obtained from a subsample of the normative group. The ACL consists of 300 adjectives that are descriptive of an individual (e.g., active, cool, lazy, reckless, tactful, versatile, zany), and respondents check those adjectives that they believe are descriptive of the target person. Then, these ratings are correlated with the obtained scores from the target on the ASPIRES scales. These adjectives are then used to help flesh out the underlying personological implications of the test score. For example, individuals scoring high on PF were seen by their raters as being contented, mature, persevering, and not being distrustful, hard-hearted, and lazy (Piedmont, 2010). The patterns of these associations reflect the social and personal impressions that someone high on PF creates in those who know him/her. The interpretive descriptions for each facet include these rater-based, adjectival descriptors.

As can be seen with our current client, being low on RI is associated with perceptions of him by others as being boastful, quarrelsome, and impatient. This low score on RI reflects a more self-centered approach to life where people are more concerned with their own needs than those of others. The high score on RC is associated with peer perceptions of being arrogant, bitter, and distrustful. High scores on RC seem to represent a person who responds to feelings of worthlessness and rejection with an almost childish, "tit-for-tat" attitude: "You do not like me, so the hell with you, I do not like you!" There is little doubt that high scores on this scale reflect a person with much internal emotional distress and conflict. After all, when one possesses a feeling of transcendent rejection, there is little perceived redress for this problem. The anger and guilt over losing one's place in the world creates a strong set of emotions that are hard to manage in a logical and rational manner. Thus, the conflict may create emotional reaction formations as a means for coping.

That is why it is not uncommon to find high RC scores with individuals who are suffering from various types of emotional problems. Especially for substance abusers, feeling this high level of social anomie may be motivating the abuse problem: The abused substances may serve to anesthetize the person from these profound feelings of dread and emptiness. Being rejected by God, one may feel driven out from the person's larger social community, forced to be alone and to wander, unable to find a place of acceptance. In some ways these feelings are similar to those experienced by Cain, as presented in the biblical texts. After Cain slew Abel, his brother, God punished him:

> Therefore you shall be banned from the soil that opened its mouth to receive your brother's blood from your hand. If you till the soil, it shall no longer give you produce. You shall become a restless wanderer on the earth.
>
> (*New American Bible* [*NAB*], 1978, Genesis, 4:11–12)

Cain was devastated by this rejection from God, and he protested, "My punishment is too great to bear. Since you have now banished me from the soil, and I must avoid your presence and become a restless wanderer on the earth, anyone may kill me on sight" (*NAB*, 1978, Genesis 4:13–14). Unlike Cain, who did receive a mark from God to prevent him from being killed by others and who was able to find a place to settle, the person scoring high on RC does not have any protective blessing to comfort him or herself. Thus, the conflict may seem irremediable.

The client's low scores on PF and UN may augment his feelings of isolation. One feature of PF is that those scoring high on this scale experience feelings of joy and contentment, even during times of stress. Low scorers do not find such emotional reprieve and instead pursue a more socially detached path. Low UN indicates feelings of detachment from others;

there are no unitive feelings or sense of common bonding with others. Our client may be perceived by others to be querulous, self-centered, and conceited. The one positive finding in this protocol is the average level score for CN. This score may indicate that the client has realized that he has some social connections to those in his family of origin and that there may have been relatives or close friends who have helped make him feel wanted, loved, and important. These individuals, living or deceased, are providing some modicum of support and personal value. Like Cain, this may be the "blessing" that can allow him to potentially overcome these feelings of isolation and rejection. Despite his mostly conflicted patterns of interaction with others, the client may realize that somewhere there is a place to settle and to call home. A therapist may want to explore these feelings of connectedness and attempt to generalize them in a way to confront the feelings of worthlessness.

Conclusions

The ASPIRES is the only trait-based measure of the numinous that is anchored within the FFM. It captures intrinsic motivations that impel individuals to seek out religious and spiritual outcomes. Because the numinous is an operant motivator, it impacts many aspects of living, including vocational choice, economic attitudes, emotional maturity, interpersonal styles, and ultimate resilience. It can also impact attitudes and values we may develop along an array of content areas (e.g., sexuality, politics). Much attention went into the development of this scale to ensure that it represented a nonredundant aspect of personality that carried a high level of interpretive and predictive value. The universal approach to understanding the numinous has gained wide traction in the field. The ASPIRES has a large, and growing, validity literature demonstrating its predictive value. The ASPIRES has been shown to provide empirically sustainable definitions of the numinous that can be useful in crafting greater definitional consensus in the field. The ASPIRES can be used to help empirically define what is and what is not a spiritual construct. It has also been translated into a number of languages and shown itself to be psychometrically robust. This creates the potential for organizing a wide, and often disparate, literature on R/S into a more cohesive fund of knowledge that can promote greater success in developing a truly cumulative database for the field.

From a clinical perspective, the ASPIRES holds tremendous potential. Its universal approach to understanding the numinous as a psychological construct makes the scale relevant for all individuals, regardless of their faith status (see Gregory, 2013). Results obtained from the scale have important implications for understanding clients and their essential orientations to the transcendent as well as for anticipating important life outcomes. Another interesting feature of the ASPIRES is that it does not top out with religiously committed individuals. Oft times, R/S measures cannot be used with clergy or vowed religious because their immersion in their own faith tradition leads to the highest scores on a scale. Ceiling effects compromise the interpretive value of any scale. Such problems have not been observed with the ASPIRES. While clergy and religious may score very high on RI, there is still variability to be found on this scale as well as on all of the ST facet scales. Its universal application makes the ASPIRES singular in the field of spiritual assessment.

Another clinical value of the ASPIRES is that it gives clients an opportunity to speak about their religious and spiritual issues in counseling. It may also stimulate clients to think about these types of topics and how they influence their feelings and actions; it can serve as an invitation to discuss these core issues. This type of discussion should not put off therapists because the constructs involved with the ASPIRES are psychological in nature and can be used as an organizing rubric for processing any religious material the client may bring up. In other words, when a client brings up religious-oriented material, the therapist should view this content through the lens of infinitude, meaning, and worthiness and frame any response in this manner.

A final value of the ASPIRES is its robust empirical structure and normative-based approach to scoring, making it an ideal tool in outcome research studies. Scores can be used to track the effectiveness of any intervention designed to impact the spiritual orientation of individuals (e.g., Griffiths, Richards, McCann, & Jesse, 2006; Piedmont, 2004) or as a consequence of specific types of therapeutic interventions (e.g., Braganza & Piedmont, 2015). Observing significant changes on numinous scores over time carries important implications for psychological growth and development. The presence of normative data and the use of standardized scores can provide a direct means for determining effect size and for characterizing how these changes will impact behavior.

References

Akyalcin, E., Greenway, P., & Milne, L. (2008). Measuring transcendence: Extracting core constructs. *The Journal of Transpersonal Psychology, 40,* 41–59.

Baron, R. (1985). *Understanding human relations.* Boston, MA: Allyn & Bacon.

Benson, P. L., Donahue, M. J., & Erickson, J. A. (1993). The Faith Maturity Scale: Conceptualization, measurement, and empirical validation. *Research in the Social Scientific Study of Religion, 5,* 1–26.

Bernt, F. (2014). Test review of Assessment of Spirituality and Religious Sentiments. In J. F. Carlson, K. F., Geisinger, & J. L. Jonson (Eds.), *The nineteenth mental measurements yearbook.* Retrieved from http://marketplace.unl.edu/buros/

Bienvenu, O. J., Nestadt, G., Samuels, J. F., Costa, P. T., Howard, W. T., & Eaton, W. W. (2001). Phobic, panic, and major depressive disorders and the Five-Factor Model of personality. *The Journal of Nervous and Mental Disease, 189,* 154–161.

Bourdeau, B., Hinojosa, O., Perez, E., & Chu, K-L. (2004). *Understanding the spirituality of gay Latino men: A cross-cultural validity study.* Paper presented at the

2nd Annual Mid Winter Research Conference on Religion and Spirituality, Columbia, MD.

Braganza, D., & Piedmont, R. L. (2015). The impact of the Core Transformation Process on spirituality, symptom experience, and psychological maturity in a mixed age sample in India: A pilot study. *Journal of Religion and Health, 54,* 888–902.

Carlson, J. F., Geisinger, K. F., & Jonson, J. L. (Eds.). (2014). *The nineteenth mental measurements yearbook* (pp. 24–28). Lincoln, NE: The University of Nebraska Press.

Chen, T. P. (2011). *Cross-cultural psychometric evaluation of the ASPIRES in mainland China.* Unpublished doctoral dissertation, Loyola University, Maryland.

Cheston, S. E., Piedmont, R. L., Eanes, B., & Lavin, L. P. (2003). Changes in clients' images of God over the course of outpatient therapy. *Counseling and Values, 47,* 96–108.

Cho, I. (2004). *An effect of Spiritual Transcendence of fear of intimacy.* Unpublished master's thesis, Torch Trinity Graduate School of Theology, Seoul, Korea.

Clark, L. A. (1993). *Schedule for nonadaptive and adaptive personality: Manual for administration, scoring, and interpretation.* Minneapolis, MN: University of Minnesota Press.

Costa, P. T., Jr., & McCrae, R. R. (1992). The Five-Factor Model of personality and its relevance to personality disorders. *Journal of Personality Disorders, 6,* 343–359.

De Conciliis, A. J. (1993/1994). Individual correlates of prosocial behavior: Comparison of three models (Doctoral dissertation, Loyola College in Maryland, 1993). *Dissertation Abstracts International, 54,* 2892.

Exline, J. J., & Rose, E. (2005). Religious and spiritual struggles. In R. Paloutzian & C. Park (Eds.), *Handbook of the psychology of religion and spirituality* (pp. 315–330). New York, NY: The Guilford Press.

First, M. B., Gibbon, M., Spitzer, R. L., Williams, J. B. W., & Benjamin, L. S. (1997). *User's guide for the Structured Clinical Interview for DSM-IV Personality Disorders (SCID-II).* Washington, DC: American Psychiatric Press.

Frankl, V. E. (1997). *Man's search for ultimate meaning.* New York, NY: Plenum Press.

Goodman, J. M. (2002). *Psychological well-being in the Jewish community: The impact of social identity and spirituality.* Unpublished doctoral dissertation, Kent State University.

Gough, H. G. (1965). Conceptual analysis of psychological test scores and other diagnostic variables. *Journal of Abnormal Psychology, 70,* 294–302.

Gough, H. G., & Heilbrun, A. B. (1983). *The Adjective Check List manual.* Palo Alto, CA; Consulting Psychologists Press.

Gregory, R. J. (2013). *Psychological testing: History, principles, and applications* (7th ed.). Boston, MA: Pearson.

Griffiths, R. R., Richards, W. A., McCann, U., & Jesse, R. (2006). Psilocybin can occasion mystical-type experiences having substantial and sustained personal meaning and spiritual significance. *Psychopharmacology, 187,* 268–283.

Hall, D. E., Meador, K. G., & Koenig, H. G. (2008). Measuring religiousness in health research: Review and critique. *Journal of Religion and Health, 47,* 134–163.

Harris, K. A., Howell, D. S., & Spurgeon, D. W. (2018). Faith concepts in psychology: Three 30-year definitional content analyses. *Psychology of Religion and Spirituality, 10,* 1–29.

Hill, P. C., & Hood, R. W., Jr. (1999). *Measures of religiosity.* Birmingham, AL: Religious Education Press.

Hill, P. C., & Pargament, K. I. (2003). Advances in the conceptualization and measurement of religion and spirituality: Implications for physical and mental health research. *American Psychologist, 58*, 64–74.

Hill, P. C., Pargament, K. I., Hood, R. W., Jr., McCullough, M. E., Swyers, J. P., Larson, D. B., & Zinnbauer, B. J. (2000). Conceptualizing religion and spirituality: Points of commonality, points of departure. *Journal for the Theory of Social Behavior, 30*, 51–77.

Hunsley, J., & Meyer, G. J. (2003). The incremental validity of psychological testing and assessment: Conceptual, methodological, and statistical issues. *Psychological Assessment, 15*, 446–455.

Insel, P. M., & Roth, W. T. (1985). *Core concepts in health* (4th ed.). Palo Alto, CA: Mayfield Publishing.

John E. Fetzer Institute. (1999, January). *Multidimensional measurement of religiousness/spirituality for use in health research.* Kalamazoo, MI: Author.

Joshanloo, M. (2012): Investigation of the factor structure of spirituality and religiosity in Iranian Shiite university students. *International Journal of Psychology, 47*, 211–221. doi:10.1080/00207594.2011.617372

Katsogianni, I. V., & Kleftaras, G. (2015). Spirituality, meaning in life, and depressive symptomatology in drug addiction. *International Journal of Religion & Spirituality in Society, 5*(2), 11–24.

Koenig, H. G. (2008). Concerns about measuring "spirituality" in research. *The Journal of Nervous and Mental Diseases, 196*, 349–355.

Lau, W. W., Hui, C. H., Lam, J., Lau, E. Y. Y., Ng, D., & Cheong, S-F. (2016). Psychometric evaluation of the Spiritual Transcendence Scale in a Chinese sample: Is there factorial invariance across gender, occupation, and religion? *International Journal for the Psychology of Religion, 26*, 136–151.

Lemos, V., & Oñate, M. E. (2018). Espiritaualidad y personalidad en el marco de los Big Five [Spirituality and personality within the framework of the Big Five]. *Ciencias Psicológicas, 12*, 59–66.

MacDonald, T. A. (2000). Spirituality: Description, measurement, and relation to the Five Factor Model of Personality. *Journal of Personality, 68*, 153–197.

Mahoney, A. (2013). The spirituality of us: Relational spirituality in the context of family relationships. In K. I. Pargament, J. J. Exline, & J. W. Jones (Eds.), *APA handbook of psychology, religion, and spirituality* (Vol. 1; pp. 365–389). Washington DC: American Psychological Association.

Maslow, A. H. (1971). *The farther reaches of human nature.* New York, NY: Viking Press.

Masters, K. S., Carey, K. B., Maisto, S. A., Caldwell, P. E., Wolfe, T. V., Hackney, H. L., France, C. R., & Himawan, L. (2009). Psychometric examination of the Brief Multidimensional Measure of Religiousness/Spirituality among college students. *The International Journal for the Psychology of Religion, 19*, 106–120.

McCrae, R. R. (1999). Mainstream personality psychology and the study of religion. *Journal of Personality, 67*, 1209–1218.

McCrae, R. R. (2010). The place of the FFM in personality research. *Psychological Inquiry, 21*, 57–64.

McCrae, R. R., & Costa, P. T., Jr., (1989). Rotation to maximize the construct validity of factors in the NEO Personality Inventory. *Multivariate Behavioral Research, 24*, 107–124.

McCrae, R. R., Herbst, J. H., & Costa, P. T., Jr. (2001). Effects of acquiescence on personality factor structures (pp. 217–231). In R. Riemann, F. M. Spinath, & F. Ostendorf (Eds.), *Personality and temperament: Genetics, evolution, and structure.* Berlin, Germany: Pabst Science Publishers.

McGinn, B. (1993). The letter and the spirit: Spirituality as an academic discipline. *Christian Spirituality Bulletin, 1*(2), 1–10.

Miller, L. H., & Smith, A. D. (1987). Vulnerability scale. *Stress Audit.* Brookline, MA: Biobehavioral Associates.

Musick, M. A., Traphagan, J. W., Koenig, H. W., & Larson, D. B. (2000). Spirituality in physical health and aging. *Journal of Adult Development, 7,* 73–86.

New American Bible (1978). New York, NY: Catholic Publishers, Inc.

Nunnally, J. C., & Bernstein, I. H. (1994). *Psychometric theory* (3rd ed.). New York: McGraw-Hill.

Parsons, N. K., Richards, H. C., & Kanter, G. D. P. (1990). Validation of a scale to measure reasoning about abortion. *Journal of Counseling Psychology, 37,* 107–112.

Piedmont, R. L. (1995). Big Five adjective marker scales for use with college students. *Psychological Reports, 77,* 160–162.

Piedmont, R. L. (1998). *The Revised NEO Personality Inventory: Clinical and research applications.* New York, NY: Plenum.

Piedmont, R. L. (1999). Does spirituality represent the sixth factor of personality? Spiritual transcendence and the five-factor model. *Journal of Personality, 67,* 985–1013.

Piedmont, R. L. (2001). Spiritual Transcendence and the scientific study of spirituality. *Journal of Rehabilitation, 67*(1), 4–14.

Piedmont, R. L. (2004). Spiritual Transcendence as a predictor of psychosocial outcome from an outpatient substance abuse program. *Psychology of Addictive Behaviors, 18,* 213–222.

Piedmont, R. L. (2007). Cross-cultural generalizability of the Spiritual Transcendence Scale to the Philippines: Spirituality as a human universal. *Mental Health, Religion, & Culture, 10,* 89–107.

Piedmont, R. L. (2010). *Assessment of Spirituality and Religious Sentiments, technical manual* (2nd ed.). Baltimore, MD: Author.

Piedmont, R. L. (2012). Overview and development of a trait-based measure of numinous constructs: The Assessment of Spirituality and Religious Sentiments (ASPIRES) scale. In L. Miller (Ed.). *The Oxford handbook of psychology of spirituality and consciousness* (pp. 104–122). New York, NY: Oxford University Press.

Piedmont, R. L., Hassinger, C. J., Rhorer, J., Sherman, M. F., Sherman, N. C., & Williams, J. E. G. (2007). The relations among spirituality and religiosity and Axis II functioning in two college samples. *Research in the Social Scientific Study of Religion, 18,* 53–73.

Piedmont, R. L., & Leach, M. M. (2002). Cross-cultural generalizability of the Spiritual Transcendence Scale in India: Spirituality as a universal aspect of human experience. *American Behavioral Scientist, 45,* 1886–1899.

Piedmont, R. L., Mapa, A. T., & Williams, J. E. G. (2006). A factor analysis of the Fetzer/NIA Brief Multidimensional Measure of Religiousness/Spirituality (MMRS). *Research in the Social Scientific Study of Religion, 17,* 177–196.

Piedmont, R. L., McCrae, R. R., & Costa, P. T., Jr. (1991). Adjective check list scales and the five-factor model. *Journal of Personality and Social Psychology, 60,* 630–637.

Piedmont, R. L., & Nelson, R. (2001). A psychometric evaluation of the short form of the Faith Maturity Scale. *Research in the Social Scientific Study of Religion, 12*, 165–184.

Piedmont, R. L., Sherman, M. F., Sherman, N. C., Dy-Liacco, G. S., & Williams, J. E. G. (2009). Using the five-factor model to identify a new personality disorder domain: The case for Experiential Permeability. *Journal of Personality and Social Psychology, 96*, 1245–1258.

Piedmont, R. L., Werdel, M. B., & Fernando, M. (2009). The utility of the Assessment of Spirituality and Religious Sentiments (ASPIRES) scale with Christians and Buddhists in Sri Lanka. *Research in the Social Scientific Study of Religion, 20*, 131–146.

Piedmont, R. L., Wilkins, T. A., & Hollwitz, J. (2013) The relevance of spiritual transcendence in a consumer economy: The dollars and sense of it. *Journal of Social Research and Policy, 4*, 59–77.

Piotrowski, J. P., Żemojtel-Piotrowska, M. A., Piedmont, R. L., & Baran, T. (2018). Polish adaptation of the Assessment of Spirituality and Religious Sentiments (ASPIRES) Scale and examining a spiritual transcendence nomological net. *Psychology of Religion and . . . Current Psychology, 2018*(2). doi: 10.1007/s12144-018-9810-1

Rayburn, C. A. (1996, August). *Religion and spirituality: Can one exist independently of the other?* Paper presented at the annual convention of the American Psychological Association, Toronto, Canada.

Rican, P., & Janosova, P. (2010). Spirituality as a basic aspect of personality: A cross-cultural verification of Piedmont's model. *The International Journal for the Psychology of Religion, 20*, 2–13.

Ruckmick, C. A. (1920). *The Brevity book on psychology.* Chicago, IL: Brevity Publishers.

Schoenrade, P. (2014). Test review of Assessment of Spirituality and Religious Sentiments. In J. F. Carlson, K. F., Geisinger, & J. L. Jonson (Eds.), *The nineteenth mental measurements yearbook.* Retrieved from http://marketplace.unl.edu/buros/

Schönemann, P. H. (1966). A generalized solution of the orthogonal Procrustes problem. *Psychometrica, 31*, 1–10.

Sheldrake, P. (1992). *Spirituality and history: Questions of interpretation and method.* New York, NY: Crossroads.

Simkin, H. (2017). Adaptación y validación al Español de la Esacla de Evaluación de Espiritualidad y Sentimientos Religiosos (ASPIRES): la transcendencia espiritual en el modelo de los cinco factores [Adaptation and validation of the Assessment of Spirituality and Religious Sentiments (ASPIRES) Scale into Spanish: Spiritual Transcendence within the Five-Factor Model. *Universitas Psychologica, 16*(2), 1–12.

Smith, G. T., McCarthy, D. M., & Anderson, K. G. (2000). On the sins of short-form development. *Psychological Assessment, 12*, 102–111.

Swap, W., & Rubin, J. (1983). Measurement of interpersonal orientation. *Journal of Personality and Social Psychology, 44*, 208–219.

Tomcsányi, T., Martos, T., Ittzés, A., Horváth-Szabó, K., Szabó, T., & Nagy, J. (2011). A Spirituális Transzcendencia Skála hazai alkalmazása: Elmélet, pszichometriai jellemz˝ok, kutatási eredmények és rövidített változat [Application of the Spiritual Transcendence Scale in Hungary: Theory, psychometric properties, empirical findings and shortened version]. *Pszichológia, 31*, 165–192.

Trull, T. J., Vergés, A., Wood, P. K., Jahng, S., & Sher, K. J. (2012). The structure of *Diagnostic and Statistical Manual of Mental Disorders* (4th edition, text revision) personality disorder symptoms in a large national sample. *Personality Disorders: Theory, Research, and Treatment, 3,* 355–369. doi:10.1037/a0027766

Walker, D. F., & Gorsuch, R. L. (2002). Forgiveness within the Big Five personality model. *Personality and Individual Differences, 32,* 1127–1137.

Wallston, K., Wallston, B., & DeVellis, R. (1978). Development of the multidimensional health locus of control scales. *Health Education Monographs, 6,* 160–170.

Wilson, T. (2004). *Ethnic identity and spirituality in the recovery from alcoholism among aboriginal Canadians.* Unpublished master's thesis, University of Windsor.

Woodworth, R. S. (1940). *Psychology* (4th ed.). New York, NY: Henry Hold & Co.

Wulff, D. M. (1997). *Psychology of religion: Classic and contemporary* (2nd ed.). New York, NY: Wiley & Sons.

Zinnbauer, B. J., Pargament, K. I., Cole, B., Rye, M. S., Butter, E. M., Belavich, T. G., Hipp, K. M., Scott, A. B., & Kadar, J. L. (1997). Religion and spirituality: Unfuzzying the fuzzy. *Journal for the Scientific Study of Religion, 36,* 549–564.

Appendix 5.A

ASPIR ES™

Assessment of Spirituality and Religious Sentiments

Scoring and Interpretive Computer Report
Version 1.0

Developed by
Ralph L. Piedmont, Ph.D.
Rose I. Piedmont

Client Information

RESULTS FOR:	Bobby T. (This name is a pseudonym.)
DATE:	6/11/2013
GENDER:	Male
AGE:	42
RACE:	Caucasian
RELIGIOUS AFFILIATION:	Methodist

The following report is based on research using normal adult samples and is intended to provide information on the basic dimensions of spirituality and religious sentiments. The interpretive information presented in this report should be viewed as only one source of information about the individual being assessed. No decisions about this person should be based solely on the results presented here. Information from this report should be combined with all other sources of information available before reaching any professional conclusions. This report is intended for use by qualified professionals.

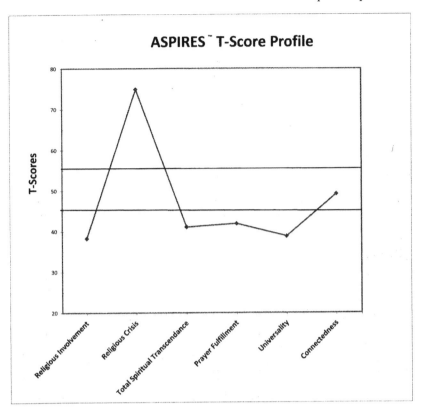

Profile Results

The following interpretations are based on scores obtained from the self report, long form of the aspires. Results are presented as T-scores, having a mean of 50 and a standard deviation of 10 based on normative data organized by age and gender.

Interpretive Context

This profile indicates an individual who has not experienced any significant changes in religious or spiritual functioning over the past year. He/she has a level of contentment and satisfaction with his/her current level of religious involvements. This score also indicates a level of stability in his/her attitudes about religion. Scores on the religious involvement (RI) scale will evidence how deeply involved in

(continued)

(continued)

those practices this person is. A high RI score may indicate a strong, continuous investment in his/her faith. A low RI score may indicate an apathy towards religious activities.

This person values their religious practices and involvements as much as the average person. Religious activities may serve as a general framework for personal identity, but there may be places in his/her life where these values may be relegated to a secondary role for determining behavior.

Religious Sentiments Scales

Religious Involvement   38   Low

This person scored in the low range for religious involvement, indicating a lack of involvement in faith-based religious activities. Low scores may indicate a person who does not conform to the established practices prescribed by a faith group and may instead prefer more personalized ways of interacting with the god of one's understanding. Or, the low score may reflect an individual who is not religiously involved at all and finds little value or use for such activities. This score may hold little interpretive value for atheists or agnostics, who do not subscribe to any such practices. With individuals for whom religion is a reality, low scorers may be found as somewhat antagonistic towards others. Low scorers on this scale are associated with higher levels of negative affect and take a more individualistic approach to life. They may be perceived by others as being boastful, dreamy, foolish, impatient, intolerant, quarrelsome, and tough.

Religious Crisis   75   Very High

This person scored high on the religious crisis scale, indicating that his/her relationship with the transcendent is disrupted and is creating emotional distress. It is likely that he or she is in a current state of crisis. This may be a crisis of faith, or it may reflect a specific conflict occurring within his/her own religious community. He/she may appear bitter and dissatisfied and be suspicious of the motivations of others. There may be a need to make a pastoral intervention. High scores on this scale are associated with higher levels of negative affect, a poor sense of life satisfaction, lowered self-esteem, and lowered psychological maturity. High scores may also be linked to an increased risk of sexually acting-out behavior. Those with a high score are perceived by others as being arrogant, bitter, distrustful, irresponsible, awkward, and dissatisfied.

Spiritual Transcendence Scales

Total Spiritual Transcendence   41   Low

Overall this person scored in the low range on the spiritual transcendence, indicating a greater focus on the tangible realities of daily living. Low scorers tend to have a more self-oriented focus to life, whereby personal concerns and issues are of greater concern than any consideration of spiritual realities that lie beyond this physical universe. This person takes a more pragmatic view of life, understanding its ebbs and flows from a more physical, mechanistic perspective. This person may evidence a difficulty in understanding failure and disappointment in life. An examination of his or her facet scores, which are presented below, may lead to a better understanding of his or her spiritual orientation.

Prayer Fulfillment   42   Low

This person scored low on the prayer fulfillment scale indicating that he/she is not much involved in meditative and reflective activities and may even shun this type of inner work. Any efforts at prayer or meditation are more haphazard in nature and superficial in depth. Low scorers are easily distracted by the immediate demands of their lives from such prayerful pursuits. Low scores on this scale are associated with high levels of negative affect, a greater sense of individualism, and more diverse sexual experiences. Individuals scoring low on this scale are perceived by others as being argumentative, distractible, distrustful, fickle, and hard-hearted. Please note that atheists, agnostics, and certain eastern religious groups frequently score low on this scale because their belief systems do not include any transcendent realities. If this is the case here, then this score may have little interpretive relevance for this person.

Universality   39   Low

On universality this person scores in the low range, which reflects a more "go-it-alone" type of attitude towards the world; a belief that each person needs to rely on him/herself. Humanity may be viewed as simply a collection of individuals, some of whom may be seen as more similar to self than others. There can be a "we versus they" mentality. Relationships to other groups may be limited to those that have personal value to the individual (e.g., work colleagues, special interest groups). Low scores on this scale are associated with higher levels of negative affect and a greater sense of individualism. Those scoring low on universality are seen by others as being complaining, conceited, greedy, quarrelsome, and self-centered.

Connectedness   49   Average

The respondent scored in the average range on connectedness, which indicates a belief that relationships are important, but one's commitments to others may be limited to certain individuals. Relationships to others may be viewed as providing some fundamental value to the person (i.e., identity definition, a place to belong) rather than reflecting a greater social interest in the well-being of the group. Feelings of independence and self-reliance may be characteristic of this person, who may have limited interest in what others (e.g., parents, friends) may have to say about their lifestyle.

6 The Logoplex as a Psychological Model for Understanding Meaning

Meaning is one of the core aspects of spirituality that is frequently studied. The reason is simple: Meaning is not only seen as the basic defining element of spirituality but also as an essential quality of the human experience. Frankl (1969) has asserted that the *will to meaning* is what drives the human experience. Park (2013) believes that individuals create an entire meaning system in an effort to organize personal experiences, to evaluate and appraise them, and to eventually construct a global sense of meaning that provides coherence, direction, and purpose. Theologians, too, also acknowledge the central role of meaning in the spiritual process and experience (Tillich, 1951, 1952/2000). How we create meaning says much about who we are as individuals and how we see the world. Meaning provides us with the overall template for organizing our experiences of the world and for creating our anticipations for the future. Meaning arrives as a consequence of our efforts at addressing core existential questions, such as "Why am I here?" "Where am I going to in life?" Because of the obvious role of meaning in the study of spirituality, frequently we are asked by students and colleagues whether the study of religiousness/spirituality (R/S) and its constructs and concepts is merely simple existentialism. In other words, is a religious or spiritual focus simply a special kind of existential meaning-making? This is an important question, one that is frequently raised by professionals from other disciplines, and one that has important consequences for the viability and importance of numinous research (e.g., Buss, 2002). Our answer to this question has always been, "No!"

There are two reasons for this answer. First, while meaning is important to the spiritual experience, it is by no means veridical with spirituality. As we saw in Chapter 2, there are three essential components to the numinous: Meaning, Infinitude, and Worthiness. Thus, to fully understand the numinous and its role in the mental life of people, one needs to appreciate all three dimensions. Second, for the existentialist, meaning is the skeleton upon which the flesh of our lives is hung. To paraphrase Frankl (1969), whoever has the "why" to life, has the who, what, and where already worked out. To the existential-ist, having meaning gives focus and direction to life. It does not matter what that meaning is, but its presence is crucial to developing a sense of purpose and resilience. As Frankl recounted in his experiences in con-centration camps during WWII, those prisoners who hated their Nazi overlords seemed more likely to survive their experience than those who seemed to simply give up and succumb to feelings of hopelessness. We believe that while meaning is important, there are different types of meaning that have varying implications for the psychological stability and numinous character of the individual.

The purpose of this chapter is to present an overview of a model of meaning-making that provides more nuance and precision to under-standing meaning. Termed *the Logoplex* (literally, meaning network), in recognition of Frankl's contribution to our thinking in this area, this model articulates that meaning is comprised of two dimensions and that their systematic combinations create very different meaning orientations (see Piedmont, 2004). Thus, not all "meanings" are the same. These two rea-sons set apart the study of the numinous from existentialism: The former includes a more developed sense of meaning than the latter. It is believed that the numinous approach to meaning will provide more insights into the psychic world of the individual as well as allow therapists to develop more specific expectations about the life directions of their clients.

Basic Assumption of the Logoplex

Meaning-making is a process by which individuals organize their percep-tions and understandings of the world they know in a way that provides a unitary structure that arranges their myriad of feelings, beliefs, and antic-ipations about their world. Meaning provides direction and coherence to life, as well as a set of values that prioritizes all aspects of functioning. Inherent to this meaning-making process is the dimension of time. Time is not well researched in the field, but how individuals address time is important for the type of meanings people create (see Zimbardo & Boyd, 1999). When we refer to the notion of time, what is being described is *psychological time* (PT). PT represents how individuals come to perceive and experience time in their lives, and such a perception may not always reflect actual time as measured by a clock or calendar. It is the context within which people situate their actions, plans, and understandings; it is a ruler against which life is evaluated and interpreted.

Lewin (1951) understood PT as "the totality of the individual's views of his psychological future and psychological past existing at a given time" (p. 75). People's PT understanding impacts choices and goals; it influences their emotional experience of events and the types of antici-pations about current and future events. Zimbardo and Boyd (1999) have developed this concept, defining PT as a "nonconscious process whereby the continual flows of personal and social experiences are assigned to temporal categories, or time frames, that help to give order, coherence, and meaning to those events" (p. 1271). For Zimbardo and Boyd, PT can be divided into five different categories (Past-Negative, Present-Hedonistic, Future, Past-Positive, and Present-Fatalistic), each with their own psychological sequelae.

From the perspective of our Logoplex model, time is an essential element underlying the meaning-making process. We assume that meaning always occurs within some kind of time frame or context, what we refer to as the *event horizon*. These event horizons can range from very short (e.g., I need to eat dinner because I am hungry) to very long (e.g., I want to get my doctorate in psychology). Our basic assumption is that the longer the event horizon for some activity, the more coherence, stability, and resilience it provides the person. Tasks that require much time to complete will confer upon people a greater ability to tolerate stressors than tasks that involve shorter time intervals. For example, if a person has the goal of getting enough money by the end of the week to pay rent, this very short time frame can be quite easily disrupted and create stress. If this fictional person is a retiree and is waiting for the first of the month so as to receive a Social Security check, and that check does not arrive, the outcome will be distress for this retiree; there is no money to pay the rent that is due.

On the other hand, consider someone who has decided to go for a graduate degree in a field of practice. This program will take 2 years of full-time work. During this time frame (or event horizon), the person works diligently towards the professional goal. While there are certainly ups and downs during this time, both in the person's general life and studies, the commitment to the final goal keeps him/her focused. The various stressors have less of a negative impact because the goal is larger and more important than any other distractions. As Adler has argued, our goals provide an organizing psychological praxis for individuals because each goal is emblematic of other, larger goals, which are themselves a component of one's style of living. For Adler, goal striving has a clear teleological character, in that we are always moving towards something larger: outcomes that call us to be better, stronger, more powerful. As Adler has noted, "that power which expresses itself in the desire to develop, to strive, and to achieve—and even to compensate for defeats in one direction by striving for success in another" (Adler, 1929, p. 1).

The creation of future goals provides a structure for moving forward despite any distractions (e.g., failures, difficulties, stressors) that are encountered. The more long-range the goal is in time (i.e., the longer the event horizon), the more stability and resilience the person experiences in living his/her life. The question arises, "How long can a time line be?" Certainly, individuals create life-long goals (e.g., graduate education and then a successful professional career), but given humans' innate ability to understand and comprehend even eternity, then the possibility exists for people to create goals that are eternal in nature. As we noted in Chapter 2, taking a transcendent perspective to creating meaning is the foundation for the numinous. When a person creates an understanding of his or her life where time is not a factor, then the most durable and resilient sense of meaning is created. In this context, viewing our current life as just one stage in a larger ontological process is the core perspective of the numinous. It is from this perspective that the individual finds the greatest level of stability and resilience.

As noted above, Zimbardo and Boyd (1999) have developed five scales to capture these different time perspectives. However, they, too, have also recognized that people do construct eternal time perspectives and have created a *Transcendental Time Perspective* scale to capture this numinous orientation as well (Boyd & Zimbardo, 1996). This scale captures the extent to which people specifically understand their sense of being within an eternal time line (scale items include: "Death is just a new beginning," and "Only my physical body will ever die"). Interestingly, when this scale was factor analyzed along with items from a Big 5 Personality scale it remained a distinct factor, leading these authors to conclude that the Transcendent Time Perspective scale "is an individual-differences dimension unaccounted for by traditional personality analyses" (Zimbardo & Boyd, 1999, p. 1284). We therefore would expect strong associations between this measure and appropriately developed numinous scales (e.g., the ASPIRES: Piedmont, 2010; see Chapter 5 as well).

The other time-perspective scales are also seen as having relevance to the numinous. Specifically, a future time orientation should be associated with Spiritual Transcendence (ST) because those scoring high on this time orientation are those who use the future to plan and organize their current life situations. Those with a future orientation seem to be embedding their personal sense of meaning within a longer event horizon. Zimbardo and Boyd (1999) demonstrated that a Future time perspective was associated with more clearly defined future goals, better problem-solving and emotional growth coping skills, higher levels of optimism, and less engagement in high-risk HIV-related behaviors. Conversely, those who have a Past-Negative time orientation were found to have minimal interpersonal relationships and be unmotivated to work for future rewards, experienced lower levels of happiness and self-esteem, and were less likely to have had sexual relations.

We hypothesized that such high levels of dissatisfaction with past events, especially as they relate to others, would be associated with higher levels of Religious Crisis (RC; a subscale of the ASPIRES). A similar association was also expected with the Present-Fatalistic group, who were found wanting to live shorter lives, to be dissatisfied with their current life and believe that their situation would never improve because their lives are predetermined by fate, and to lack the desire to spend time with friends (Zimbardo & Boyd, 1999). Such a fatalistic sense of unworthiness would also seem a correlate of RC.

In an effort to test these hypotheses, the NAG (Numinous Assessment Group; see Chapter 7) members collected a sample of 711 adults (416 women and 295 men) with a mean age of 35.48 ($SD = 12.26$) using the MTurk platform of workers. The sample was largely Caucasian (76%) with 8% African-American, 6% Asian, 6% Hispanic, and the remaining 4% representing other categories. These individuals completed the Zimbardo Time Perspective Inventory (ZTPI) and the Transcendental-Future Time Perspective Scale (TFTPS: Boyd & Zimbardo, 1996) along with the ASPIRES, and the results are presented in Table 6.1. As can be seen, time perspective does have many significant associations with the numinous. As expected, the Transcendental Time Perspective (TTP) is very strongly associated with all of the ASPIRES' scales, except RC. The item content of the TTP is very closely associated with aspects of Prayer Fulfillment and overall Spiritual Transcendence Scale (STS) scores. The magnitude of these associations is so high that one may consider the two scales as capturing a common construct.

As anticipated, Future time perspective was positively correlated with the STS scales and was negatively related to RC. Having a forward focus in creating meaning is associated with a more transcendent perspective. While expectations for the other time perspective scales were not made, the observed patterns do make conceptual sense. Those who held Past-Negative and Present-Fatalistic perspectives tended to also score higher on the RC scale; negative experiences from the past and current negativism all relate to feelings of rejection and personal unacceptability. As noted above concerning the Present-Fatalistic perspective, high-scoring

Table 6.1 Correlations between the Time Perspective Scales and the ASPIRES.

ASPIRES *Scales*	*Time Perspective Scales*					
	Transcendent	*Past-Negative*	*Present-Hedonistic*	*Future*	*Past-Positive*	*Present-Fatalistic*
Prayer Fulfillment	.77***	-.03	.14***	.10**	.27***	.07
Universality	.55***	-.09*	.22***	.12***	.28***	-.08*
Connectedness	.30***	.07*	.16***	.10**	.32***	-.08*
Total STS	.72***	-.03	.20***	.13***	.33***	.01
Religious Involve	.69***	.01	.15***	.03	.21***	.11**
Religious Crisis	-.08*	.34***	-.02	-.15***	-.19***	.23***

$N = 711$, * $p < .05$, ** $p < .01$, *** $p < .001$, two-tailed.

individuals feel that their lives are based on fate; there is a very low sense of personal agency. Yet, despite feeling trapped in an unacceptable life process, high scores on this scale were also associated with higher scores on Religious Involvement (RI). This is a curious finding because if one believes that life is predetermined, why involve oneself in religious rituals? What purpose does prayer to a higher power serve? This finding may underscore our earlier interpretation of the RI scale as reflecting efforts to reduce negative affect through the performance of repetitive rituals. Perhaps the association with RI reflects a belief that while things may not get better or change, ritual activities may provide some degree of emotional succorance and assuage personal disappointment and pain.

These data demonstrate the essential role of time perspective in the creation of meaning. One cannot understand meaning without knowing how time is being involved in the perceptions of reality. We find empirical support for our assumption that the longer the event horizon within which meaning is created, the more stability and resilience a person maintains. When this event horizon takes on an eternal perspective, an individual should experience the highest levels of well-being and complete life satisfaction. There is an unperturbability that is encountered with this sense of PT that is difficult for negative events to disrupt. In discussing Adler's notion of fictional goals and their impact of behavior, Bischof (1970, p. 180) noted, "The past may set the stage and thus limit the actions of the actors, but the future determines what the players will do. The past is prologue, but the future is the scene."

The next section will present the structure and function of the model itself. The Logoplex is a circumplex model that provides a framework for understanding the different types of meaning that individuals develop for construing their lives. The model appreciates the inherent multidimensionality of meaning formation, including not only the role of ST but aspects of the personality dimensions of Agreeableness and Extraversion. This model, which is presented graphically below in Figure 6.1, identifies two broad domains that we hypothesize to underlie the different meaning orientations that individuals can develop: *Transpersonalism versus Materialism* and *Relationalism versus Intentionalism*.

The Logoplex

A circumplex represents a circular ordering of traits around two independent dimensions. These traits represent varying amounts of the two defining constructs. Scales that are closer together in space on the circumplex are more related than scales that are farther apart. Scales that are 90 degrees apart are independent of one another, while those 180 degrees apart are negatively related. What the model illustrates is that there are multiple ways in which individuals create meaning and that there exist certain relationships among these various outcomes. As noted above, the most salient aspect of meaning-making is the event horizon within which the meaning is constructed. We hypothesize that the broader the frame of reference (i.e., the longer the time frame), the richer and more durable the resulting meaning (i.e., one's sense of self remains stable and satisfied in the face of existential challenges and physical hardships). Because a numinous orientation involves some relationship or connection to an eternal reality and/or being, its event horizon is the broadest and therefore is considered to provide the highest level of meaning organization.

The first major dimension of the Logoplex is Transpersonalism versus Materialism. Transpersonalism represents Frankl's (1959) motivational construct of a will to meaning. It is the effort to create a personal sense of meaning and purpose. There are two components to creating meaning. First, there is the recognition that "life is a time gestalt, and as such becomes something whole only after the life has been completed" (Frankl, 1966, pp. 99–100). This perspective enables a view of one's life as an emerging entity that fills a need in nature. Second, as Frankl (1966) stated, "being human is directed to something other than itself" (p. 102). Thus, Transpersonalism allows an individual to construct meaning that transcends his or her immediate sense of time and self. In contrast, Materialism maintains a focus on the immediate and the concrete. The materialist is primarily concerned with that which can be possessed and/or consumed in the here and now. Meaning is found only in terms of mechanical, tangible operations that follow prescribed paths; there are limits in vision, purpose, and meaning. The materialist maintains a very strong self-focus.

The second major dimension of the Logoplex is the Relationalism versus Intentionalism dimension. The Relational orientation reflects a desire for involvement in, communion with, and connection to larger social groups. It is a personal response to care for larger organizations or institutions and to see that they are affirmed. What Adler referred to as *Gemeinschaftsgefühl*, or social interest, very much embodies this orientation. In contrast, the Intentional orientation reflects a much more self-centered, interpersonally cynical position. Intentionalism reflects a desire to put the interests of the self above any other considerations; one's own personal needs are seen as being paramount. Another way to conceive of this domain is as a group versus individual focus.

These two domains comprise the Logoplex, which is presented in Figure 6.1. The Logoplex marks off four distinct quadrants that represent the various combinations of the two defining constructs. The *Solipsism* quadrant reflects the Material-Intentional combination. Individuals in this quadrant are hypothesized to be very much self-focused and self-involved. Their worlds are comprised of their range of immediate

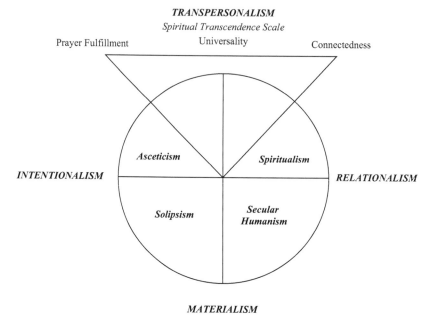

Optimal Levels of Human Functioning

Figure 6.1 Proposed Logoplex Model

This figure is reproduced from Piedmont (2004) from *Research in the Social Scientific Study of Religion*, volume 15. Copyright 2005 by Koninklijke Brill NV, Leiden, The Netherlands. Reproduced with permission of publisher.

experiences. Their sense of meaning is wrapped around their own sense of self. These individuals tend to focus only on their own needs, feelings, and aspirations. They distrust the motivations of others and tend to avoid getting involved with people. Because the event horizon for creating meaning is the most restricted, individuals in this category are prone to experience high levels of mental distress as a consequence of being easily cut off from the nurturing experiences of both other people and social institutions. Their lives lack broad perspective, and therefore stressful events can easily upset their lives.

Secular Humanism represents the Material-Relational quadrant. Individuals maintaining this orientation are hypothesized to be very much concerned with their own immediate needs and concentrate on realities that are experienced through their senses; however, they do have a broader orientation that includes larger social institutions. Individuals who are committed to social institutions or to the larger social good fall into this category. They have found a place for themselves in a larger group or society and are able to find personal satisfaction in these groups. However, as far as personal meaning goes, these people do not find value beyond their social institutions. They carry with them a sense of civic-mindedness and social responsibility; their service to these organizations helps to maintain a sense of purpose and contributes to their ongoing survival. Individuals in this quadrant may have a highly developed social ethic and may recognize their responsibility to not only those in their own life cohort but to those who come after them. Their experiences represent mental health as traditionally defined (i.e., the absence of any debilitating symptoms). In fact, this lower half of the circumplex represents minimum levels of well-being and marks out the area traditionally studied by psychology.

The upper half of the circumplex contains those qualities that are at the center of more optimal levels of human functioning. The two quadrants here are perhaps the least well researched in the social sciences but have the most to contribute to expanding our understanding of people and the goals they pursue. The *Asceticism* quadrant reflects a Transpersonal-Intentional orientation to finding meaning. Such individuals are assumed to be quite concerned about developing a broad sense of personal meaning within a transcendent context; there is the recognition that one is a member of a larger community of believers that transects both the material and spiritual worlds. However, these individuals remain detached from involvement in larger communities and social groups. The prototypes for this quadrant are the Desert Fathers and Mothers, cloistered monks and nuns, or hermits. People in this category experience very intimate relations with a larger, Ultimate Reality, but this relationship with their God is a very personal and singular one. Although there is a broad concern and care for all of humanity, and perhaps a desire to witness this sacredness to larger communities, they create a very self-contained, and perhaps insulated, social world.

Finally, the Transpersonal-Relational quadrant defines *Spiritualism.* These are individuals who are hypothesized to have a broad sense of transcendent meaning and develop and/or express this understanding within a defined community. It is important to note here that the community is an essential element of their meaning processes. Unlike the Ascetic (AS), connections with others, groups, or institutions become the foundations upon which meaning is developed and personal value is assessed. Unlike the Secular Humanist (SH), there is a realization that their involvement with others arises from strong teleological convictions. Individuals such as Mother Teresa of Calcutta or Mahatma Gandhi ideally represent this category. Like the AS, these individuals bear witness to larger, transcendent realities, but unlike the AS they are enmeshed in a ministry that directly bonds them daily to the larger secular world.

We hypothesize this quadrant as representing the most durable level of personal fulfillment and meaning.

The triangle depicted in Figure 6.1 represents the substantive aspect of the circumplex that is captured by the STS of the ASPIRES. It is clear that the STS does not represent the totality of the Transpersonal/Transcendent domain (i.e., the top half of the circumplex). Certainly, there are other variables that would be needed in order to better nuance and reflect the role of the numinous in the meaning process. Although general scores on the STS can give a sense of how a person may be oriented towards developing a sense of meaning, without consideration of the other dimension of the model (e.g., Relational vs. Intentional), one cannot determine the specific form this transcendent motivation will take.

Interpretive Approach to the Logoplex

The value of a circumplex model is that it clearly illustrates that the phenomenon under study is one that involves two independent dimensions interactively combining to produce specific behaviors. In other words, outcomes based on the model need to appreciate the different blends of the underlying defining dimensions. This is also the case for the Logoplex. The definitions presented above for each quadrant ought to be seen as heuristics: broad explanations designed to highlight the essential qualities present in each area. However, actual interpretations need to be more nuanced. Within each quadrant there exists a wide range of meaning-making outcomes, depending where on the outer circle one falls. Consider the Secular Humanism quadrant. Overall, this section reflects a meaning-making orientation that incorporates a clear social element to it. However, how much social interest there may be depends on where in the quadrant the person falls. For example, someone who falls near the 6:00 position (i.e., on the border between Solipsism and Secular Humanism) may have an orientation to others that may be more manipulative and exploitive. The concern for others is based on a perceived need to use them for his or her own purposes and support. Others are seen as resources that the person can extract for his/her own goals.

However, as the meaning orientation moves along the circumference of this model towards the 3:00 position, there are very clear changes in meaning. Someone at the border with the Spiritualism quadrant would appear quite different from the previous person. This individual may be someone who is very altruistically oriented, maintaining a concerned and involved social interest, such as a financial donor, volunteer for social groups/endeavors, or a worker in service professions (e.g., teaching, helping fields). Think of those young men and women serving in the military today. These people are committed to the ideals of their nation and the values it represents. This deep commitment is expressed in their willingness to put their own lives on the line for the safety and security of their fellow citizens. As we noted in an earlier chapter, spirituality can be found in the values for which one is willing to die. Clearly, the SH in this place on the circumplex may closely resemble the Spiritualist (SP); the one distinction is that the former may not have a larger transcendent perspective or commitment underlying this willingness to sacrifice oneself.

As one moves around the circumference of this circumplex, it must be kept in mind that the two major qualities being combined are always being blended together. Their relative incidence in the combination is a function of where precisely someone is located in the model. Especially as one moves closer to the inter-quadrant boundaries, it needs to be recognized that the features of both areas will become mixed into a kind of hybrid form. It is also important to recognize that while we hypothesize increasing positive meaning-making as one moves out of the Solipsism quadrant into the Secular Humanism quadrant and then into the upper half of the circle, with Spiritualism representing the most durable meaning level, there are both strengths and weaknesses associated with each of these categories. Being a SP, as we argued in Chapter 5, does not necessarily protect one from emotional pain and distress. Bad things can and do happen, and being spiritually oriented does not provide protection from life's ups and downs. Similarly, Solipsists (SOs) create a fragile interpretive context where meanings are easily disrupted, and personal coherence can quickly fray. Yet, there are strengths associated with this orientation. SOs can be imaginative in solving problems in parsimonious ways and can act creatively and decisively when confronted with choices. Any interpretation of a person's meaning orientation needs to appreciate both the positive and negative aspects of each quadrant. Table 6.2 presents an overview of these positive and negative features, and each quadrant will be discussed in turn.

The Spiritualism quadrant is hypothesized to represent the highest level of meaning-making. The integration of a transpersonal orientation with a focus on people and groups provides an opportunity to become

Table 6.2 Overall Strengths and Weaknesses for Each of the Logoplex Quadrants.

Quadrant	Strength	Weakness
Solipsism	Goal Focused	Psychological Distress
Secular Humanism	Socially Generative	Cynicism
Asceticism	Wise and Insightful	Crisis of Meaning
Spiritualism	Capacity to Transform	Crisis of Relevancy

completely absorbed in the human experience. Individuals in this category exhibit a selflessness and absorption into a community because
their transcendent values provide a very universal understanding of relationships, which enables these individuals to completely embrace their
communities with passion, care, and love. It is this "all in" approach
that makes possible their ability to transform communities in ways that
develop and exercise the group's strengths. This can only happen when
a person finds his/her identity embedded in the identity of humanity.
Recall the images of the Buddhist monk, who, protesting the Vietnam
War, poured gasoline on himself and turned himself into a human
torch. His sacrifice made evident and tangible, to those who watched,
the tragedy of war and its senseless killing of people and of the immeas-
urable injury suffered by the community with each loss of life. SPs can
have profound effects on groups.

However, there is also a dark side to this quadrant. As noted in
Table 6.2, the potential weakness is the *crisis of relevancy*. Those high on
Spiritualism may come to believe that they do not have the necessary
skills, abilities, or talents to meet the social needs they encounter. As a
result, they may question their own sense of meaning and mission. They
may develop what Maslow (1971) has referred to as meta-pathologies,
which include feelings of senselessness, nihilism, cessation of striving,
and a loss of feeling needed. A glimpse into this crisis is seen in a letter
from Mother Teresa of Calcutta to her spiritual advisor as she considered beginning her ministry with the poor in India:

> Pray for me—for I am really unworthy of all He is doing for me and
> in me. I have asked Father to tell you all my many great sins—so that
> you will ask Our Lord—if the work is to be done—to give you a more
> worthy person.
>
> (Kolodiejchuk, 2007, p. 58)

If the Spiritualism quadrant represents the optimal orientation, then
its opposite quadrant, Solipsism, represents the least effective orientation. Individuals in this category experience high levels of psychological
distress, mostly due to the inability to construct a useful, reassuring
sense of personal meaning that can endure the many contradictory
and fragmenting forces endemic to society (Allport, 1950). Unlike the
self-enhancing virtues of the meaningful and purposeful life characteristics of the Spiritualism quadrant, the SOs experience *existential
disappointment* (Tillich, 1951) or *noögenic neurosis* (Frankl, 1959) as a
result of their efforts to extol their own impulses. Their glass house of
meaning easily shatters and results in despair and inertia. As Emmons
(1999) noted in his analysis of personal strivings, "individualistic, self-
oriented spiritual strivings outside of faith-based communities may not
be associated with adaptive psychological, physical and interpersonal

outcomes" (p. 111). Their self-focus on personal needs and desires also pre-empts their ability to establish and maintain emotionally satisfying, intimate relationships with others, both people and groups. This deprives SOs from accessing and enjoying the positive succoring effects of social support.

The Solipsism quadrant represents psycho-spiritual immaturity, so movement out of this quadrant, in either direction, results in higher levels of meaning-making. There are several forces that may operate to keep an individual in the Solipsism quadrant. First, Frankl (1966) has noted that a continual focus on reductionistic thinking fosters an empty existentialism. According to Frankl, a strong life is built upon strong ideas. Without such large, overarching values life collapses into the atomistic world of basic impulses and immediate gratification. We hypothesize that another factor is narcissistic injury experienced at the hands of important emotional care givers, such as parents. Individuals hurt by life at a young age will tend to retreat into themselves and find recourse in their own efforts and strivings. An emotional rebuff from a powerful transferential object will sever the person's emotional links to others as he or she matures. Thus, the outer world of people and groups becomes too threatening and is perceived as being unable to provide the consistent positive regard and validation the child and subsequent adult requires. Such a painful experience forces the individual to retreat into and rely on only oneself. For better or worse, the person needs to develop an inner sense for discerning outcomes that will fulfill his or her needs. As a consequence, the SO can create clear, short to mid-term goals that will provide satisfaction to one's needs. The SO can be clever and insightful, creatively identifying opportunities that can provide the reward for the current need.

The Secular Humanism quadrant reflects individuals who are able to make reasonably robust emotional connections with their environments. Involvements with civic and social organizations make these individuals vibrant, involved citizens committed to bringing about specific social ends. However, because these individuals do not have a teleological vision of the world that both celebrates their own humanity and affirms their own dignity and worth, the social ends pursued can be quite varied and chillingly pragmatic. What separates this quadrant from Spiritualism above it, is the immediacy of focus. The practical realities of tangible, social structures are the center of attention, possibly resulting in the development of very parochial attitudes and allegiances. Yet, individuals in this quadrant can also express a deep sense of nobility and selfless dedication. Patriots who, as Abraham Lincoln described in his Gettysburg Address, gave their last full measure of devotion to their country certainly represent the best of this category. Individuals in this sector can have an event horizon for construing meaning that spans generations. As such, they may aspire to create a personal legacy to reach that distance through time. Then there are the political ideologues and fanatics who work to sculpt people to fit their ideal civic organization. Fascists and Communists are those who ruthlessly pursue the creation of a durable social order.

Both the SH and SP can be motivated by a common sense of commitment and concern for their social worlds. Both may find value to communities and wish to support, encourage, and develop these social resources so that they can be healthy and vibrant moving through time. However, a distinguishing feature of the SH from the SP is the focus of their efforts. The SHs involve themselves in community processes because there is a pay-off for them. This could be social recognition for their material support of the group, increased status and prestige, or even a personal dividend as the desired results solve some personal issue or problem. SPs, on the other hand, because of their transcendent perspective, which gives them an eternal view of their lives, are more able to empty themselves of their own personal needs and more fully submit themselves to the needs of the group. Their endless perspective on life enables them to invest in the community, not for personal gain or status, but because they truly wish for the betterment of the group. This helps to explain why the potential weakness of SHs is cynicism. They believe in their own abilities to provide added value to the community, but they may find that the community is not worthy of their investments. The cynicism arises out of personal disappointment with how the social world responded to their efforts, either by rejecting their offers of assistance or by squandering the investment. The SHs can develop a sense of disappointment, betrayal, or disdain for those they intended to help

Asceticism is the opposite pole of Secular Humanism and is distinguished from the latter by its belief in the wholeness of nature and its movement towards ultimate realities that transcend ordinary material existence. These groups are similar in that both may have ideologies that give a direction and purpose to existence. What separates the AS is the larger event horizon that defines his or her ideological agenda. The cosmology of the AS concerns itself with a reality that emerges once the material experience passes away. Meaning for the AS begins where Secular Humanism ends. Another important difference between these two groups is the more solitary or detached existence of the AS. He or she does not share the same absorption in larger social groups that characterizes both the SH and the SP. The AS feels in the world but not of it. Further, the prototypical AS evidences a single-minded effort to find an individual connection with the divine or ultimate reality. Nonetheless, the transcendent, eschatological nature of the ASs imbues them with a broader, more integrated and durable sense of self.

It is the AS's efforts at making a solitary connection to the transcendent that characterizes this quadrant and also creates the potential weakness, which is personal distress and a loss of meaning. The individualistic approach that characterizes this domain prevents the AS from establishing meaningful, supportive relationships with others. Connecting with the transcendent can bring many issues to the fore-front of consciousness, some of which can be distracting and personally disappointing. The AS has a strong inner focus on desires, beliefs, and character, which are all brought up for examination and analysis. The goal is to perfect oneself and find the personal worthiness that enables an emotionally close and fulfilling relationship with the transcendent. Two possible issues can negatively impact the AS. The first relates to feelings of personal unworthiness. The AS may find that he or she has many flaws and physical desires that can distract from the transcend-ent relationship, making the person feel inadequate and unworthy. The second issue emerges from a loss of perspective that can develop when one becomes too focused on a specific image. Spiritual development entails balance and discernment, an ability to accept one's weaknesses and needs as part of being human, which may be a challenge as one attempts to find spiritual perfection. Reconciling these competing and oft times conflicting motivations can create emotional dysphoria and cognitive confusion. Without external resources to help provide con-text and balance to this process, one can quickly become discouraged and defeated. As a result, the AS may experience a crisis in meaning-making, what St. John of the Cross (1935/2003) referred to as the *dark night of the soul.* This results when the secular, temporal meanings and values one had created for living become stripped away and replaced by more divine meanings and values. The synapse between these two states is where current meaning breaks down, and the person is left to create a new interpretive framework for living.

Both the ASs and SPs find their weakness surrounding their own sense of meaning. The SPs question their relevance and ability to impact the community, while the ASs question their own sense of personal mean-ing. There is a lack of purpose to behavior that the SP never experiences. What differentiates the SO from the AS is that for the SO, external events can overwhelm plans and expectations, resulting in the loss of needed resources, which leads to distress. The ASs are not overtaken by events, rather losing their foothold on the ground of their constructed meaning. The organization that gave them direction and purpose now seems lost or empty. Any resulting emotional distress surrounds a lack of knowing or understanding, what Frankl referred to as a noölogical crisis. Thus, the AS experiences a numinous crisis, while the SO experiences emotional frustration due to a lack of need fulfillment.

Clinical and Practical Considerations

Given the presented model in Figure 6.1, it is hypothesized that indi-viduals in the upper half of the Logoplex ought to have higher levels of ST than those in the lower half. What is less obvious is how the facet scales of ST apply to those in the AS and SP quadrants. We hypothesize that Prayer Fulfillment ought to be most relevant to those in the AS category because of their strong focus on the personal relationship with the Transcendent. Relatedly, those in the SP category ought to find Connectedness as being more relevant for them because of their strong personal centering within community. Universality should be equally relevant for both groups. It is not clear whether one would expect these two groups to show significant mean level differences on the ST facet scale; after all, ST is a dimension that characterizes both quadrants. This would need to be a question for future research.

Working from the ontological perspective presented in Chapter 2, it is clear that issues related to Meaning and its ancillary value of purpose would be most relevant to the AS sector while Worthiness and its ancillary value of acceptance would be most relevant to the SP domain. Elements of Infinitude, representing personal abundance and durability, would be the key issue for those in the SO and SH quadrants. Meeting personal needs and imbuing the environment with added value and resources all hinge on an internal belief that one has the necessary resources, skills, and abilities to obtain important goals, especially in a temporally consistent manner. If one does not believe that he or she has what it takes to make a difference or to be an asset in life, then one is left to anxiously forage for needed resources, never feeling personally secure in knowing that success can be reliably repeated. As will be shown in Chapter 7, these broad assignments can and do carry significant clinical value for understanding a client's meaning orientation.

Developmental Issues

ST is hypothesized to increase with age. Age brings with it the growing inevitability of death and thus the pressing need for the individual to construct a sense of meaning and purpose. This change is usually expressed in concerns about creating a legacy, mentoring, and finding personal closure. These tasks coincide with Erikson's (1950) notions of generativity and ego integrity, the final two psychosocial stages of life. Individuals can only come to see the inevitability of their own lives and their place in the greater scheme of life by adopting a transcendent orientation. Brown, Chen, Gehlert, and Piedmont (2013) found a significant age effect for total ST, with scores increasing from adolescence/young adulthood to middle age, when scores leveled off and did not change into old age. Therefore, the natural movement of numinous growth over time is away from the self-involved impulses of the SH and SO toward the broader, transcendent goals of the SP and AS. However, when growth is either delayed or pre-empted, the Logoplex can provide a conceptual paradigm for constructing intervention strategies. For example, techniques aimed at developing a sense of mindfulness, gratitude, and self-acceptance could be used to help individuals move toward understanding their lives from a spiritual perspective.

The dimensions of Transpersonalism and Relationalism are the guideposts for signaling directions for growth. From a clinical perspective, the Logoplex can help therapists identify the ways in which clients are constructing their sense of personal meaning. Being solipsistic, ascetic, spiritual, or humanistic carries with it particular styles of interaction with the world, along with its own potential strengths and weaknesses. More than just providing insight into clients, the Logoplex can also serve as a focus for making interventions aimed at promoting a more durable, resilient, and engaging meaning-making style.

Conclusions

Meaning is a very salient construct for both psychology and theology. It is seen as a centerpiece of human functioning. As human beings we have an essential need for structure, organization, and synthesis. We do not like loose ends or incomplete tasks. There needs to be synergy and coherence in our thoughts, plans, and actions. Chaos is the bane of our existence. It is difficult for us to accept that there could be no purpose or meaning intrinsic to life. To accept that our presence here on earth, both corporately and individually, is a result of chance events and that there is no rhyme or reason for our lives and what happens in them is quite a challenge. We need meaning because it gives us purpose and direction to life, but more than that, it provides us with a sense that there is value in the things we do. Our work, our hobbies, the things we volunteer our time for, all of them have a larger value. When that assessed value is being made by a Transcendent Being or Reality, then life becomes very important to us and carries a deep worth that makes us feel significant and important. Feeling important makes us feel content with our lives and motivates us to engage life fully and to make a difference in it through our actions.

This is only one type of meaning-making, and the Logoplex outlines other levels of existential understanding, each with their own worth and liability. While this chapter implied that individuals have only one meaning-making style, the reality is that people may employ different meaning styles with different aspects of their lives. Personally, one may be spiritual in style, but from a financial perspective, more of a secular humanist and vocationally, solipsistic. Similarly, the time lines used to make meaning, the event horizons, can also vary across goals and aspects of life. So, when assessing clients, it is important to select the aspect of life that is most central to treatment and evaluate meaning-making style at that level or from that perspective. By understanding the multi-level nature of meaning-making, one can develop a much more sophisticated understanding of a person, being able to appreciate how the many facets to a person's life as well as how seemingly contradictory and perhaps incompatible aspects of his or her personality all fit into a single, cohesive, multidimensional characterological style.

While a tremendous amount of energy has been devoted to the understanding of meaning-making and its centrality for successful human existence, this chapter should also make us mindful of the reality that while meaning is a key numinous construct, it is not the only one. The study of the numinous, as stated earlier, entails an examination of at least three motivations: Meaning, Infinitude, and Worthiness. Each carry important personological weight and have tremendous implications for adaptation and resilience. Each can contribute to dysphoria and emotional fragility. Each needs to be assessed and considered in its own right. Yet, ultimately, it will be an appreciation of their interrelated influences that will be of most consequence for the successful therapist.

References

Adler, A. (1929). *The science of living.* New York, NY: Doubleday.

Allport, G. W. (1950). *The individual and his religion.* New York, NY: MacMillan.

Bischof, L. J. (1970). *Interpreting personality theories* (2nd ed.). New York, NY: Harper & Row.

Boyd, J. N., & Zimbardo, P. G. (1996). Constructing time after death: The transcendental-future time perspective. *Time & Society, 6,* 35–54.

Brown, I. T., Chen, T., Gehlert, N. C., & Piedmont, R. L. (2013). Age and gender effects on the Assessment of Spirituality and Religious Sentiments (ASPIRES) scale: A cross-sectional analysis. *Psychology of Religion and Spirituality, 5,* 90–98.

Buss, D. M. (2002). Sex, marriage, and religion: What adaptive problems do religious phenomena solve? *Psychological Inquiry, 13,* 201–203.

Emmons, R. A. (1999). *The psychology of ultimate concerns: Motivation and spirituality in personality.* New York, NY: Guilford Press.

Erikson, E. H. (1950). *Childhood and society* (2nd ed.). New York, NY: Norton.

Frankl, V. E. (1959). *From death camp to existentialism.* Boston, MA: Beacon Press.

Frankl, V. E. (1966). Self-transcendence as a human phenomenon. *Journal of Humanistic Psychology, 6,* 97–106.

Frankl, V. E. (1969). *The will to meaning.* New York, NY: New American Library.

Kolodiejchuk, B. (2007). *Mother Teresa come be my light: The private writings of the "Saint of Calcutta."* New York, NY: Doubleday.

Lewin, K. (1951). *Field theory in the social sciences: Selected theoretical papers.* New York, NY: Harper & Brothers.

Maslow, A. H. (1971). *The farther reaches of human nature.* New York, NY: Viking Press.

Park, C. L. (2013). Religion and meaning. In R. F. Paloutzian & C. L. Park (Eds.), *Handbook of the psychology of religion and spirituality* (2nd ed.; pp. 357–379). New York, NY: The Guilford Press.

Piedmont, R. L. (2004). The logoplex as a paradigm for understanding spiritual transcendence. *Research in the Social Scientific Study of Religion, 15,* 263–284.

Piedmont, R. L. (2010). *Assessment of Spirituality and Religious Sentiments, technical manual* (2nd ed.). Baltimore, MD: Author.

St. John of the Cross. (1935/2003). *Dark night of the soul.* Mineola, NY: Dover Publications.

Tillich, P. (1951). *Systematic theology I.* Chicago, IL: University of Chicago Press.

Tillich, P. (1952/2000). *The courage to be* (2nd ed.). New Haven, CT: Yale University Press.

Zimbardo, P. G., & Boyd, J. N. (1999). Putting time in perspective: A valid, reliable individual-differences metric. *Journal of Personality and Social Psychology, 77,* 1271–1288.

7 Clinical Assessment of Clients that Includes the Numinous

Introduction to and Validation of the *Comprehensive Psycho-Spiritual Clinical Interview* (CPSCI)

With the explosion of interest in the numinous over the past 30 years came a corresponding clinical sensitivity to these issues among a wide range of professionals, both in the social sciences and health care fields. A variety of professional organizations have developed guidelines for the systematic incorporation of numinous information in the assessment and treatment processes. For example, the Substance Abuse and Mental Health Services Administration's (SAMHSA, 2017) Wellness Initiative emphasizes the importance of utilizing a holistic approach and identifies eight dimensions that should be acknowledged, including physical, emotional, social, environmental, intellectual, occupational, financial, and spiritual areas. The emphasis in the spiritual domain is on "expanding a sense of purpose and meaning in life" (paragraph 5).

The Council for Accreditation for Counseling and Related Educational Programs (CACREP, 2015) updated the latest set of standards to note that faculty should include spirituality as a multicultural aspect addressed in the curriculum and should train students to take a spiritual history, although that assessment technique is only included in reference to the field of addiction treatment. In their *Code of Ethics*, the American Counseling Association (ACA, 2014) has included spiritual well-being as part of a counselor's responsibility to attend to one's own self-care, and additional sections highlight the importance of religiousness/spirituality (R/S) networks, the imperative to avoid discrimination based on R/S (as well as other areas), and the need for exercising caution in assessment. In addition, the ACA has endorsed the competencies identified by the Association for Spiritual, Ethical, and Religious Values in Counseling (ASERVIC, 2009), and Cashwell and Young (2011) have published a guidebook suggesting ways that counselors can address each of the 14 identified areas. See http://www.aservic.org/resources/spiritual-competencies for a complete list of the competencies.

The ethics code of the American Psychological Association (APA, 2017) includes similar warnings against discrimination and notes the necessity to work within the boundaries of competence, including obtaining sufficient training before treating clients. APA has published multiple books to assist clinicians with such training, including *Spiritually Oriented Psychotherapy* (Sperry & Shafranske, 2005), *Spiritual Practices in Psychotherapy* (Plante, 2009), and *Handbook of Psychotherapy and Religious Diversity* (Richards & Bergin, 2014).

While the ethical demands made by these professional organizations are to obtain and incorporate this information into the clinical process, two issues continue to plague the field in its ability to acquire and apply such information. One issue concerns when to measure these constructs. The timing of such assessment has much to do with the overall strategic view held concerning R/S issues, which is related to the level of assessment being employed (e.g., demographic, cultural, organismic). R/S constructs may be assessed only once, most frequently at the beginning of treatment, or several times (e.g., pre- and post-treatment). A second difficulty concerns how to measure these constructs. As we have already noted in Chapter 5, there is little consensus on how to define R/S constructs and, consequently, on which measure(s) to employ. The purpose of this chapter is to present the *Comprehensive Psycho-Spiritual Clinical Interview* (CPSCI), a wide-ranging interview schedule designed to assess all the clinically relevant dimensions of a client, including numinous orientations. It can be used regardless of which level of analysis is being taken or one's theoretical orientation. The information contained in this measure can help structure therapists' acquisition of all relevant information and can help to promote the development of a multidimensional view of clients.

Development of the CPSCI

The most common moment for collecting systematic data on clients is usually at the time of intake. Here, clients provide relevant data across a variety of content areas that are necessary for informing therapists about presenting problems, past treatment history, psychosocial status, and personality. Intake assessments are a crucial and indispensable part of the treatment process. However, in working with our students in regard to their clinical practicums, two significant issues emerged. The first was the size of the intake forms used at many of their placements. In reviewing a number of these forms, one common characteristic was their sheer volume. In many cases, the intake form was over 20 pages in length! Our clinicians-in-training would spend anywhere from 1 to 3 hours speaking with clients in order to complete the document. Questions were numerous, specific, and required the interviewer to write out answers in longhand. While certainly such documents were thorough, they did have some limitations. Oft times, students would tell us that the information would be collected and then just unceremoniously placed in the client's file. Other than just some basic information, this document was not used much after its completion. While demographic information was clear and specific, the clinically oriented information usually required the interviewer to provide some written explanations about clients and their responses to the questions, which were phrased to be open-ended. As such, there were no algorithms for extracting relevant information from the written responses. Thus, no deeper, systematic inferences were able to be harvested from this information.

The second issue, which was of greater concern, related to the assessment of R/S material. In some instances, clinics did not ask any questions about this aspect of their clients, other than perhaps what their religious denomination was. In those instances where more attention was devoted to this content, the questions were simplistic, descriptive, and factual. The focus was on whether someone had a faith commitment, how frequently they may attend religious services, and an overall question as to how important these involvements were. While the intake process may include the administration of various psychological tests (e.g., MMPI-2), no specific R/S measures were ever given. Thus, there was a dearth of numinous-related information available for use. If our students wanted this information, then frequently they would have to devote treatment time to collect it.

These two issues, the unwieldiness of the intake form and the lack of any developed numinous material, create impediments to treatment by either forcing clinicians to reassess this information during therapy or forgoing this information entirely. This makes for a very haphazard approach for collecting both numinous and relevant background information, with no assurance that a complete assessment was done. The need was identified for an intake form that would be efficient, comprehensive, and allow for the drawing of relevant clinical inferences from clients. Working with our *Numinous Assessment Group* (NAG), a program of research was initiated to develop a useful intake form that used items/scales that were clinically relevant and empirically valid in order to obtain information that was both comprehensive and went beyond mere description to allow users to derive important clinical inferences.

The value of an intake form is that it provides a structured context wherein therapists can systematically obtain relevant clinical data in a standardized manner. This information provides a larger context for understanding clients' issues, and the document is used by therapists to form an understanding of their clients and what is driving their visit to the clinic. With many intake forms being open-ended, there are no empirically or rationally developed procedures for abstracting, summarizing, and interpreting this information. Thus, much of the collected information is taken at face value. This is what we consider to be a descriptive approach. There are no normative data to allow clinicians to determine whether a client is high or low on some relevant dimension. For example, some intake forms ask the question, "Do you consider yourself to be religious?" If a client responds, "yes," what does this mean? Survey research (Pew Research Center, 2014) has shown that 77% of the people in the US endorse the importance of religion in their lives as being *very important* (53%) or *somewhat* important (24%). So when clients say they are religious, how is this to be interpreted?

We believed that a good intake form needed to have several key features. First, it should be relatively brief, so that the information in it can be easily reviewed and processed. Second, the form needs to be comprehensive, in that it addresses client issues from a variety of perspectives. Third, there needs to be numinous information contained in the interview that reflects concepts that have been empirically determined as being interpretively and clinically useful. Fourth, the intake should include closed-ended questions (i.e., questions that have a fixed set of standardized responses) so that the information could be easily quantified and stored for future analysis. Finally, it would be helpful if some of the information relating to personality and the numinous were normed so that inferences could be drawn from the data about the client. As noted in the example above, it is important to know if a person is religiously oriented but of more consequence would be to know just how strong or weak the religious sentiments are. It would also be useful to have a meaningful way of extracting information on clinically relevant personality traits (e.g., Five Factor Model [FFM] domains) as well. Wherever possible, having information that provides insights into the bio-psycho-social-numinous functioning of the client would help better inform therapists of the person to be counseled and would allow therapists to anticipate the course of treatment.

With those objectives established, NAG reviewed a number of already existing intake forms and the clinical literature, focusing on constructs that would be helpful to have for an initial assessment. Of particular concern was the numinous area of the document, where the need was to identify relevant constructs that would help to provide a useful orientation to the client's ultimate level of functioning. The result of our work was the creation of the CPSCI. This document is only five pages in length and includes items that are descriptive of clients' status as well as incorporating scales with normative data that allow for the drawing of inferences about underlying motivational strivings. Most items are closed-ended and allow for a quick and efficient documentation of relevant information. The structure of the form allows clinicians to complete it in less than an hour. This information can be easily stored in electronic databases and is easily amenable to statistical analyses that can support program evaluations. Finally, the CPSCI contains several, validated, numinous scales that address key aspects of clients' ultimate psychological functioning. The goal of the CPSCI is to provide an overall assessment that allows therapists to make clinical inferences about clients in a manner that can help direct the focus of treatment as well as to suggest additional assessment measures that can more specifically target clients' particular issues.

Basic Structure

Four basic dimensions for assessment, termed "axes," were identified and used to organize the material in the CPSCI. Appendix 7.A contains a copy of the final document. The authors invite interested readers to feel free to use this form in their own intake assessment process. In doing so, it is requested that the user include both the name of the scale and the author in its presentation. Also, it would be helpful if the actual copy presented in the Appendix were used. Potential users can contact the first author (ralphpiedmont01@gmail.com) for an electronic copy, which can be reproduced. The CPSCI is an evolving document, so the authors are open to any feedback or suggestions for improvement.

The first axis is *The Presentation*. This section concerns the client's demographics, such as gender, age, ethnic background, education level, etc. As can be seen in Appendix 7.A, every effort was made to provide predetermined options for each item. This was done to support any attempts at quantifying this information for entry into a database or for later program evaluation purposes. Mental Status is the second section and contains traditional questions included in the majority of such screeners currently available. The response formats are established such that as you move to the right, the level of impairment increases. For example, concerning the item "Appearance," the answer options start at *well-groomed* (representing the most adjusted category) and end at *inappropriate* (indicating the least well-adjusted response).

Axis II is *The Problem* and focuses on the types of issues that the client may be experiencing and that are the current reason for treatment seeking. This section examines past psychiatric history as well as presenting complaints. The section also includes a consideration of physical symptoms and lists all currently used medications. The beginning of page 3 includes two sections, one that examines the number and type of current social support systems that represent potential resources for treatment and one that examines potential barriers to treatment. These two questions assess the client's contextual situation to determine what factors are influencing his/her involvement in treatment. Finally, this section ends with four global questions concerning overall psychological functioning.

Axis III is *The Person* and focuses on maladaptive aspects of personality. Using the FFM as the guide and definitions of pathological character traits outlined by Widiger, Costa, and McCrae (2013), dysfunctional aspects for each personality domain were identified and items written. The focus of these items is on those aspects of each factor linked with general levels of impairment (e.g., High Neuroticism [N], and low levels of Extraversion [E], Openness [O], Agreeableness [A], and Conscientiousness [C]). The response format for these items is set so that moving from left to right, the rating scale indicates greater impairment.

Finally, four rating scales assessing overall elements of functioning (e.g., identity, self-direction, empathy, and intimacy) are provided, which were based on information from the *Diagnostic and Statistical Manual of Mental Disorders, 5th edition* (*DSM*-5; American Psychiatric Association, 2013, p. 762). Responses to these items should coincide with the definitions presented in that document.

The Final Axis is termed *The Predicament* and addresses the numinous qualities of the individual. This Axis is labeled The Predicament because it addresses the ultimate levels of self-understanding and relational timber, qualities that set the tone and context for all other aspects of functioning. The first nine items are devoted to measuring the constructs of Religious Involvement (RI), Spirituality (S), and Religious Crisis (RC). These scales were selected to parallel information that is obtained with the ASPIRES (see Chapter 5). The next item concerns the overall meaning orientation of the client. This item is based on the Logoplex, which was presented in Chapter 6. The therapist selects that box that appears to characterize the client's preferred model of viewing life. The final section concerns the *Pastoral Themes*. In considering the three basic numinous motivations outlined in Chapter 2, the NAG group considered what types of personal themes, images, and memes would be indicative of these different motivations. These perspectives would be identified through the *pastoral reflection process* (see Chapter 3), whereby clients would describe those larger images that seemed to be most salient in defining their sense of being and personhood. The items reflect beliefs, hopes, self-perceptions, and behaviors that are currently quite salient to the client. The relative number of themes identified for each motivation category can help gauge how important or salient the motivation(s) may be, thus providing an avenue for discussion and intervention.

Using, Scoring, and Interpreting the CPSCI

In developing the CPSCI, it was important that the document not only comprehensively overview the psychosocial status of the client but that the form would allow for the derivation of inferences about the client as well. To this end, a focus was placed on collecting data that would serve two functions: a) to provide a normative perspective on relevant scales (e.g., personality, the numinous), and b) to provide evidence of their construct validity. Data were acquired from a small sample ($N = 14$) of our graduate counseling students and clinical faculty who were recruited to complete CPSCIs on up to five of their clients. In order to participate, the counseling students needed to have completed their first year of clinical practicum. There were four men and 10 women therapists who participated and provided protocols for 65 clients. Our therapists completed the CPSCI; the Global Pathology Index from the Derogatis Psychiatric Rating Scale, which is an overall assessment of client pathology on a 9-point Likert-type scale from 0 *absent* to 8 *extreme*; and a rater version of the Ten Item Personality Inventory (TIPI: Gosling, Rentfrow, & Swann, 2003), which is a measure of the FFM domains.

The therapists provided ratings on 40 women and 25 men, ages 13 to 72 (mean age = 40 years). Clients had been in treatment with therapists from 1 month to 5 years (mean treatment length = 10 months). Therapists rated how well they believed they knew the client on a 1 *not very well* to 7 *very well* scale, with an overall rating of 4.66 (range 2 to 7). Most clients were Caucasian (75%), and 14% were African-American. The remaining 11% were split among Arab (2%), Asian (3%), Hispanic (5%), and Other (1%). The top four most common presenting problems were: Depression (80%), Anxiety (57%), Sleep Problems (37%), and Substance Abuse Issues (20%).

These data need to be considered preliminary given the relatively small sample size and restricted number of clinical issues. Nonetheless, these data provide some evidence of mean levels for various scales that can be helpful for developing inferential hypotheses about clients. Not all items need normative information, such as the Mental Status questions, which are all self-evident and idiographic in nature (i.e., they are focused on the unique descriptions of a particular client, and scores do

Table 7.1 Preliminary Normative Information for the Comprehensive Psycho-Spiritual Clinical Interview (CPSCI) Scales.

CPSCI Scale	Mean	SD	Scores	
			Low (Below)	High (Above)
History of Psychiatric	3.96	2.29	2	6
Problems	3.29	1.91	1	5
Presenting Complaints	1.18	1.57	0	3
Health Issues				
Support-Barriers to Treatment	1.31	1.94	0	3
Dysfunctional Neuroticism	12.66	2.81	10	16
Dysfunctional Extraversion	7.32	2.07	5	9
Dysfunctional Openness	7.48	1.77	5	9
Dysfunctional Agreeableness	3.51	1.38	2	5
Dysfunctional Conscientiousness	6.35	1.98	4	8
Religiousness	8.42	2.64	5	11
Spirituality	8.88	3.06	6	12
Religious Crisis	5.22	2.72	3	8
Infinitude Themes	5.90	4.16	2	10
Meaning Themes	6.68	4.42	3	11
Worthiness Themes	9.54	5.34	5	15

not need to be compared to others in order to be considered interpretively valuable). The remaining parts of this chapter will examine each of the sections where normative data would be helpful, provide relevant validity information, and overview the kinds of interpretations that can be drawn. Table 7.1 presents the preliminary normative information.

Actual means and standard deviations are given for each scale so that users can calculate more specific measures of relative standing, which may be very useful for any research application of this form. To facilitate clinical use, the last two columns of Table 7.1 are the scores either below which or above which indicate low vs. high values, respectively. For example, in the row for "History of Psychiatric Problems," scores between 2 and 6 are considered average. Thus, for the sample included here, the majority of clients presented with this range of past issues. However, if a client had a score greater than 6, that would be considered a relatively high value for a current therapy client. Such a client ought to be considered as someone who is experiencing a very high level of emotional difficulties across a number of problem areas and would need to be examined carefully. Conversely, a client with less than 2 previous problems may suggest that he/she has a very specific concern, of perhaps more recent occurrence, that is pressing him/her to seek treatment.

The first section, Axis I, has no need for any normative information; it is all descriptive in nature. The Mental Status section can be interpreted in the manner that such scales are usually evaluated (e.g., Folstein, Folstein, & Fanjiang, 2001). Axis II, The Problem has several dimensions that will benefit from normative data. The first set includes Psychiatric History, Presenting Complaints, and Health Issues. For each section, a number of salient symptoms and conditions are listed. It is recognized that these sections are not comprehensive, so space was reserved for therapists to enter specific features of the conditions or to enter any symptoms not listed. It was believed that some indication of an expected number of problems and disorders that treatment-seeking clients would experience would be welcome. Symptom experience has been shown to be related to the personality disposition of N (e.g., Costa & McCrae. 1980), so high levels of symptom reporting may be indicative of this personality trait and therefore may not always be a reflection of actual pathognomonic processes (e.g., Costa & McCrae, 1987). As can be seen in Table 7.1, the majority of clients reported from 1 to 5 current problems and from 0 to 3 health issues. Therefore, a client endorsing more than 5 current problems, and/or more than 3 health issues, ought to be examined in more detail. Are these indicated problems more of a somatic issue or truly identifying of serious, underlying emotional/physical issues?

This section also contains two questions focusing on how much social support the client enjoys and what possible barriers to treatment may exist. The former is a resource for treatment, and higher scores (more sources of support) would indicate that the client has a social context that will accept and encourage his/her treatment efforts. The latter scale examines real-life issues that can impede the client from getting to treatment and seeing it through. The presence of some issues (e.g., homelessness, disability, and insurance) may necessitate the involvement of other professionals (e.g., social workers, health care agents) to address and help resolve these difficulties. While it would be easy to examine normative values for each item, we thought that it would be more efficient to create a combined index of scores, where the number of barriers to treatment would be subtracted from the number of current support systems. This difference score would provide more of a "relative risk" for treatment continuation, with larger values suggesting a more positive balance of issues that would facilitate ongoing treatment, while lower, negative scores would indicate more potential impediments.

As can be seen in Table 7.1, most of the clients had difference scores between 0 and 3. Thus, scores greater than 3 indicate a very positive treatment context, while scores lower than 0 would indicate the presence of serious difficulties for the client. As a way of validating this index, the difference score was correlated with several other CPSCI scales: the four overall ratings in section 2, the five FFM dysfunctional personality scores in section 3, and four overall personality assessment factors at the end of section 3. The results of this analysis are presented in Table 7.2. As can be seen, some very interesting patterns of association emerged in the data. Clients who scored *low* on the Support-Barriers difference score received higher ratings on Global Pathology and Social Impairment. It appears from these data that those experiencing higher levels of emotional distress and pathology are the ones also encountering more barriers to receiving the treatment they need. Interestingly, those with lower scores were also rated as having greater problems with self-direction as well as experiencing more difficulties with self-organization and self-discipline. This underscores the possibility that one major contributor to the experience of obstacles to treatment is personality weaknesses of the client. These individuals are those who have problems coping with difficulties (high N), lack the necessary personal focus and discipline to harness and direct their efforts at identifiable goals (low C), and lack an ability to plan, organize, and direct their behavior at short-term life goals (low levels of Self-Direction). Therefore, clients having negative values on this index may require more support, both emotional and logistical, from the therapist in the planning and execution of the treatment protocol.

Axis III contains information about dysfunctional personality. Our aim in creating these scales was not to merely reinvent the FFM personality dimensions; there are already a number of well-constructed versions of these constructs that capture normal personality variations. Rather, the focus was on identifying dysfunctional aspects of personality: more

Table 7.2 Correlations between Various CPSCI Scales and Support-Barriers to Treatment Difference Score.

CPSCI Scale	Support-Barriers Difference Score
Global Pathology Index	-.31*
Axis II: Dysphoria	-.14
Axis II: Social Impairment	-.26*
Axis II: Perceptual Aberration	-.13
Axis II: Cognitive Distortion	-.08
Axis III: Identity	-.18
Axis III: Self-Direction	-.45***
Axis III: Empathy	-.27*
Axis III: Intimacy	-.22
CPSCI-Neuroticism	-.37**
CPSCI-Extraversion	-.22
CPSCI-Openness	-.31*
CPSCI-Agreeableness	-.16
CPSCI-Conscientiousness	-.48***

$N = 65$. * $p < .05$. ** $p < .01$. *** $p < .001$, two-tailed.

extreme variants of their normal-based cousins that are implicated in characterological impairment (e.g., Piedmont, Sherman, & Sherman, 2013). In order to accomplish this task, there were two pieces of information that would be essential for demonstrating the construct validity of these new scales. The first would be to show that the new scales do correlate in appropriate ways with current measures of the FFM, which focus on normal levels of functioning. The underlying content of these new scales ought to have significant overlap with the basic content of these already validated instruments. The second piece of information needed would be to demonstrate the incremental validity of these new scales over the existing FFM scales in predicting relevant psychosocial ratings. If these new scales do indeed capture dysfunctional tendencies, then they should predict impairment incrementally over scales that are only designed to measure more adaptive personality traits. Both questions were addressed in the current data set.

Table 7.3 presents the intercorrelations between the TIPI and the new CPSCI FFM scales. Table 7.3 provides three points of interest. First, each of the CPSCI FFM scales correlates with its TIPI cousin negatively (with the exception of N). This is because high scores on the CPSCI scales are capturing impaired aspects of functioning, which are typically represented on the lower poles of each FFM domain (with the exception of N, where dysfunctionality is represented by high scores). Thus, the CPSCI scales are representing these nonadaptive aspects of character. Second, with the exception of O, each of the CPSCI scales has its highest loading (in its respective column and row) with its intended TIPI counterpart.

Table 7.3 Correlations between the Ten Item Personality Inventory FFM Scales and the New CPSCI Dysfunctional FFM Scales.

CPSCI Scale	Ten Item Personality Inventory Scale					
	N	E	O	A	C	α
Dysfunctional Neuroticism	.71***	.13	.30*	.23	.54***	.79
Dysfunctional Extraversion	-.03	-.70***	-.36**	-.01	-.08	.75
Dysfunctional Openness	-.16	-.39***	-.34**	-.05	-.30*	.62
Dysfunctional Agreeableness	-.37**	-.03	-.29*	-.47***	-.13	.80
Dysfunctional Conscientiousness	-.51***	-.06	-.32**	.37**	-.75***	.89

$N = 65$. * $p < .05$. ** $p < .01$. *** $p < .001$, two-tailed.

Note: N = Neuroticism; E = Extraversion; O = Openness; A = Agreeableness; C = Conscientiousness.

This provides evidence of both convergent and discriminant validity for the new scales. The one exception here is O, which has a stronger association with the TIPI E scale. It is not immediately obvious why this pattern of association was found. The two TIPI items for E are "extraverted, enthusiastic" and "reserved, quiet." How these items compare to the CPSCI O items that focus on personal rigidity, need for structure, and personal insight is not clear and certainly more research is needed on this aspect of the scale. Finally, the last column in Table 7.3 presents the alpha reliability estimates for scores on the CPSCI scales. Given that four of these five scales have only three items, the observed alphas are

Table 7.4 Results of Hierarchical Multiple Regressions Examining the Incremental Predictive Validity of the CPSCI Dysfunctional FFM Scales over the Ten Item Personality Inventory.

Criterion Rating	FFM R^2	CPSCI FFM ΔR^2	CPSCI Predictors
Global Pathology Index (GPI)	.29***	.26***	N
Axis II Personal Dysphoria	.17*	—	
Axis II Social Impairment	.26***	.23***	N, O, C
Axis II Perceptual Aberrations	.35***	.17**	O
Axis II Cognitive Distortion	.33***	.24***	O
Axis III Identity	.35***	.18**	N, O
Axis III Self-Direction	.31***	.29***	N
Axis III Empathy	.41***	.13*	A
Axis III Intimacy	.33***	—	

Note: N = Neuroticism; E = Extraversion; O = Openness; A = Agreeableness; C = Conscientiousness. * $p < .05$. ** $p < .01$. *** $p < .001$, two-tailed.

indeed quite robust. Clearly, O has the lowest value and may suggest that the therapists rating their clients may have held different understandings of these terms than what was intended by the author. Nonetheless, the data certainly provide support for viewing these scales as representing qualities associated with the FFM.

In order to examine the incremental validity of the new scales, a series of hierarchical multiple regression analyses was conducted. The criterion variables were the Global Pathology Index and scores on the two sets of four overall functioning ratings found in Axes II and III. On step 1 of the analysis, all of the TIPI scales were entered simultaneously. On step 2, all of the CPSCI scales were also entered simultaneously. A partial F – test was conducted to determine whether the CPSCI scales significantly improved the amount of predicted variance. Table 7.4 presents the results of these analyses.

As can be seen, the TIPI FFM scales, which are measures of normal-range personality traits, were all significantly related to the clinical outcome ratings. Column 3 presents the incremental predictive results for the new CPSCI FFM scales. In all but two instances, the CPSCI scales added significant *additional* explained variance to the criteria. The pattern of results also supports the construct validity of the new scales. For example, in predicting the GPI rating, it was the CPSCI N scale that was the only significant predictor. In predicting ratings of cognitive and perceptual issues, it was the CPSCI O scale that was the only significant predictor. Thus, not only do the CPSCI scales capture qualities not contained by the TIPI, the observed pattern of associations provides additional construct validity evidence for the new scales.

Of concern are the two criteria that were not predicted by the CPSCI: Axis II Personal Dysphoria and Axis III Intimacy. At first glance one may argue that the CPSCI scales only contain two or three items and as such may not have enough statistical power to correlate with these single-item ratings. There are two reasons to discount this argument. First, the alpha reliabilities for the CPSCI scales were all adequate for research purposes. Second, it must be noted that the TIPI only has two items per scale. Why would the briefer TIPI evidence more predictive power than the longer CPSCI scales? A more in-depth analysis is warranted.

In examining the results for Personal Dysphoria, while the TIPI scales together accounted for a significant amount of the variance, an examination of the individual beta weights revealed that none of the individual TIPI scales was significantly related to the criterion. This suggests two hypotheses. First, when this counter-intuitive finding is encountered, it represents a situation where none of the variables has a unique overlap with the outcome: Rather it is what all the variables share in common that is driving the observed predictiveness. Given the putative distinctiveness of the FFM domains, that a common feature of all scales is underwriting the association may suggest that some type of methodological artifact is operating in this circumstance. A second interpretation is that because the CPSCI scales did not replicate this finding with the TIPI, it may be a Type I error, especially because the total amount of explained variance by the TIPI just exceeds the alpha = .05 level.

The results found with Intimacy indicate a different set of issues. The TIPI scales very substantially predicted this rating, and it was the A scale that was the significant predictor. None of the CPSCI scales was found to be related. In this instance, the results may be due to the differential content of the two A scales. The TIPI A scale contains the items "critical, quarrelsome" and "sympathetic, warm." Both of these items carry with them specific relationship content and reflect how one may interact with others in relationship. Therefore, it is not surprising that this scale was strongly related to Intimacy. The CPSCI A scale, on the other hand, does not directly capture aspects of relationship texture. The two A items are "orientation to others" which is responded to on a caring – disingenuous scale, and "interpersonal orientation" which is assessed on an other-oriented – uninterested in others scale. The CPSCI A scale does not contain any content that specifically addresses the quality and/or depth of relationships, like the TIPI. Therefore, users of this new scale need to be mindful that the CPSCI A scale assesses more of the broad, general attitudes one has towards others, rather than the more typical FFM A scale, which may also examine the style of relationship.

Overall, these data provide positive support for the contention that the CPSCI FFM scales do capture dysfunctional aspects of personality. High scores on these scales indicate the presence of motivational patterns that lead to maladaptive outcomes. It must also be kept in mind that these scales are also very selective in what areas of personality they assess: They capture the high end of N and the low poles of the other four domains. These qualities have traditionally been associated with impairment (e.g., Miller, 1991), although impairment can be found at both poles of each domain (Widiger et al., 2013). Thus, users should not rely on these brief indices as substitutes for more rigorous clinical assessments of both temperament and symptom experience.

The normative values presented in Table 7.1 for these FFM scales can be helpful in two ways. First, identifying high scores on the various personality dimensions can alert therapists to potential motivational dynamics that may complicate treatment. For example, clients who score high on the CPSCI C scale may evidence problems in personal reliability, focus, and follow through. These weaknesses are particularly salient if the treatment is one with large amounts of homework between sessions. Second, finding clients high on all of these CPSCI personality scales may also indicate the presence of a personality disorder; follow-up with an appropriate measurement would be recommended. Finding low scores across these five scales may also suggest the presence of a number of temperamental resources that can be drawn upon in treatment and that may serve to facilitate the entire process.

The final set of scales is found in the last section of the intake form, Axis IV, The Predicament. This section is entirely focused on the numinous. Items 1, 2, and 4 comprise a measure of religiousness (R), while items 3, 5, and 6 represent spirituality (S), and the final three items, 7, 8, and 9 make up the religious crisis scale (RC). Scores on these scales can range from 3 to 15. As can be seen in Table 7.1, mean scores for R and S hover between 8 and 9, suggesting that the clients being assessed in this data set do have some level of interest in these areas. Mean score on the RC scale is lower (5.22), indicating less distress associated with numinous conflicts. What is interesting here is that this is a treatment-seeking sample, where individuals do have significant emotional distress and conflict in their lives. Clearly, emotional distress and RC are not isomorphic constructs; each seems to have its own influence on impairment, conflict, and emotional pain.

The next item refers to clients' status on the Logoplex (see Chapter 6); each of the four quadrants are presented, and therapists select which of the four best represents how clients view their worlds on a broad level. Each of these quadrants represents a different orientation to creating personal meaning, from a very restricted and limited view of life that centers on the fulfillment of personal needs (the Materialistic quadrant), to those whose orientation to meaning is transpersonal, communal, and transcendent (the Spiritual/Transpersonal quadrant). It is expected that those in the different quadrants will demonstrate differences on the R, S, and RC scales, the dysfunctional FFM scales, and levels of personal problems, both current and historical. It is expected that those in the more transcendent quadrants (Self-Directing and Spiritual/Transpersonal) will exhibit better levels of emotional well-being than those in the more secular quadrants.

The final section of Axis IV concerns Pastoral Themes. These themes were selected as representative allegories or metaphors of each of the basic numinous motivations that characterize the major dimensions and qualities of clients' lives. What is important about these themes is that they capture and organize broad aspects of living in summary form and represent the overall demands clients perceive being placed on them by life. These themes can be both positive (e.g., positive Infinitude themes include adoration, eternal perspective, mysticism), which reflect a sense of fulfillment for the numinous motivation, and negative (e.g., negative Infinitude themes include fear of death, greed to feel secure, need for certainty), which reflect a current sense of crisis or conflict surrounding this motivation.

Identifying clients' engagement with these numinous motivations can be found in the pastoral reflection process. Pastoral reflection is an essential component to treatment processes that include the numinous dimension. Pastoral reflection entails a discussion with clients concerning how they create ultimate meaning in their lives. It examines the metaphors and parables clients use to represent how they situate themselves within their life context. Numinous-based counseling employs pastoral reflection as an essential therapeutic tool that seeks to uncover how the various numinous motivations are being expressed and managed in clients' lives. Oft times clients may rely on parables, terms, and stories that are part of their wisdom tradition to convey their spiritual strivings. This is the value of religious traditions: They provide easy-to-grasp, simple stories to address complex existential issues. Understanding these wisdom tales provides therapists with keys to unlocking the underlying psychological, numinous motivations that may be most salient in clients' current life situations.

Much care and attention went into identifying pastoral themes that were linked specifically to each of the numinous motivations. To accomplish this, the NAG group created a list of relevant pastoral themes. These themes were obtained from various pastoral counseling courses, clinical practice, and personal familiarity with various wisdom traditions. A long list of over 150 such motifs and metaphors was identified by the group. A study was then conducted where various students and faculty were given the list of numinous motivations and their definitions and were asked to assign each of the themes to these motivations. Themes could be assigned to more than one motivation. These data were then analyzed to determine which items were associated with one and only one of the numinous motivations. Further, a theme needed to be endorsed by more than 50% of the subjects as being a reflection of that specific numinous dimension in order to be included in this list. This resulted in 98 themes that could be clearly assigned to a single numinous domain.

The value of this list is twofold. First, on a descriptive level, it identifies specific personal motifs that clients are using to understand and describe their current overall life situations. These items can be informative about the issues, struggles, and adaptations clients are making, and they can provide a platform for larger clinical discussions on the direction, tenor, and ultimate outcome of such perspectives. Second, the number of themes clients identify in each category can be diagnostic of the types of ultimate concerns and psychological investments that are being made. For example, a client who has a large number of Worthiness themes may suggest that this person is struggling with or most concerned about this specific motivation. Sections with few identified themes may suggest areas of growth and exploration. Such a lack of interest may represent a direction for therapy in order to develop the lacking motivation(s) and bring more balance among the three motivations.

Given that all the scales in this section are numinously oriented, it is expected that there should be a number of positive associations among them. The first set of analyses examined the correlations between the R, S, and RC scales and the Pastoral Themes and Personality. These results are presented in Table 7.5. As can be seen, the numinous scales correlated with moderate to strong effect sizes with the different types of Pastoral Themes. The RI and S scales appeared independent of the Worthiness group, while RC was independent of the Infinitude items. It is interesting to note that RC and S both correlated positively with higher ratings on the Meaning section. While this may appear counter-intuitive (i.e., why would someone experiencing this extreme existential crisis indicate higher concern with meaning, just like someone who is high on S?), an examination of the selected items reveals different patterns of association. As noted above, each of these Theme sections contains both positive and negative items. In comparing the ratings for those high on S and low on RC with those who are low on S and high on RC, a differential pattern emerges. In short, those high on S were more likely to receive ratings of "feeling blessed," while those high on RC were more likely to receive ratings on "ambiguity" and "disillusionment." A similar pattern was also found for Worthiness; those high on S were more likely to receive a rating on "self-compassion," while those high on RC were more likely to be rated on "alienation" and "brokenness/unfixable." More work needs to be done exploring how these positive and negative elements are differentially related to other numinous constructs.

Concerning the dysfunctional personality scales, the numinous scales were mostly independent, with only three of the 15 correlations emerging to be significant. The patterns of association do make conceptual sense, in that RC was correlated with higher levels of N while the S scale correlated with more adaptive levels of A and C (see Saroglou, 2010).

Table 7.5 Correlations between the Religiousness, Spirituality, and Religious Crisis Scales and the Pastoral Themes, FFM Personality Domains, and Emotional Problems Scales.

Outcome Criteria	CPSCI Numinous Scale		
	RC	RI	S
Total Infinitude Themes	.22	.39***	.56***
Total Meaning Themes	.30*	.38**	.44***
Total Worthiness Themes	.48***	.10	.19
Dysfunctional Neuroticism	.27*	-.15	-.24
Dysfunctional Extraversion	.11	-.07	-.11
Dysfunctional Openness	.18	.01	-.14
Dysfunctional Agreeableness	-.08	-.13	-.25*
Dysfunctional Conscientiousness	.02	.16	-.26*
Total Psychiatric History Complaints	.33**	-.10	-.19
Total Presenting Complaints	.38**	-.13	-.08
Total Health Complaints	.21	-.19	-.02

$N = 65.$ * $p < .05.$ ** $p < .01.$ *** $p < .001$, two-tailed. Note: RC = Religious Crisis; RI = Religious Involvement; S = Spirituality.

All correlations with the maladaptive personality scales were less than 0.30 in magnitude. Given that these scales were based on the corresponding ASPIRES versions, this is not surprising. Finally, RC was significantly related to both the number of presenting problems and the number of problems experienced in the past. This supports our contention that RC represents another pathway to emotional distress. These significant associations continue to hold even after the predictive effects of the Dysfunctional FFM scales are partialed out (RC partial correlations with History of Complaints and Presenting Complaints: prs = .28 and .31, respectively, ps < .05, two-tailed). None of the scales was related to the number of current health problems. These data provide some initial convergent and discriminant validity to these new numinous scales.

The next scale to examine is the global rating of Meaning Orientation. The content describing each category was provided by the definitions given by the Logoplex Model. Clients could be assigned to one and only one category. Interestingly, the number of clients assigned to the Materialistic, Humanistic, Self-Directed, and Transpersonal categories were relatively uniform (ns = 10, 25, 17, and 13, respectively). Four dichotomous variables were created to contain this information for analysis (i.e., those who were assigned to a category received a value of "1" while those not assigned to this category received a value of "0"). These four variables were correlated with a number of the other CPSCI scales, and these results are presented in Table 7.6 below.

The four meaning orientations are designed to reflect increasingly sophisticated understandings of ultimate meaning that are associated with greater resiliency, deeper enmeshment with the totality of one's life space, and a core sense of well-being, coherence, and thriving. This development occurs as an individual gains a deeper transcendent perspective that centers itself within a broadly defined sense of community. As such, it is expected that, at a minimum, there should be identifiable differences between those at the lowest level (e.g., Materialistic) and those at the highest level (e.g., Spiritual/Transpersonal) of development. An inspection of Table 7.6 provides support for this hypothesis. In examining Meaning Level with the Pastoral Themes, the Materialistic clients have lower endorsements of Infinitude and Meaning than the Transpersonal clients. Curiously, Worthiness issues seem most related to the intermediate Meaning categories: Humanists are rated as having lower concerns with Worthiness, while Self-Directed individuals have more concerns. Conceptually, this is consistent with the underlying model: Humanists are concerned with their community and supporting its growth and health in ways material and personal. Individuals so motivated may have less concerns with Worthiness because these individuals already believe they are acting as positive agents in their communities. Self-Directed individuals, on the other hand, have a more developed sense of Spiritual Transcendence, but their connection to the Ultimate

Table 7.6 Correlations between the Logoplex-Based Meaning Orientation Ratings and the Pastoral Themes, FFM Personality Domains, Emotional Problems Scales, and Axis III Personality Disorder Scales.

Outcome Criteria	Logoplex-Based Meaning Orientation			
	Materialistic	Humanistic	Self-Directed	Transpersonal
Total Infinitude Themes	-.26*	-.13	-.09	.49***
Total Meaning Themes	-.39***	-.07	-.02	.46***
Total Worthiness Themes	-.02	-.25*	.26*	.04
Religious Crisis	-.10	-.18	.14	.16
Religious Involvement	-.38**	-.07	.11	.31*
Spirituality	-.38**	-.17	.13	.41***
Dysfunctional Neuroticism	.24ª	-.06	.12	-.27*
Dysfunctional Extraversion	.08	-.20	.25*	-.10
Dysfunctional Openness	.25*	-.07	.14	-.29*
Dysfunctional Agreeableness	.40***	.01	-.09	-.27*
Dysfunctional Conscientiousness	.31*	-.13	.20	-.35**
Total Psychiatric History Complaints	.27*	-.05	.01	-.19
Total Presenting Complaints	-.07	-.09	.11	.05
Total Health Complaints	.17	-.07	-.03	-.04
Axis III Identity	.26*	-.17	.16	-.20
Axis III Self-Direction	.31*	-.14	.20	-.32**
Axis III Empathy	.42***	-.08	.07	-.36**
Axis III Intimacy	.33**	-.08	.10	-.31**

$N = 65$. ª $p < .06$. * $p < .05$. ** $p < .01$. *** $p < .001$, two-tailed.

is based on a personal relationship with the divine, as they understand it. Such individuals usually avoid communities and focus more on their own efforts at encountering and distributing the benefits of their transpersonal perspective. Given this very idiocentric perspective, issues about self-worthiness become salient. These individuals are hypothesized to be working to purify and perfect themselves so as to find their ultimate "salvation."

A similar pattern of associations is found with the numinous R/S scales. Those classified in the Transpersonal category have higher scores on these scales (with the exception of RC), while those in the Materialistic category have lower scores. In fact, those in the Transpersonal group were rated as having significantly higher levels of RI [Mean = 10.0 vs 6.1; $t(21) = 4.78$, $p < .001$] and S [Mean = 11.31 vs 6.2; $t(21) = 4.99$, $p < .001$] than those in the

Materialistic category. Surprisingly, no significant difference between these two groups was observed with RC. The Logoplex model hypothesizes that those in the Materialistic category, having a fragile and limited sense of meaning that can be easily disrupted by life events, would experience more emotional distress. While Materialism was found to associate with negative affect (see below), such vulnerability to distress does not seem to extend to feelings of rejection from the God of their understanding.

With the dysfunctional FFM scales, those in the Materialistic groups have more characterological weaknesses associated with O, A, and C. This personality profile suggests individuals who are rigid, untrusting, and selfish, reflecting a very "me first" attitude. Those in the Transpersonal category show greater personal adaptiveness: They evidence a personality profile indicating greater emotional control and an empathic embracing of others that includes compassion and an active altruistic orientation. There is some indication of emotional difficulties for the Materialistic group, as the correlation with N trends towards significance [$r(63) = .24$, p < .06]. The two middle categories demonstrate few associations with these personality constructs. The one exception is for the Self-Directing group, who are rated higher on dysfunctional E. This is consistent with the description of this category: The self-focus of these individuals may be a consequence of their own lack of interpersonal skills and emotional capacities. This would explain why these individuals center the focus of their numinous strivings within their own personal relationship with the Transcendent instead of situating themselves within a community context.

Correlations with the mental and physical health complaints yield only one significant result: between the Materialistic group and the total number of psychological problems experienced. This provides evidence supporting that those in this category experience an emotionally tenuous relationship with their environment. The fragility of their meaning-making paradigms is easily challenged and disrupted by life events. To follow up this perspective, a comparison of the mean ratings on the GPI between the Materialistic and Transpersonal categories resulted in a significant difference with the former scoring higher than the latter group [$t(21) = 2.27$, $p < .05$]. The mean score for the Materialistic clients was 5.0 and is associated with a "substantial" level of pathology, which is described on the rating form as: "Adjustment is marginal. Manifest symptoms cause the client considerable distress. Intrapsychic processes show signs of disruption, and interpersonal functioning is impaired. Mood tends to be dysphoric, and need for treatment is obvious." As expected, those in this meaning category are likely to experience high levels of emotional distress.

The Transpersonal clients had a mean rating of 3.54, which is associated with a "mild" level of distress and is described by the rating form as: "General functioning is somewhat disturbed. Client complains of certain distressing symptoms, and mood is slightly irregular; however, social and intrapsychic processes appear normal."

Keeping in mind that the data presented here are obtained from a clinical, in-treatment sample where some level of clinical impairment is expected, this finding clearly supports the hypothesis of a higher incidence of mental issues with the Materialistic group. They do experience higher levels of pathology, but this emotional distress does not seem to generalize to a level of numinous distress (e.g., higher levels of RC). Those in the Materialistic category are apparently unconcerned with connections with an Ultimate reality; it may be seen as irrelevant to them as they actively pursue fulfillment of their basic physical and emotional needs. One may need a more developed sense of Transcendent meaning before such issues become relevant.

The final set of correlates in Table 7.6 relates to the Axis III personality disorder ratings. As illustrated, the Materialistic group is rated as having more impairment than the Transpersonal group across all of the ratings. An independent samples *t*-test indicated that there were significant differences in the mean ratings between these two groups on all four scales (the Materialistic group was rated as experiencing "moderate impairment" while the Transpersonal group was rated as having "some impairment"). No effects were observed for the two intermediate groups: Humanistic and Self-Directed. A direction for future research would be to focus more on empirically developing and testing these meaning orientations in order to better delineate their personological implications.

The final set of scales to evaluate for Axis IV are the Pastoral Themes. Some of their associations with other CPSCI scales have already been presented in previous tables. Table 7.7 provides those associations not yet examined. Overall, greater engagement of clients in Pastoral Themes surrounding Infinitude and Meaning was associated with less pathology globally and in the area of characterological impairment. Interestingly, no associations were found on the Axis II overall ratings for these two content categories. Instead, having more Worthiness issues was associated with higher ratings on the overall dimensions of Personal Dysphoria and Social Impairment. As done above, it would be interesting to explore those aspects of Worthiness associated with these ratings; it may be possible that the negative Worthiness themes (e.g., false self, shame, social isolation) are responsible for these correlations. Finally, Infinitude and Meaning were also associated with the Support-Barriers Difference Score. This suggests that those who are engaged in these issues find less barriers to treatment than those who are less concerned with these themes. It is not clear from these data what the essential pathways are underlying this effect. It may be that those who are more numinously inclined develop better relationships with others so that they find the necessary social support to find treatment. They may also be more psychologically

Table 7.7 Correlations between the Pastoral Themes Categories and the GPI, Axis II and Axis III Emotional Problems Scales, and the Dysfunctional FFM Scales.

Outcome Criteria	CPSCI Pastoral Themes		
	Infinitude	Meaning	Worthiness
Global Pathology Index (GPI)	-.33**	-.32**	.15
Axis II Personal Dysphoria	.13	.20	.31*
Axis II Social Impairment	-.07	-.01	.30*
Axis II Perceptual Aberrations	-.06	-.05	.03
Axis II Cognitive Distortion	-.02	-.02	.19
Axis III Identity	-.37**	-.27*	.10
Axis III Self-Direction	-.44***	-.44***	.02
Axis III Empathy	-.38**	-.33**	.11
Axis III Intimacy	-.54***	-.46***	.01
Dysfunctional Neuroticism	-.38**	-.37**	.17
Dysfunctional Extraversion	-.34**	-.21	.13
Dysfunctional Openness	-.36**	-.34**	.02
Dysfunctional Agreeableness	-.38**	-.35**	-.17
Dysfunctional Conscientiousness	-.45***	-.52***	-.20
Support-Barriers Difference Score	.31*	.45***	.04

$N = 65$. * $p < .05$. ** $p < .01$. *** $p < .001$, two-tailed.

well adjusted, which enables them to more easily identify issues when they arise and to be motivated to address them.

As was shown in Table 7.5, the Pastoral Themes were also associated with scores on the R/S scales, providing additional evidence for construct validity. Clearly, those high on RI and S tend to be more likely to develop metaphors and scripts that define their lives in terms of these numinous qualities. Even those high on RC also struggle with these same themes, albeit with their negative sides. The Pastoral Themes were related to the overall character ratings, both the Dysfunctional FFM scales and the overall personality disorder ratings. We are encouraged by these findings because they suggest that the Pastoral Themes are important psychological representations that have an impact on the totality of our character. The themes reflect our capacities to relate to ourselves and to establish durable relationships with others. They also are associated with a more productive personality orientation enabling individuals to develop and maintain an internal characterological structure that is efficient and adaptively oriented. We hypothesize that these numinous qualities help individuals to develop and maintain a resilient approach to life because these themes represent ultimate meaning; they are the psychological lodestars that guide individuals and help keep the course of their lives on track.

We also hypothesize that changes in these themes (i.e., focusing more on the positive aspects and avoiding the negative poles) will have important positive consequences for adjustment. They represent ultimate sources of influence on psychic functioning and should serve as a starting point for understanding clients. Clients' perspectives as reflected by these numinous concepts ought to have important implications for the types of pathology that develop and the internal qualities that are operating to maintain these dysfunctional patterns. Because the Pastoral Themes were found to be mostly independent of the overall mental status ratings found on Axis II, this suggests that while numinous images have an overarching influence on the basic structure and expression of personality, they are not related to those situational processes that may define the expression of pathology at any given point in time. How individuals think about and perceive ultimate meaning represent systems different from, and at a higher level than, these contextual processes. The numinous is hypothesized to contribute to pathology or may influence these situational processes as they degenerate into dysregulation. Psychiatric status may contain a strong exogenous component, and as these data indicate, will have little to do with the endogenous, numinous processes that operate continuously.

Caveats and Conclusions

The data evaluated here provide support for the utility of the CPSCI as a useful platform for drawing insights and inferences into the psychological and numinous functioning of clients. The patterns of findings offer initial confirmation of a number of underlying assumptions to the numinous model presented in this volume. The Numinous domain represents an internal set of motivations and expectancies that help shape and direct those long-term psychological structures that give continuity and bearing to the life course. They operate in conjunction with other psychosocial processes, with varying levels of engagement. Assessing numinous qualities in clients can help therapists foster an understanding of the meta-perspectives held by clients that may be operating to create and maintain pathognomonic processes that undermine their ability to find ultimate satisfaction and coherence for their lives.

The items on the CPSCI are valuable in their own right and provide useful insights into the overall levels of functioning of clients. The basic descriptions they provide can serve as a foundation for developing a useful clinical profile. However, the normative information presented here for the CPSCI scales should provide additional assistance to therapists as they formulate broader conceptualizations of the underlying motivations and dynamics that may be driving the behavior of clients. The organization of the CPSCI is efficient and provides useful ways of organizing a wide array of salient clinical information. This document can and should be used throughout the therapeutic process, as a diagnostic indicator, assessment tool, and even as an outcome measure (the CPSCI can be given at the beginning and end of treatment). We believe that its greatest strength is its systematic inclusion of numinous material.

While all the data are based on therapist ratings of real clients in treatment and should be relevant to results found in other clinical contexts, it must be remembered that the data are based on a relatively small sample. This makes issues of representativeness and statistical power germane. It is not clear how many of the null findings presented above represent Type II errors, or how many of the observed relationships would continue if a more diverse clinical sample were used. Some test of replication would be desirable employing larger samples.

The analyses that were conducted were selected on the basis of their straightforwardness and alignment with the basic assumptions of the numinous model presented here. There are many more questions that need to be addressed that were not covered here. For example, as noted earlier, some examination of the positive and negative Pastoral Themes would be helpful. There may be differential patterns of relations with the other clinical scales that are diagnostically and/or prognostically relevant. This is clearly a direction for future work on this instrument. The R/S scales also need additional validation work. In the current study, the observer form for the ASPIRES was not given. Its inclusion would have provided useful validity information for the RI, S, and RC scales. Do they really provide a reasonable representation of the constructs identified by the ASPIRES? Such findings would be helpful for understanding the results presented in Table 7.5. Certainly, more work needs to be directed towards the Logoplex-derived meaning categories. Of particular interest are the two intermediate categories, Humanistic and Self-Directed. A fuller empirical development of these orientations and their implications for treatment need further explication.

The CPSCI ought to be viewed as a living document, a form that needs to be used and experienced by therapists so that its strengths and weaknesses can be identified for future modification. The document was developed to reflect our particular orientation to both treatment and the numinous; the members of NAG were all counselors and so were able to comment on the clinical value, relevance, and efficiency of the form. While we believe the CPSCI has a great deal of ecological value (i.e., it captures important clinical dynamics in a manner that clinicians can appreciate), we are open to feedback that can be used to improve it. We included the instrument here and encourage its use in the hope that over time we will receive evaluations of its practical and clinical value from those working in the field.

Suggestions for Use

The CPSCI is designed as a structured intake form. The items and questions should be seen as a framework to guide an initial conversation with clients that identifies the key issues to be addressed. While much of the needed information can be gleaned from that initial conversation, some material, especially that related to the numinous, may need more than one session. Learning about clients' Pastoral Themes and meaning orientation may require an extended dialogue that occurs over the first few weeks of treatment. Given the structured format for many of the response categories, it should be easy to record responses to each item, helping to keep the therapist focused more on the discussion than on completing the form. All information should be gathered within three sessions. Going longer may only serve to confound current status with treatment effects. It is also possible to use the form at the end of treatment, as one way to quantify therapeutic change in the client. Because several of these scales have normative data, it is possible to examine how much clients have changed and in what ways.

Although the CPSCI is mostly a screener in nature, the information it yields can be very helpful for alerting therapists to potential issues that will need to be followed up, either with additional assessments or in conversation with clients during treatment. The CPSCI can help make the initial exploratory phase of therapy less like a search for a "needle in a haystack," and more of a focused exchange, which makes for a better utilization of everyone's time. The brevity of the CPSCI should make it easy for therapists to refer to in an ongoing manner. Finally, what is valuable about the CPSCI is that it does include questions about clients' numinous motivations. As such, it meets the recommendations by many professional organizations (e.g., ACA, APA) to specifically address and include numinous information in any treatment process. Further, by directly bringing these questions up, therapists convey to their clients that such material is okay for discussion in therapy and that therapists are open to discussing such issues as part of the process. This may help facilitate greater involvement of clients in the session because they do not feel that some personal content (especially something as important as their R/S sentiments) is "off limits" for consideration. The more clients reveal about themselves, the more honest the sessions, and the more engaged with, and committed to, the process they become.

References

American Counseling Association. (2014). *2014 ACA code of ethics*. Alexandria, VA: Author.

American Psychiatric Association. (2013). *Diagnostic and statistical manual of mental disorders* (5th ed.). Washington, DC: Author.

American Psychological Association. (2017). *Ethical principles of psychologists and code of conduct*. Washington, DC: Author. Retrieved from www.apa.org/ethics/code/ethics-code-2017.pdf

Association for Spiritual, Ethical, and Religious Values in Counseling. (2009). Competencies for addressing spiritual and religious issues in counseling. Retrieved from www.aservic.org/resources/spiritual-competencies/

Council for Accreditation for Counseling and Related Educational Programs. (2015). *2016 CACREP standards.* Alexandria, VA: Author.

Cashwell, C. S., & Young, J. S. (Eds.). (2011). *Integrating spirituality and religion into counseling: A guide to competent practice* (2nd ed.). Alexandria, VA: The American Counseling Association.

Costa, P. T., Jr., & McCrae, R. R. (1980). Somatic complaints in males as a function of age and neuroticism: A longitudinal analysis. *Journal of Behavioral Medicine, 3,* 245–257.

Costa, P. T., Jr., & McCrae, R. R. (1987). Neuroticism, somatic complaints, and disease: Is the bark worse than the bite? *Journal of Personality, 55,* 299–316.

Folstein, M. F., Folstein, S. E., & Fanjiang, G. (2001). *Mini-Mental State Examination: Clinical guide.* Lutz, FL: Psychological Assessment Resources.

Gosling, S. D., Rentfrow, P. J., & Swann, W. B., Jr. (2003). A very brief measure of the Big Five personality domains. *Journal of Research in Personality, 37,* 504–528.

Miller, T. R. (1991). The psychotherapeutic utility of the Five-Factor Model of Personality: A clinician's experience. *Journal of Personality Assessment, 57,* 415–433.

Pew Research Center. (2014). Religious Landscape Study: Importance of religion in one's life. Retrieved from www.pewforum.org/religious-landscape-study/importance-of-religion-in-ones-life/

Piedmont, R. L., Sherman, M. F., & Sherman, N. C. (2013). Maladaptively high and low Openness: The case for Experiential Permeability. *Journal of Personality, 80,* 1641–1668. doi:10.1111/j.1467-6494.2012.00777.x

Plante, T. G. (2009). *Spiritual practices in psychotherapy: Thirteen tools for enhancing psychological health.* Washington, DC: American Psychological Association.

Richards, P. S., & Bergin, A. E. (2014). *Handbook of psychotherapy and religious diversity* (2nd ed.). Washington, DC: The American Psychological Association.

Saroglou, V. (2010). Religiousness as a cultural adaptation of basic traits: A five-factor model perspective. *Personality and Social Psychology Review, 14,* 108–125.

Sperry, L., & Shafranske, E. P. (2005). *Spiritually oriented psychotherapy.* Washington, DC: American Psychological Association.

Substance Abuse and Mental Health Services Administration. (2017, October 24). *The eight dimensions of wellness.* Retrieved from www.samhsa.gov/wellness-initiative/eight-dimensions-wellness

Widiger, T. A., Costa, P. T., Jr., & McCrae, R. R. (2013). Diagnosis of personality disorder using the Five-Factor Model and the proposed DSM-5. In T. A. Widiger and P. T. Costa (Eds.), *Personality disorders and the Five-Factor Model of Personality* (pp. 285–310). Washington, DC: American Psychological Association.

Appendix 7.A
A Comprehensive Psycho-Spiritual Clinical Interview

Comprehensive Psycho-Spiritual Clinical Interview

Ralph L. Piedmont, Ph.D.

NAME: _____

AXIS I: THE PRESENTATION
Demographics:

Age: _____ Gender Orientation: _____ Sexual Orientation: _____

Ethnicity: . . . . ❏ *Arab* ❏ *Asian* ❏ *Black* ❏ *Caucasian* ❏ *Hispanic* ❏ *Mixed* ❏ *Other*

Marital Status: . . . . ❏ *Single* ❏ *Married* ❏ *Divorced* ❏ *Committed Relationship* ❏ *Widow/Widower*

Education Level:

❏ *Elementary School* ❏ *Some college* ❏ *Some graduate school* ❏ *Trade School*
❏ *Some high school* ❏ *AA degree* ❏ *Masters Degree*
❏ *High School grad* ❏ *BA/BS degree* ❏ *Doctoral Degree*

Employment
Status: . . . . ❏ *Full Time* ❏ *Part Time* ❏ *Unemployed* ❏ *Homemaker* ❏ *Disabled* ❏ *Student*

Current Occupation: _____

Religious Affiliation: _____

Mental Status:

Appearance: . . . . ❏ *Well-groomed* ❏ *Disheveled* ❏ *Bizarre* ❏ *Inappropriate*

Attitude: . . . . ❏ *Cooperative* ❏ *Guarded* ❏ *Suspicious* ❏ *Uncooperative* ❏ *Belligerent*

Motor Activity: . ❏ *Lethargic* ❏ *Calm* ❏ *Hyperactive* ❏ *Agitated* ❏ *Tremor/Tic* ❏ *Muscle Spasms*

Affect: . . . . ❏ *Appropriate* ❏ *Labile* ❏ *Expansive* ❏ *Constricted* ❏ *Blunted* ❏ *Flat*

Mood: . . . . ❏ *Normal* ❏ *Depressed* ❏ *Anxious* ❏ *Euphoric*

Speech:

❏ *Normal* ❏ *Soft* ❏ *Slurred* ❏ *Pressured* ❏ *Incoherent* ❏ *Poverty of*
❏ *Delayed* ❏ *Loud* ❏ *Excessive* ❏ *Perseverating* *Speech*

Thought Process: . ❏ *Intact* ❏ *Circumstantial* ❏ *Loose Associations* ❏ *Tangential* ❏ *Flight of Ideas*

Hallucinations: . . . . ❏ *Not Present* ❏ *Auditory* ❏ *Visual* ❏ *Tactile* ❏ *Olfactory*

Delusions:

❏ *Not Present* ❏ *Being Controlled* ❏ *Ideas of Reference* ❏ *Thought*
❏ *Persecutory* ❏ *Bizarre* ❏ *Grandiose* *insertion/deletion*

Orientation: . . . . ❏ *Fully oriented x3* ❏ *Partially oriented* ❏ *Disoriented*

Insight: . . . . ❏ *Intact* ❏ *Impaired*

Describe impairment: _____

Judgment: . . . . ❏ *Intact* ❏ *Impaired*

Describe impairment: _____

Memory: Immediate . . . .   ❏ *Intact*   ❏ *Impaired*

Memory: Recent . . . .   ❏ *Intact*   ❏ *Impaired*

Memory: Remote . . . .   ❏ *Intact*   ❏ *Impaired*

AXIS II: THE PROBLEM

Psychiatric History:

Does the client have a history with any of the following problems?

❏ *None by Client Report*	❏ *Suicide attempts*	❏ *Inattention*
❏ *Depression*	❏ *Psychosis*	❏ *Irritability*
❏ *Anger*	❏ *Sleep problems*	❏ *Impulsive*
❏ *Mania*	❏ *Memory*	*(gambling/sex/shopping)*
❏ *Anxiety*	❏ *Repetitive thoughts/behaviors*	❏ *Trauma/Abuse*
❏ *Somatic symptoms*	❏ *Dissociation*	❏ *Sexual/Physical/Emotional Abuse*
❏ *Suicidal ideation*	❏ *Personality disorder*	❏ *Grief & Loss*
❏ *Homicidal ideation*	❏ *Substance abuse*	

Symptom Specifics: _____

Has the client experienced any of the following interventions?

❏ *Inpatient Psych/Substance Abuse TX*	❏ *Outpatient Psych/Substance Abuse TX*	❏ *Incarcerated*
		❏ *Family History of Treatment*
❏ *ER Visits or Crisis Episode prior 12 months*	❏ *Psychiatric Medication*	❏ *No Previous Treatment*
	❏ *Arrested*	

Treatment Specifics: _____

Presenting Complaints:

Indicate the client's presenting problems:

❏ *None by Client Report*	❏ *Suicide attempts*	❏ *Inattention*
❏ *Depression*	❏ *Psychosis*	❏ *Irritability*
❏ *Anger*	❏ *Sleep problems*	❏ *Impulsive*
❏ *Mania*	❏ *Memory*	*(gambling/sex/shopping)*
❏ *Anxiety*	❏ *Repetitive thoughts/behaviors*	❏ *Trauma/Abuse*
❏ *Somatic symptoms*	❏ *Dissociation*	❏ *Sexual/Physical/Emotional Abuse*
❏ *Suicidal ideation*	❏ *Personality disorder*	❏ *Grief & Loss*
❏ *Homicidal ideation*	❏ *Substance abuse*	

Symptom Specifics: _____

List Relevant Z-codes: _____

List All Current Medications: _____

Indicate health-related issues currently affecting the client:

❏ *Cancer,*	❏ *Stomach issues*	❏ *Head trauma/injury*
type:_____	❏ *Neurological condition,*	❏ *Asthma*
❏ *Diabetes*	*type:_____*	❏ *Hearing-related problems*
❏ *Cardiovascular*	❏ *Sleep disturbances*	❏ *Allergies,*
❏ *Hepatitis*	❏ *Weight management*	*type:_____*
❏ *High blood pressure*	❏ *Vision-related problems*	❏ *AIDS/HIV/STD*
❏ *Epilepsy*	❏ *Kidney/bladder*	❏ *Tuberculosis*
❏ *Digestive issues*	❏ *Reproductive issues*	
❏ *Other:*		

Current Support Systems:

❏ *Family*　　　　　　　　❏ *Spouse/Significant Other*　　❏ *Hobbies/Interests*
❏ *Faith Group*　　　　　 ❏ *Work*　　　　　　　　　　　 ❏ *Living Context*
❏ *Friends*　　　　　　　 ❏ *Recreation*
❏ *Other:*

Barriers To Treatment:

❏ *Homelessness*　　　　　❏ *Safety*　　　　　❏ *Motivation*
❏ *Transportation Issues*　❏ *Health*　　　　　❏ *Financial*
❏ *Food*　　　　　　　　　 ❏ *Disability*　　　 ❏ *Insurance*
❏ *Other:*

Please rate the client on the following dimensions using the scale provided.

Degree of personal dysphoria	❏ *None*	❏ *Mild*	❏ *Moderate*	❏ *Severe*	❏ *Extreme*
Degree of psychosocial impairment	❏ *None*	❏ *Mild*	❏ *Moderate*	❏ *Severe*	❏ *Extreme*
Degree of perceptual aberration	❏ *None*	❏ *Mild*	❏ *Moderate*	❏ *Severe*	❏ *Extreme*
Degree of cognitive distortion	❏ *None*	❏ *Mild*	❏ *Moderate*	❏ *Severe*	❏ *Extreme*

AXIS III: THE PERSON

This section assesses stable attributes of the client. As such, your responses should indicate how the client is generally or usually. What is his/her overall level of each of these qualities?

Coping Ability	❏ *Strong*	❏ *Average*	❏ *Weak*	❏ *Impaired*
Self-Esteem	❏ *Strong*	❏ *Average*	❏ *Weak*	❏ *Impaired*
Ability to Tolerate Frustration	❏ *Strong*	❏ *Average*	❏ *Weak*	❏ *Impaired*
Ability to Control Cravings	❏ *Strong*	❏ *Average*	❏ *Weak*	❏ *Impaired*
Level of Negative Affect (e.g., depression, sadness, anxiety)	❏ *None*	❏ *Some*	❏ *Moderate*	❏ *High*

Sociability	❏ *Gregarious*	❏ *Approachable*	❏ *Loner*	❏ *Detached*
Personal Energy Level	❏ *Energetic*	❏ *Active*	❏ *Relaxed*	❏ *Sluggish*
Level of Positive Affect (e.g., joy, enthusiasm)	❏ *High*	❏ *Moderate*	❏ *Some*	❏ *None*

Level of Personal Rigidity	❏ *None*	❏ *Some*	❏ *Moderate*	❏ *High*
Need for Structure	❏ *None*	❏ *Some*	❏ *Moderate*	❏ *High*
Level of Personal Insight	❏ *High*	❏ *Moderate*	❏ *Some*	❏ *None*

Orientation to Others	❏ *Caring*	❏ *Considerate*	❏ *Manipulative*	❏ *Disingenuous*
Interpersonal Orientation	❏ *Other-oriented*	❏ *Responds to Appeals*	❏ *Self-focused*	❏ *Uninterested in Others*

Self-Discipline	❏ *Strong*	❏ *Average*	❏ *Weak*	❏ *Impaired*
Personal Organization	❏ *Strong*	❏ *Average*	❏ *Weak*	❏ *Impaired*
Personal Competence	❏ *Strong*	❏ *Average*	❏ *Weak*	❏ *Impaired*

Please evaluate the level of clinical impairment the client exhibits on each of the following aspects of personality functioning.

Identity: Ability to experience oneself as unique, with clear boundaries between self and others; stability of self-esteem and accuracy of self-appraisal; capacity for, and ability to regulate, a range of emotional experiences

❑ *Little or no impairment*   ❑ *Some impairment*   ❑ *Moderate impairment*   ❑ *Severe impairment*

Self-Direction: Ability to pursue a coherent and meaningful set of short-term and life goals; utilization of constructive and prosocial internal standards of behavior; ability to self-reflect productively

❑ *Little or no impairment*   ❑ *Some impairment*   ❑ *Moderate impairment*   ❑ *Severe impairment*

Empathy: Ability to comprehend and appreciate other's experiences and motivations; tolerance of different perspectives; understands the effects of one's own behavior on others.

❑ *Little or no impairment*   ❑ *Some impairment*   ❑ *Moderate impairment*   ❑ *Severe impairment*

Intimacy: The depth and duration of connection with others; desire and capacity for closeness; mutuality of regard reflected in interpersonal behavior.

❑ *Little or no impairment*   ❑ *Some impairment*   ❑ *Moderate impairment*   ❑ *Severe impairment*

AXIS IV: THE PREDICAMENT

How frequently is the client involved in the practice of his/her faith tradition (this includes any aspect, attending services, reading religious literature, involvement in faith groups).

❑ *Never*   ❑ *Rarely*   ❑ *Occasionally*   ❑ *Often*   ❑ *Quite Often*   ❑ *N/A*

How important are the client's RELIGIOUS beliefs?

❑ *Not at all important*   ❑ *Somewhat unimportant*   ❑ *Fairly important*   ❑ *Extremely important*   ❑ *N/A*

How important are the client's SPIRITUAL beliefs?

❑ *Not at all important*   ❑ *Somewhat unimportant*   ❑ *Fairly important*   ❑ *Extremely important*   ❑ *N/A*

Over the past 12 months, has the client's religious and/or spiritual interests and involvements:

❑ *Decreased*   ❑ *Stayed the Same*   ❑ *Increased*

To what extent does the client have a personal, unique, close relationship with a Transcendent Reality and/or God?

❑ *Not at all*   ❑ *Slight*   ❑ *Moderate*   ❑ *Strong*   ❑ *Very Strong*

To what extent does the client feel a union with a Transcendent Reality and/or God that provides him/her with spiritual truth?

❑ *Not at all*   ❑ *Slight*   ❑ *Moderate*   ❑ *Strong*   ❑ *Very Strong*

To what extent does the client feel that God is punishing him/her?

❑ *Not at all*   ❑ *Slight*   ❑ *Moderate*   ❑ *Strong*   ❑ *Very Strong*

To what extent does the client believe he/she has been abandoned by God?

❑ *Not at all*   ❑ *Slight*   ❑ *Moderate*   ❑ *Strong*   ❑ *Very Strong*

To what extent does the client feel rejected by God?

❑ *Not at all*   ❑ *Slight*   ❑ *Moderate*   ❑ *Strong*   ❑ *Very Strong*

Overall meaning-making orientation of client:

❏ *Materialistic:Very self-focused, narcissistic, distrusts others, cut-off from nurturance of others, oriented towards short-term goals*
❏ *Humanistic: Concerned with own needs and realities that are experienced through senses; is socially responsible and civic minded, socially generative*

❏ *Self-Directing: Concerned about personal meaning and transcendence, however focus is on self; relationship to transcendent is personal/singular*
❏ *Spiritual/Transpersonal: Broad sense of personal meaning that is expressed within defined community; Relationship with transcendent defined in/with/by connection to community*

PASTORAL THEMES:

Personal Durability and Infinitude Themes (check all that apply):

❏ *Adoration*
❏ *Benevolence*
❏ *Creating/Continuance*
❏ *Determination*
❏ *Development*
❏ *Endurance*
❏ *Eternal Perspective*
❏ *Fear of Death*
❏ *Finding Wisdom in Past*
❏ *Greed to Feel Secure*

❏ *Growth*
❏ *Initiative*
❏ *Loyalty to Ideals*
❏ *Miracles*
❏ *Mourning*
❏ *Mysticism*
❏ *Need for Certainty*
❏ *Patience*
❏ *Perserverence in Face of Fear*
❏ *Prayer*

❏ *Protection*
❏ *Resurrection*
❏ *Securing a Legacy*
❏ *Sense of Personal Abundance*
❏ *Shepherd*
❏ *Stewardship*
❏ *Transform for Lasting Change*
❏ *Trust in Ultimate Reality*
❏ *Vision*

Meaning Themes (check all that apply):

❏ *Ambiguity*
❏ *Care-giving*
❏ *Conformity*
❏ *Contemplation*
❏ *Discernment*
❏ *Disillusionment*
❏ *Exploring the Shadow*
❏ *Faith*
❏ *Feeling Blessed*
❏ *Grief/Loss*

❏ *Identity*
❏ *Justice*
❏ *Meditation*
❏ *Mission*
❏ *Morality*
❏ *Nature*
❏ *Order*
❏ *Purpose*
❏ *Quest*
❏ *Rebirth*

❏ *Reverence*
❏ *Risk*
❏ *Sacrifice*
❏ *Self-Identity/Purpose*
❏ *Simplicity*
❏ *Surrender*
❏ *Temptation*
❏ *Thanksgiving*
❏ *Wisdom*

Worthiness Themes (check all that apply):

❏ *Abandonment*
❏ *Alienation*
❏ *Betrayal*
❏ *Brokenness, Unfixable*
❏ *Despair over Lack of Self-worth*
❏ *Discipleship*
❏ *Envy*
❏ *Evil*
❏ *False Self*
❏ *Genuineness*
❏ *Gluttony*
❏ *God Forgiveness*
❏ *Goodness*
❏ *Guilt*

❏ *Humiliation*
❏ *Isolation*
❏ *Judgment*
❏ *Loneliness*
❏ *Mercy*
❏ *Obedience*
❏ *Penitence*
❏ *Perfection*
❏ *Personal Brokenness*
❏ *Personal Suffering*
❏ *Prodigal: Hope Despite Failure*
❏ *Reconciliation*
❏ *Redemption*
❏ *Repentance*

❏ *Sanctification*
❏ *Self-Acceptance*
❏ *Self-Compassion*
❏ *Self-Condemnation*
❏ *Selflessness*
❏ *Shame*
❏ *Sin*
❏ *Sloth*
❏ *Social Isolation*
❏ *Superiority*
❏ *Supplication*
❏ *Woundedness*

Other Relevant Observations:

_____
_____
_____
_____
_____

8 Clinical Case Presentation

Assessment is a vital aspect of all elements related to our work with clients. We have found that both formal and informal assessments provide us with critical data and assist us in multiple areas. They can enhance our understanding of a client's worldview and life story, can direct us toward a diagnosis, can provide a foundation for treatment planning, and can assist us in our efforts to advocate for a client. Assessment includes more than testing, though. While the results from administration of a single instrument may be illuminating, any decision made must be based on data gathered from multiple areas, including life outcomes, observer ratings, self-report, and tests (John & Soto, 2007). When a client first arrives in our office, we know very little other than what might have been gathered during a telephone conversation. Engaging in appropriate exploration during an intake and then continuously throughout a series of sessions can provide us with substantial information, which can be supplemented with reports from other providers and from people close to the client.

From which areas, then, should we endeavor to gather data that can provide the basis for statistical prediction? We have found that tools measuring spirituality and personality cover a wide range and can be supplemented as needed with instruments that address other issues pertinent to particular clients (e.g., depression, anxiety, substance abuse). The Comprehensive Psycho-Spiritual Clinical Interview (CPSCI, see Chapter 7) and the ASPIRES (see Chapter 5) are our preferred methods of examining religiousness/spirituality (R/S), and the NEO PI-3 (McCrae & Costa, 2010) consistently provides us with helpful information about personality. The NEO PI-3 addresses personality within a normal range, though, so the Millon Clinical Multiaxial Inventory-IV (MCMI-IV; Millon, Grossman, & Millon, 2015) or the Minnesota Multiphasic Personality Inventory-2 (MMPI-2; Butcher et al., 2001) would be appropriate tools to measure psychopathology. We also understand the importance of a providing a mental status examination and exploring any symptoms endorsed by the client.

Good assessment is a key component of the clinical process. Standardized, normed instruments are the core elements to this process in addition to any other information available (e.g., peer ratings, previous clinical records, clinical judgment). The purpose of this book is to advance an understanding of the numinous as a scientific construct with important implications for psychological functioning. Part of our argument for this position was the presentation of two different instruments that have been shown to be psychometrically valid, norm-referenced, and relevant to clinical work. This chapter is devoted to providing a clinical demonstration of the value of these measures in the therapeutic process. To this end, we contacted a therapist-colleague and asked her to select a new client for whom a consideration of the numinous would seem relevant for his/her treatment and to invite that person to complete some scales at both the beginning and end of the treatment process. Also, we wished to gather some clinical information from the therapist herself, again at the beginning and end of the process. We hope that this information will help to put some "flesh on the bones" of our approach and help to elucidate the kinds of information numinous assessment provides and demonstrate how this knowledge can add significantly to the therapeutic encounter.

The Assessment Process

As we noted in Chapter 4, there are four information sources that professionals should assess when examining a client: self-report, observer-rating, test data, and life outcome. Because there is no gold standard for determining the accuracy of any one assessment method, we can only view information from tests as hypotheses that need to be confirmed through other information sources. When findings converge across different methods (e.g., self-reports correlate with observer-ratings), then one can have increased confidence that a finding may be accurate. At the very least, psychological tests can provide a counterpoint to clinicians' ratings/observations. Tests can provide broader interpretive perspectives on clients' issues in a manner that goes beyond how the clients phenotypically present themselves.

Costa and McCrae (1992) have identified six ways that test information can be fruitfully employed in clinical work. The first value of testing is *understanding the client.* The use of personality and numinous scales can provide a broad-based assessment of clients' personality, which includes a thorough understanding of their strengths and weaknesses. These scales can provide relevant information on interpersonal style, meaning-making orientation, emotional well-being, and ultimate levels of well-being, among others. The second value of testing concerns *differential diagnosis.* While measures of temperament and the numinous are not necessarily designed to capture pathology, they can be useful for providing information relevant to making a diagnosis or for ruling one out. For example, a high score on the personality domain of extraversion would rule out a schizoid personality disorder (see Trull, 1992). However, including measures of symptom experience or dysfunctional personality styles (as found with the CPSCI) can provide more information about the extent of emotional impairment.

A third value for assessment is *empathy and rapport.* Information from test scores can provide professionals with insights into the client that can support an empathic orientation towards the client. Scales can outline clients' conflicts, struggles, and aspirations and can present a more nuanced personological portrait of those issues surrounding the need for treatment in ways clients just cannot convey. The use of personality and numinous scales can provide a more holistic, person-centered orientation towards clients that can reflect their growth potential as well as their growing edges. *Feedback and insight* is the fourth value for assessment. The results of testing can, and perhaps ought to be, shared with clients at appropriate times in treatment. This information can help provide a language to clients to use in expressing and describing their issues. Many times, clients feel distress or conflict but do not have the words to fully articulate their difficulties. Often, these individuals may feel that their problems are unique, not understood, and therefore untreatable. Seeing how well the measures reflect their inner dynamics, clients may develop a sense of hope that treatment, and change, are possible.

The fifth value for testing described by Costa and McCrae (1992) is *anticipating the course of therapy.* Successful psychotherapy depends not only on a therapist's skill but also on clients' cooperation, motivation to work, and capacity for therapeutic change. No matter what a therapist's theoretical orientation, clients bring unique characteristics that need to be accommodated in treatment. These qualities may create potential impediments to change, while others may serve as potential therapeutic resources. These qualities of clients can also set expectations for the amount and type of change that can be expected from therapy. *Matching clients to treatments* is the final value and is perhaps the most important contribution testing can provide practitioners. It has long been known that some people benefit more from certain therapies than others. For example, individuals high on extraversion, who are sociable and talkative, will find therapies that require interpersonal interactions more helpful than do introverts, who may prefer and benefit from behavior therapy or Gestalt approaches. Individuals who score high on Religious Involvement may prefer some explicit inclusion of their faith orientations. Assessment tools can provide a wealth of useful, clinical information about clients that can help expedite the treatment process.

Assembling a Testing Protocol

We have always told our students when teaching psychological assessment, that the use of well-crafted instruments can be of great value to the clinical process. Ideally, we believe that any useful protocol should provide enough information, in terms of depth and breadth, that is consistent with having spent 6–8 hours in conversation with a client. This is a tall order, expecting that a set of self-report scales can give insights and understandings about a client that would only emerge after a lengthy personal conversation across multiple sessions. I remember one of my (RLP) counseling students who was taking my assessment class and interning at a clinical placement. Under supervision, he gave the NEO PI-3 (a measure of the Five Factor Model [FFM] personality domains; McCrae & Costa, 2010) to one of his clients as part of his paper for the course. He selected this client because he had worked with her for about 10 sessions and thought that there was some issue impeding progress that was not obvious to him. When he got the results of the test, it indicated that his client might have been sexually or physically abused at a younger age. He was surprised because this issue never was shared throughout their many sessions. When he brought it up with the client, she did acknowledge being abused as an adolescent. He was quite surprised that something so important remained hidden for so long. Once brought to light, treatment moved more quickly thereafter. As he said to me, "I wish I had this test at the beginning of treatment, we could've saved a lot of time!"

While the selection of instruments depends on many factors, we believe having a core set of scales for all clients can be helpful in two ways. First, it ensures that a reasonably comprehensive set of instruments have been assembled, providing some assurance that a complete description of the client will be obtained. Second, having a core set of scales can provide the basis for a clinical data set that can be used for therapists to undertake evaluations of their own practices to determine overall levels of treatment effect, how much change clients experienced, and in what ways clients change. In this age of managed care, such information can be helpful for therapists to demonstrate their clinical value.

We believe that for numinous-oriented therapy, there are some standard scales that ought to be considered as part of an assessment protocol. First, as we noted above, we recommend the NEO PI-3 and the ASPIRES – two well-designed measures that together provide a comprehensive description of personality. Further, both scales have documented clinical utility and validated observer-rating forms. Adding to this core would be a measure of symptom experience, such as the *Brief Symptom Inventory-18* (BSI-18; Derogatis, 2001). This provides information on three scales (Somatization, Depression, and Anxiety) as well as an overall Global Severity Index (GSI). Finally, we would include a measure of personal problems: the *Personal Problems Check List* (PPCL; Schinka, 1985). This scale includes over 200 personal problems that are organized around 13 different domains (e.g., Family, School, Religious, Health). The scale can be very helpful in identifying specific areas where clients are experiencing problems in adaptation; such information would serve as an initial place to start any treatment. Research has provided normative data concerning endorsement rates so that some assessment of just how much difficulty clients are experiencing can be obtained (Piedmont, Sherman, & Barrickman, 2000).

Rounding off the assessment battery would be the CPSCI (see Chapter 7). The CPSCI is an observer-based scale, so it provides a different perspective on clients and can be used to help frame interpretations from the other scales. For example, information on the R/S section can be helpful in evaluating results from the ASPIRES, and information from Axis II, Presenting Problems, can be compared to information from the BSI-18 and PPCL. Areas of convergence should provide therapists with confidence in the accuracy of the self-report findings. Areas of disagreement would be ideal places of departure for discussion in treatment. Usually, such disagreements can provide very important interpretive material. While there may be non-substantive reasons for disagreement (e.g., the rater only knows the target in a very specific context, or the rater may not know the target well enough), oft times such divergence may reflect how the target does not really understand the type of social impression he or she makes on others or does not understand the larger social implications of his/her behavior. Such reasons can be the basic content for a useful therapeutic discussion (see Piedmont & Rodgerson, 2017 for an overview of such comparisons with couples).

Using the above instruments as a core battery for assessment should provide a rather comprehensive and interpretively valuable set of client information. Using these scales, we present below a case study of one individual receiving outpatient counseling. We will present the results of his assessment as well as therapist ratings on the CPSCI. It is left to the reader to determine the overall utility of these scales.

Case Study

After receiving approval from our university's Institutional Review Board, we approached a licensed psychotherapist, who is a graduate of our program and who specializes in anxiety disorders. She agreed to identify a candidate, administer a battery of tests, and then provide feedback to the client and to us. Both the therapist, whom we will call Claire, and the client, whom we will call Zach (not their real names), were provided with informed consent forms that they read and signed. They were both compensated for their time and efforts.

The battery of tests included the NEO PI-3, the BSI 18, the PPCL for Adults, the Adjective Check List (used to capture the client's Image of God; Gough & Heilbrun, 1983), the CPSCI, and the ASPIRES (both self-report and observer-ratings forms). Zach agreed to have a close companion (his wife) complete the observer ratings form for the ASPIRES, and both the client and the therapist completed a brief treatment outcome questionnaire as well. Claire also provided us with a written report addressing additional questions we had, and she met with us for a debriefing session as well.

The duration of the first bout of treatment was approximately 3 months long, with a total of five sessions. The client, a 28-year-old, Caucasian, heterosexual, married, medical professional who was also enrolled in a program to become a nurse practitioner, had sought assistance for his anxiety symptoms and compulsions. He endorsed fears of contamination and noted engaging in excessive handwashing. He was interested in a therapist who was receptive to his faith beliefs and who was open to including that part of his worldview into the sessions.

While there are many ways to present this information, we will start with the self-report (and associated observer ratings where available) results first and then present the CPSCI. In this manner, we hope to gather a sense of how the client sees himself across the domains of personality, symptom experience, and personal problems. Then, this information will be compared to and contrasted with information obtained from the CPSCI. Our hope is that readers will get to view how the CPSCI complements these other assessments. We also hope that our interpretive remarks will highlight some of the intrinsic strategies for harvesting these scales for useful information.

NEO PI-3 Results

The results of the NEO-PI-3 are presented in Table 8.1. Results are given as *T*-scores (a *T*-score has a mean of 50 and a standard deviation of 10 and is based on normative data provided by McCrae & Costa, 2010), and the interpretive meaning of each score is also presented. Concerning Neuroticism, this individual is anxious, generally apprehensive, and prone to worry. He often feels frustrated, irritable, and angry at others, but he has only the occasional periods of unhappiness that most people experience. Embarrassment or shyness when dealing with people, especially strangers, is only occasionally a problem for him. He reports being poor at controlling his impulses and desires, but he is able to handle stress as well as most people. We should expect that he has a number of symptom complaints, both mental and physical.

With regards to Extraversion, Zach is very warm and affectionate toward others, and he usually enjoys large and noisy crowds or parties. He is forceful and dominant, preferring to be a group leader rather than a follower. The individual has a high level of energy and likes to keep active and busy. Excitement, stimulation, and thrills have great appeal to him, and he frequently experiences strong feelings of happiness and joy. Zach has a profile that ought to raise some clinical concern. He is someone who has high levels of both positive and negative affect. Such

Table 8.1 NEO PI-3 Results for Zach.

Scale	T-Score	Range	Facets	T-Score	Range
Domains			**Facets con't.**		
Neuroticism (N)	71	Very High	O1 Fantasy	74	Very High
Extraversion (E)	75	Very High	O2 Aesthetics	69	Very High
Openness (O)	64	High	O3 Feelings	79	Very High
Agreeableness (A)	50	Average	O4 Actions	53	Average
Conscientiousness (C)	55	Average	O5 Ideas	55	Average
			O6 Values	31	Very Low
Facets			A1 Trust	44	Low
N1 Anxiety	78	Very High	A2 Straightforwardness	56	High
N2 Angry Hostility	78	Very High	A3 Altruism	60	High
N3 Depression	47	Average	A4 Compliance	53	Average
N4 Self-Consciousness	47	Average	A5 Modesty	43	Low
N5 Impulsiveness	**72**	Very High	A6 Tender-Mindedness	71	Very High
N6 Vulnerability	48	Average	C1 Competence	51	Average
E1 Warmth	62	High	C2 Order	30	Very Low
E2 Gregariousness	59	High	C3 Dutifulness	50	Average
E3 Assertiveness	70	Very High	C4 Achievement Striving	59	High
E4 Activity	73	Very High	C5 Self-Discipline	**44**	Low
E5 Excitement-Seeking	**64**	High	C6 Deliberation	45	Average
E6 Positive Emotions	68	Very High			

Note: T-scores in bold indicate aspects of impulsive triad.

individuals usually present as outgoing and charming and seem to have an upbeat approach to life. While this is the social face he presents to the world, it is also clear that he has much negative energy as well, qualities that usually do not come out immediately and remain buried underneath the warmth that he exudes. As such, many people may miss the interior, personal pain he has. Clinicians may have to work to get behind the positive presentation and look for these darker, deeper feelings of anger and anxiety.

In experiential style, Zach is generally open. He has a vivid imagination and an active fantasy life. He is particularly responsive to beauty as found in music, art, poetry, or nature, and his feelings and emotional reactions are varied and important to him. He sometimes enjoys new and different activities and has a moderate need for variety in his life. He has only a moderate level of intellectual curiosity, and he is conservative in his social, political, and moral beliefs. The low score on Values indicates that he has a core set of values, specifically his religious beliefs, that are very important to him and which are held to very strongly. Faith issues will certainly be a part of his treatment experience.

Zach scores average overall on the Agreeableness domain, although there is much inter-facet scatter on this factor. Zach tends to be cynical, skeptical, and suspicious, and he has a low opinion of human nature. He is very candid and sincere and would find it difficult to deceive or manipulate others, and he goes out of his way to be thoughtful and helpful to others; he is quite generous. Zach holds his own in conflicts with others, but he is also willing to forgive and forget. He is quite proud of himself and his accomplishments and happy to take credit for them. Compared to other people, he is particularly sympathetic to those in need, and his social and political attitudes reflect this concern.

Finally, on Conscientiousness, Zach is reasonably efficient and generally sensible and rational in making decisions. He can be sloppy and disorganized, but he is usually dependable and reliable in meeting his obligations. He has a high aspiration level and strives for excellence in whatever he does. He sometimes finds it difficult to make himself do what he should, and he tends to quit when tasks become too difficult. Zach is reasonably cautious and generally thinks things through before acting.

According to his NEO Interpretive Report, Zach's profile matches closely with those obtained from individuals with a Histrionic Personality Disorder (PD). While the NEO cannot diagnose PDs, it does raise an issue that should be explored further in treatment. It may be warranted to follow up with an MMPI-2 or MCMI-IV. However, given his presenting complaints (i.e., his obsessive-compulsiveness and high symptom experiences), this issue does make sense. While his PD status is unclear, this finding should be viewed, at a minimum, as reflecting a tendency to have many physical complaints.

Another aspect of his profile is the presence of an impulse control issue. His high scores on Impulsiveness (N5) and Excitement Seeking (E5) and low score on Self-Discipline (C5) indicate this tendency (see Piedmont, 1998; Piedmont & Ciarrocchi, 1999). Usually, individuals with this profile experience difficulties in controlling behaviors around substance abuse, alcohol usage, gambling, sexual behavior, and spending. It would need to be explored how Zach manages these issues, especially given his strong commitment to his religious beliefs. While he scores low on Values (O6), he scores average on Dutifulness (C3), which examines how well an individual follows through on his commitments. It will be important to examine his levels of Worthiness on the CPSCI; sometimes when individuals are confronted with strong beliefs and have problems in following through behaviorally, there can be strong self-recriminations centering on personal worthiness.

PPCL Results

The results of the PPCL were examined and his scores for each problem domain, and overall number of checked issues, were converted to *T*-scores based on data presented by Piedmont et al. (2000). Reviewing his scores indicated that Zach had specific concerns related to health, unlike some who report to therapy with a broad set of concerns. His *T*-score for Health/Habits was 56, which was high. His score for Emotions was 54, which was average. While he endorsed some problems in Vocational, Legal, Attitude, Appearance, and Social, none of the *T*-scores in those areas fell into the high range. He did not endorse any problems related to other areas, and in fact, his overall *T*-score for the instrument was 42, which was low. This is an interesting finding given Zach's high scores on the Neuroticism domain. Thus, while he may experience high levels of negative affect, these feelings of anger and anxiety do not seem, from his perspective, to be causing any specific behavioral problems in his life. This reinforces the average score for Vulnerability (N6), demonstrating that Zach is able to control these negative feelings. Also, it reveals that he sits with these feelings inside and may not share them with others.

Adjective Checklist Results

The results of the Adjective Checklist can be seen in Table 8.2. They converged with the results of the NEO PI-3 in several areas, including Masculine Attributes (79, the highest *T*-score) and Femininity (36, one of the lowest *T*-scores). He also scored high in the areas of Achievement (60), Autonomy (65), Dominance (67), and Aggression (70). His numbers indicated someone with a tendency to express himself directly, to emphasize actions and rewards, to be ambitious and stubborn, to insist

Table 8.2 Adjective Check List Results for Zach.

Scale/Need	T-Score	Range
Achievement	60	High
Dominance	67	Very High
Endurance	44	Low
Order	60	High
Intraception	38	Low
Nurturance	43	Low
Affiliation	43	Low
Heterosexuality	60	High
Exhibition	42	Low
Autonomy	65	High
Aggression	70	Very High
Change	36	Low
Succorance	40	Low
Abasement	34	Very Low
Deference	51	Average
Topical		
Counseling Readiness	34	Very Low
Self-Control	57	High
Self-Confidence	64	High
Personal Adjustment	45	Average
Ideal Self	50	Average
Creative Personality	37	Low
Military Leadership	43	Low
Masculine Attributes	79	Very High
Feminine Attributes	36	Low
Transactional Analysis	56	High
Critical Parent		
Nurturing Parent	39	Low
Adult	45	Average
Free Child	45	Average
Adapted Child	56	High
Origence-Intelligence		
A-1 (High Origence, Low Intelligence)	54	Average
A-2 (High Origence, High Intelligence)	55	Average
A-3 (Low Origence, Low Intelligence)	45	Average
A-4 (Low Origence, High Intelligence)	42	Low

Note: Number Checked = 104

on attaining goals, and to keep others at a distance. In addition, he appeared as fault-finding, hard-headed, and opinionated. Such data could specify a critical parent, as well as someone distrustful, skeptical, quick to anger, and not easily impressed.

BSI Results

His *T*-scores on the BSI 18 for Somatization (73), Anxiety (79), and total GSI (69) aligned with his presenting remarks, as all were well above the norm. Interestingly, his score for Depression was 42, which was low. These scores are consistent with the NEO PI-3 results where Zach scored high on Anxiety and Anger but average on Depression. The overall GSI is consistent with the high overall *T*-score for Neuroticism ($T = 71$).

CPSCI Results

During data gathering for the CPSCI, Claire completed each of the four axes. For Axis I, The Presentation (see Appendix 8.A at the end of this chapter to view the completed CPSCI), she filled out the demographics portion and noted in the mental status section that his presentation was normal, with no obvious aspects of impairment in any of the categories, He was oriented x4.

For Axis II, The Problem, she ascertained that in addition to high anxiety, he endorsed a history of depressive, somatic, and attention-related symptoms, as well as obsessive handwashing and fear of contamination, which were interfering with his ability to complete work-related tasks. He endorsed some current (and past) medications (Luvox, Klonazepam, and Methylphenidate), but he still experienced OCD and anxiety symptoms. His presenting complaints paralleled his historical problems, with the exception of dissociation, inattention, and irritability; they were not part of his rationale for seeking treatment. His current health-related issues included problems related to digestion, his stomach, sleep disturbances, weight management, asthma, seasonal allergies, and an allergy to bee stings. In comparing the ratings in this section to the normative data for the CPSCI (presented in Table 7.1 in Chapter 7), we see that with regards to both Psychiatric History and Health-Related Issues, he is in the high range while he is on the cusp of being high for the Presenting Complaints section. On a positive note, in evaluating his score on the Support-Barriers to Treatment index, his score is very high indicating few barriers to treatment. Given Zach's scores on the NEO Neuroticism domain and BSI-18, it is not surprising that he has so many personal issues in his life. The convergence of these findings on this portion of the intake form provides evidence of convergent validity for the results of the CPSCI.

As Claire completed Axis II of the CPSCI, she documented the client's multiple support systems, including family, spouse, faith group, friends, work, and hobbies (specifically fishing). Claire rated his level of psychosocial impairment as moderate, and she noted an absence of personal dysphoria, perceptual aberration, and cognitive distortion. Again, the results of the BSI 18 converged. While he had endorsed a few problems in some other areas, he had noted no difficulties in domains such as Family/Home, School, Finances, Religion, Sex, and Crisis. This suggested that he had a strong support system, sufficient resources, and a stable relationship.

Claire then moved on to Axis III, The Person. She noted some difficulty with the ability to control cravings, but she rated the majority of the categories as average or better. Per her assessment, Zach's personality functioning was not impaired in any of the following areas: identity, self-direction, empathy, or intimacy. His stable attributes included strong coping ability and self-esteem, a caring orientation towards others, and high levels of personal insight. She noted some negative affect, which was supported by his scores on the NEO PI-3 and his completion of the PPCL in the area of Emotion, where he had acknowledged several items related to his presenting problems (e.g., "worrying about diseases or illness"). His *T*-score (54) for that dimension was within the normal range, though, providing additional evidence for the validity of the CPSCI.

In evaluating ratings on the Dysfunctional FFM Personality scales, Zach was rated low on all domains except Extraversion, where his total score was in the average range. This presents some very intriguing interpretations that can complement those found with the NEO PI-3. As we have already noted, the NEO does not capture dysfunctional elements of personality. However, the CPSCI scales are intended to do so. It is interesting to note that on the NEO, Zach scored high on Neuroticism, yet on the CPSCI his score is in the low range. This is not a contradictory finding. What we learn from the NEO is that Zach has large amounts of negative affect, especially anxiety and anger. These feelings, while more intense than the average person, are all within normal limits. The low ratings on Dysfunctional Neuroticism on the CPSCI indicate that whatever negative affect Zach has, it is not creating clinical issues for him in his life. This is consistent with his average score on Vulnerability, which indicates Zach's ability to control and manage whatever emotional dysphoria he has. Claire seems to agree that Zach's emotional distress is not in any manner negatively affecting his life.

However, a different pattern emerges with Dysfunctional Extraversion. Again, Zach scored high on Extraversion on the NEO, indicating high levels of positive affect across all facets. While such scores usually indicate more positive aspects of interpersonal functioning, there are negative dimensions to Extraversion (Widiger, Costa, & McCrae, 2013). Claire's ratings on the CPSCI place Zach in the average range for Dysfunctional Extraversion. Keep in mind that scores on this scale are being normed against other outpatient clients, so an average rating indicates that Zach has as much impairment interpersonally as the average client. The point here is that the rating, while "average," indicates some level of difficulty in this area. Claire's rating on Intimacy suggests that whatever interpersonal issues Zach has, they are not negatively impacting his relationship with his wife. When interpreting the CPSCI Dysfunctional Personality scales, remember that scores that are average *do* indicate some level of difficulty. The question to address is, where in Zach's life can we find these interpersonal difficulties?

As we noted above regarding Zach's scores on the Impulsive Triad on the NEO PI-3 (very high impulsiveness, high excitement seeking, and low self-discipline), and its implications for substance abuse, gambling, sex, and/or spending, Zach had not acknowledged concerns related to any of those areas. However, Claire disclosed to us, during the debriefing, that the arena for possible impulsive acting-out appeared to be when he was driving, as he would get angry with himself and with other motorists. While some flawed thinking was apparent (e.g., "a good Christian guy should not get angry"), Claire attributed his ability to restrict himself from engaging in "road rage" to his strong moral code, and she noted his tendencies toward scrupulosity.

While Claire rated his self-discipline, personal organization, and personal competence on the CPSCI as high, some of the results of the other tests diverged from her assessment in those particular areas. Of additional interest were low to very low scores on Order, Modesty, Trust, and Values on the NEO PI-3. As noted above, a *T*-score of 31 for Values did not indicate a lack of values but rather a strong commitment to his belief systems. Coupled with high to very high scores on Anxiety, Angry Hostility, all of the facets of Extraversion, Fantasy, Aesthetics, Feelings, Straightforwardness, Altruism, and Tendermindedness, a picture emerged of a man who was fun-loving, highly strung, conservative, skeptical, and rational.

The final section addressed in the CPSCI was Axis IV, The Predicament. Claire noted Zach's frequent involvement in the practice of his faith, the extreme importance of his spiritual and religious beliefs, his very strong relationship with the God of his understanding, and his denial of feeling punished, rejected, or abandoned by God. When evaluating his scores on these items in light of the norms for the Spirituality, Religiousness, and Religious Crisis scales, he was rated high on the first two and average on the last. This indicates that Zach was perceived as being very religiously and spiritually oriented, a finding consistent with his low score on the Openness to Values scale on the NEO. His Religious Crisis score was average, indicating that he does not feel rejected or punished by God any more than the average person. This is an important finding given that Zach scored, overall, very high on the Neuroticism dimension. Thus, while Zach may experience high levels of emotional distress, these feelings are different from any types of transcendent feelings of rejection from God. As we have argued in Chapter 5, Religious Crisis is *not* merely feelings of negative affect. Rather, this dimension represents an entirely different pathway for experiencing distress. As such, never assume that scores on these two scales should move in tandem with one another.

Table 8.3 Comparison of Self-Report and Observer Ratings T-Scores for Zach.

ASPIRES Scale	ASPIRES T-Scores	
	Zach's Report	Wife's Rating
Religious Involvement	61	71
Religious Crisis	39	41
Prayer Fulfillment	64	66
Universality	62	68
Connectedness	52	66
Total Transcendence	63	71

ASPIRES Results

Zach's T-scores on the ASPIRES (presented in Table 8.3) converged with the information obtained on the CPSCI. Religious Involvement was high (61), Religious Crisis was low (39), and Total Spiritual Transcendence was high (63). Zach's scores were in the high range for both Prayer Fulfillment (64) and Universality (62), and average for Connectedness (52). This indicates a man satisfied with and actively engaged with his religious community (Zach was Catholic), as well as a man concerned with actions congruent with his belief system, fortified by his relationship with God, and connected to all of life.

The observer ratings of the ASPIRES provided by his wife indicated strong agreement with both the self-report and the CPSCI. The results showed high T-scores for all areas except Religious Crisis, which was quite low (41). See Table 8.3 for a comparison of the couple's scores. Interestingly, his wife rated his level of Religious Involvement, Connectedness, and Total Transcendence much higher than he did, although all scores are in the same interpretive region (i.e., Zach's scores on Religious Involvement, 61 and 71, are different but carry the same interpretation: Zach is very much involved in his religious commitments, more than 85% of the normative samples). The profile agreement correlation (see McCrae, 2008) was .85, showing a very strong convergence between the self and the observer ratings. Such convergence provides strong support for viewing Zach's self-report findings as being accurate. That both his wife and therapist agree similarly on these dimensions rules out any suggestion that his findings are a product of some kind of response error (e.g., social desirability, acquiescence).

Pastoral Themes

As Claire completed Axis IV of the CPSCI, she assessed his overall meaning-making orientation as spiritual/transcendent and indicated that multiple pastoral themes were apparent. In the areas of Personal Durability and Infinitude, 18 items were chosen, which when compared to the normative data for this scale puts him in the high category: He noted more items than other outpatient clients. This score indicates that Zach situates his current sense of the numinous within this category. His focus is on eternity, and he tries to live his life accordingly. Claire endorsed only 9 items on the Meaning Themes, which is in the average category, and he received only 3 endorsements on Worthiness, which is in the low category. This type of endorsement pattern suggests that Zach does not appear to have a balanced sense of the numinous. His current focus is strongly on Infinitude, which carries with it an eternal time perspective and provides Zach with a sense of resilience and hope in the face of struggle as well as encouraging personal feelings of abundance, value, and deep engagement with life. The intensity of such focus restricts his attention to issues of Meaning and Worthiness. Especially the latter domain is relevant here. As we mentioned at the beginning of this chapter, Zach is studying to be a nurse practitioner, a very caring and other-oriented profession. Individuals in this job category have been shown to possess higher levels of spirituality (Piedmont, Wilkins, & Hollwitz, 2013). However, the lower endorsement rate for Worthiness may indicate that this is a particular area of spiritual need.

In seeking help with his obsessive behaviors, he may be thinking to himself that this truly is an irony: a care giver who himself is damaged and in need of care. Usually when ministering to others, we believe that we are coming from a position of strength or stability, otherwise what would lead us to believe that we had something to give to those who are in need? One of the items Claire selected for Zach was *self-condemnation.* Zach may hold himself in contempt, to some degree, because he may not see himself worthy enough to provide practical help to others in need. After all, he is damaged himself, having a reduced capacity to manage the anxieties that lead to his excessive handwashing. On the CPSCI, Claire noted that he is fearful that these behaviors will interfere with his occupational activities. As a consequence, Zach focuses on the hope of eternity with God and avoids dealing with his inner questioning of his essential fitness for that experience.

An unequal endorsement rate for items on these three scales does carry with it important interpretive value. In the case of Zach, the pattern of endorsements is the opposite of that found in our normative group (mean number of ratings were 5.9, 6.7, and 9.5, for Infinitude, Meaning, and Worthiness, respectively). Something is occurring with this client that is important and needs to be addressed clinically because it is impacting his core numinous sense. He is counting on a relationship with God as the answer to his concerns, but he does so at the cost of his sense of Worthiness. It is hard to stand tall spiritually if one believes himself to be broken and damaged. It signals the need for a spiritual crutch to survive. What is needed is a spiritual empowerment that enables him to feel accepted despite the weaknesses and brokenness, that one is adequate and of value. Clearly, one focus of treatment will need to include these aspects of the numinous. While remediating the psychological problem, it will also be important to open up Zach's feelings of worthiness; doing so may help teach him that while some may be broken physically, our spirituality can remain intact.

Overall, the entire battery of tests showed that Zach was dealing with an average amount of dysfunction for a clinical client. His scores were typical of someone presenting for outpatient treatment, and he appeared to have an average amount of interpersonal problems. While he experiences more emotional and physical problems than outpatient clients in our normative sample, his CPSCI indicates that he does not seem to have a wide array of psychological problems and issues, and he seems to be adapting well overall. Such a pattern usually indicates a client who has a very specific set of issues in need of management. Such is the case here: Zach is seeking treatment only for his compulsive behaviors.

Treatment Outcome Information

At the end of treatment, both Claire and Zach completed a short questionnaire that queried their perspectives on the treatment process and how effective each felt it to be. This section will review these comments.

Claire utilized CBT with Exposure and Response Prevention (ERP) and reported rapid improvement. She also expressed concern that after Zach saw such a drop in his symptoms, he stopped therapy too quickly and did not address some of his subtler compulsions. In his outcome questionnaire, Zach noted that he had experienced "large growth" over the course of his time with Claire and wrote, "This was my first experience with ERP. I found the therapy model to be very effective and helpful. I easily applied the technique outside the office and improved greatly." He also endorsed "some growth" in the R/S arena.

Claire also asserted that even though he had only completed five sessions, she recognized slight growth for him in the numinous domain. She reported that after a 6-month hiatus, Zach returned for treatment when he had a resurgence of some OCD symptoms. In our debriefing session, she stated that while it might have been helpful to receive some training before utilizing the CPSCI, she found that, even for a naïve user, it provided an abundance of data that assisted her in conceptualizing his case and in providing effective interventions. Upon re-examination of the materials when Zach returned for treatment, she acknowledged that his tendency toward scrupulosity was quite strong and that she was going to "re-think and re-evaluate" her approach about addressing that area.

As we discussed her impressions of the CPSCI, it became apparent that the instrument's results dovetailed with the NEO PI-3, the ASPIRES, and the other assessments and provided us with substantial information that could assist Claire in her continuing work with Zach. The combination of high Extraversion with high Neuroticism could have been an additional catalyst for his seeking out her support again. With that combination, a client may come across as emotionally needy because he seeks out others to gain emotional support and succorance. High Neuroticism tends to play out with symptoms continuing over the lifespan. At first glance, high Extraversion may seem to be quite positive, but in Zach's case, these two personality factors provided rich interpretive material for his previous and current presentations to therapy.

During the beginning of treatment, he was enrolled in higher education classes and interacting with colleagues, instructors, and other students. For someone highly extraverted, he was in a supportive milieu, surrounded by people who could provide nurturance for his need to connect. After completing his degree, he began working in the field in a small community and had to set boundaries to eliminate possible dual relationships. The succorance he had previously received was no longer coming from his working environment. Claire noted his continued desire for friendships but that he struggled due to his professional status and due to his peers not being at the same intellectual level. With high levels of anxiety, anger, and impulsiveness, Zach's insecurities were quite evident. However, his outgoing nature and low level of vulnerability provided him with some coping skills. He could use his Extraversion traits (e.g., Warmth, Gregariousness, Assertiveness, Activity Level, Excitement Seeking, and Positive Emotions) as tools to help him manage his negative affect. While high Neuroticism captures high levels of distress and may "account for the predictive utility of depressive symptoms" (Zonderman, Herbst, Schmidt, Costa, & McCrae, 1993, p. 550), it does not necessarily indicate pathology. Per Claire, he was "incredibly functional in many ways."

We asked Claire several other questions about her perceptions regarding Zach's growth, emphasizing dimensions of R/S, especially in the areas of Infinitude, Meaning, and Worthiness. She noted that during the initial completion of the CPSCI, she had endorsed multiple themes related to Infinitude. This was during a period when he was obtaining new skills and training and the emphasis on this area made sense due to the prominence of the theme of abundance. Claire had rated him as average on Meaning and low on Worthiness. During the debriefing, she acknowledged that Worthiness was still an area where her client showed some deficits. She asserted that he doubted his own clinical skills, although there was substantial evidence to support that he was a very good practitioner. Zach appeared to question if he were good enough and if he would live up to expectations. Claire added that his scrupulosity played into this as well. She declared that his religious standards were set so high that she knew she would not be able to live up to them herself. His emphasis was on having to do a good job, having to be moral, and having to set rigid boundaries, without giving himself any leeway.

Therapist Debriefing

After all the data were collected for this chapter, we asked Claire a number of questions about her treatment with Zach. We wished to clarify and expand on some of her comments on the CPSCI as well as to get her take on the assessment results from Zach (Claire received copies of his results during treatment). We are grateful for the feedback she provided to our questions in written form, which we have included below:

1 How did spirituality filter into treatment? Spirituality was an important component of treatment, as many of his obsessive intrusive thoughts were about a scrupulous need to do what is right and moral.
2 How was spirituality used as a resource? Spirituality is an important moral compass for the patient, as his religious beliefs inform his interactions with his clients, his family, and his peers. It is also a source of strength for him and a guiding light.
3 To what extent did spirituality contribute to finding growth? Without acknowledging his strong sense of spirituality and incorporating it into treatment, it would have been impossible to do effective ERP with this client. It was important to him to have a therapist who had at least some understanding of his worldview so that ERP exposures would not be in direct conflict with his deeply held beliefs. We were able to incorporate his belief that God knows he has OCD as a way to help him engage in the hard work of ERP.
4 What was the client strongly committed to? He was strongly committed to becoming more functional in his work environment and not letting OCD get in the way of his job performance. He was willing to do the hard work of ERP in order to get better and saw significant success in a very short amount of time. This gave him the courage to continue doing ERP as needed.
5 How did spirituality play out in the sessions? Aspects of how his faith informs his life choices were brought up by the client in almost every single session. How scrupulosity interferes with faith was also a factor, as the patient was avoiding "passing the peace" at church due to contamination fears, which then resulted in him feeling as if he were sinning because he was appearing to be unfriendly to those around him.
6 Did you see any gaps related to spirituality or other issues? No.

7   What was your experience of the client when he first began treatment? My first experience of this client was that here was someone who was feeling highly distressed due to how his OCD was interfering with his everyday life. There was also a sense of excitement that this was a client who would be open to exploring spirituality in treatment, as it related to his OCD and in general. He is a likeable young man, devoted to his faith and his family, with a ready smile and a willingness to engage in the hard work of therapy.

8   Did additional issues pop up? Yes, in addition to having OCD, the patient was studying for medical exams in his field and was trying to balance work, life, and school. He passed his license during treatment and had at least one job change during the course of treatment, during the survey period. All of this was also discussed in treatment. We also had several discussions on ethics as it related to his job performance and workplace environments. He lost his job shortly after he completed the surveys, which resulted in him terminating treatment early. He was, at that stage, doing very well, and was able to come up with his own ERP as needed for his OCD, so I did not feel the need to refer him elsewhere. (Added to this is that fact that there are, to my knowledge, no other therapists in our area who are knowledgeable about the nuances of treating OCD efficaciously that I felt I could refer him to). The patient took a 6-month hiatus in treatment and returned after a flare-up of OCD symptoms.

9   How did symptoms change from the beginning to the end of treatment, and how was spirituality part of this? When the patient first presented for treatment, he was washing his hands more than 100 times daily. By the time the survey was completed, he was down to only washing them 10 to 20 times per day, which was a significant improvement. The other issue he was experiencing was scrupulous worry about whether or not he was making the right decisions regarding meds management with his own patients, and during the course of treatment he was able to be more comfortable with the uncertainty that he may have mis-prescribed. He was also able to slightly speed up the time it took to see his patients, which resulted in him being more efficient in the workplace. (Note that he lost his job due to the facility mismanaging resources, not through any fault of his own). Spirituality allowed him to dream bigger, and he is now in the process of opening his own practice with another psychiatrist in the area.

10 What was your experience of the client at the end of the first round of treatment? It was gratifying to see a client make such significant progress in such a relatively short time span. Since he has come back this year for additional treatment, I relish the opportunity to work with him again.

11 Did spirituality augment or get in the way of treatment (or not matter at all)? Spirituality definitely augmented treatment, for the most part. There were one or two occasions where it did get in the way

of treatment, for example, his need to confess "possible sins" to his priest despite not knowing for sure if he had actually committed a sin that needed to be addressed. However, because we come from different denominational backgrounds, the patient was loath to take my treatment suggestion that he practice not confessing anything other than sins he was certain he had committed.

12 If you were to complete another CPSCI at the end of treatment, what do you think might have changed? He is definitely in a much better place at this point and has improved significantly from when we first began treatment.

13 What do you think his prognosis is, moving forward? The patient has an excellent prognosis, as he is engaged and willing to return to treatment as needed for future OCD flare-ups. He understands the principles of good ERP work and is able to implement them on his own, for the most part, only returning for treatment now because he needed a bit of a refresher.

The above answers, graciously provided by Claire, underscore our point that we are not spiritual directors. Our clients report to us for assistance in the mental health arena. The inclusion of the numinous helps to augment clinical understandings and to suggest different approaches for implementing treatment.

Conclusions

We hope that this case presentation sheds light on the utility of the measures we created to capture numinous functioning. It is one thing to present group data evidencing general patterns of association, it is quite another to evaluate a real profile and note the internal consistency found in the pattern of scores. Zach's case not only reinforces many of the claims made in Chapters 5, 6, and 7 but also provides interesting twists and turns in the scale results that help to reinforce the interpretive value of the measures. While this is only one case and is presented in a limited space format, we do believe that some of the basic interpretive strategies surrounding these measures were clearly presented for the reader. We also acknowledge that there may be other insights and potential interpretations in these scales, and they are left for the reader to harvest.

Another value of this presentation is that it also demonstrated many of the features presented in Chapter 3 about using the numinous as a psychological construct in treatment. As we saw here, Claire was always addressing the psychological issues that Zach presented. The goal of treatment was strictly psychological in nature, even though there was a substantial numinous component to the work that was done. Including numinous material does not mean that treatment is becoming less psychological and more theological in focus. Rather, when understood as a psychological construct, the numinous can be easily folded into any established treatment protocol. Further, as we saw here, the numinous dimension was not only appropriate material to be addressed for someone who is as religiously committed as Zach, but its consideration also provided useful insights into his inner core being, and these insights led to other, important psychological understandings that were not available through other measures (e.g., NEO PI-3).

If time permitted, it would have been ideal to obtain some post-treatment or follow-up data on the numinous scales from Zach, to see if there were any noticeable changes from his therapy. The numinous measures included here can also serve as useful outcome measures for gauging the impact of treatment across identified, clinically salient areas. It would be helpful to learn if Zach comes to better balance out his numinous motivations and to document the impact of such action on his professional feelings of competence and his other interpersonal relationships. For now, though, we can feel comfortable in knowing that the numinous scales we developed and presented in this book appear to be working as planned and can provide clinicians with useful information about their clients. Every element included herein has been empirically developed and validated; at the very least, these instruments cannot be faulted for being fanciful, unverifiable, or unscientific. Correspondingly, while these scales meet current standards of psychometric integrity, their structured format cannot be dismissed as presenting clients as static, superficial, or sterile. As these data documented, the scores from these assessments accurately captured the subtleties and nuances of a real person in terms that were clinically meaningful.

References

Butcher, J. N., Graham, J. R., Ben-Porath, Y. S., Tellegen, A., Dahlstrom, W. G., & Kaemmer, B. (2001). *Minnesota Multiphasic Personality Inventory-2 (MMPI-2) manual*. Minneapolis, MN: Pearson Assessments.

Costa, P. T., Jr., & McCrae, R. R. (1992). Normal personality assessment in clinical practice: The NEO Personality Inventory. *Psychological Assessment, 4*, 5–13.

Derogatis, L. R. (2001). *Brief Symptom Inventory 18: Administration, scoring, and procedures manual*. San Antonio, TX: NCS Pearson, Inc.

Gough, H. G., & Heilbrun, A. B. (1983). *The Adjective Check List manual*. Palo Alto, CA; Consulting Psychologists Press.

John, O. P., & Soto, C. J. (2007). The importance of being valid: Reliability and the process of construct validation. In R. W. Robbins, R. C. Fraley, & R. F. Kreuger (Eds.), *Handbook of research methods in personality psychology* (pp. 461–494). New York, NY: The Guilford Press.

McCrae, R. R. (2008). A note of some measures of profile agreement. *Journal of Personality Assessment, 90*(2), 105–109. doi:10.1080/00223890701845104

McCrae, R. R., & Costa, P. T., Jr. (2010). *NEO Inventories: Professional manual.* Odessa, FL: Psychological Assessment Resources.

Millon, T., Grossman, S., & Millon, C. (2015). *Millon Clinical Multiaxial Inventory–IV manual.* Minneapolis, MN: Pearson Assessments.

Piedmont, R. L. (1998). *The Revised NEO Personality Inventory: Clinical and research applications.* New York, NY: Plenum.

Piedmont, R. L. (1999). Does spirituality represent the sixth factor of personality? Spiritual transcendence and the five-factor model. *Journal of Personality, 67,* 985–1013.

Piedmont, R. L., & Ciarrocchi, J. W. (1999). The utility of the Revised NEO Personality Inventory in an outpatient, drug rehabilitation context. *Psychology of Addictive Behaviors, 13,* 213–226.

Piedmont, R. L., & Rodgerson, T. E. (2017). Cross-over analysis: Using the Five-Factor Model and NEO Personality Inventory-3 for assessing compatibility and conflict in couples. In T. A. Widiger (Ed.). *The Oxford Handbook of the Five Factor Model of Personality* (pp. 423–448). New York, NY: Oxford University Press.

Piedmont, R. L., Sherman M. F., & Barrickman, L. (2000). Brief psychosocial assessment of a clinical sample: An evaluation of the Personal Problems Checklist for adults. *Assessment, 7,* 177–187.

Piedmont, R. L., Wilkins, T. A., & Hollwitz, J. (2013) The relevance of spiritual transcendence in a consumer economy: The dollars and sense of it. *Journal of Social Research and Policy, 4,* 59–77.

Schinka, J. A. (1985). *Personal Problems Checklist for Adults.* Odessa, FL: Psychological Assessment Resources.

Trull, T. J. (1992). DSM-III-R personality disorders and the five-factor model of personality: An empirical comparison. *Journal of Abnormal Psychology, 101,* 553–560.

Widiger, T. A., Costa, P. T., Jr., & McCrae, R. R. (2013). Diagnosis of personality disorder using the Five-Factor Model and the proposed DSM-5. In T. A. Widiger and P. T. Costa, (Eds.), *Personality disorders and the Five-Factor Model of Personality* (pp. 285–310). Washington, DC: American Psychological Association.

Zonderman, A. B., Herbst, J. H., Schmidt, Jr., C., Costa, Jr., P. T., & McCrae, R. R. (1993). Depressive symptoms as a nonspecific, graded risk for psychiatric diagnoses. *Journal of Abnormal Psychology, 102,* 544–552.

APPENDIX 8.A
A CPSCI for Zach

Comprehensive Psycho-Spiritual Clinical Interview
Ralph L. Piedmont, Ph.D.

NAME: _____ _Zach S._____

AXIS I: THE PRESENTATION

Demographics:

Age: _28_   Gender Orientation: _Male_   Sexual Orientation: _heterosexual_

Ethnicity: . . . . ❏ Arab ❏ Asian ❏ Black ☒ Caucasian ❏ Hispanic ❏ Mixed ❏ Other

Marital Status: . . . . ❏ Single ☒ Married ❏ Divorced ❏ Committed Relationship

Education Level:

❏ Elementary School ❏ Some college ☒ Some graduate school ❏ Trade School
❏ Some high school ❏ AA degree ❏ Masters Degree
❏ High School grad ☒ BA/BS degree ❏ Doctoral Degree

Employment
Status: . . . . ☒ Full Time ❏ Part Time ❏ Unemployed ❏ Homemaker ❏ Disabled ❏ Student

Current Occupation: _Registered Nurse & in school to become an NP_

Religious Affiliation: _Catholic_

Mental Status:

Appearance: . . . . ☒ Well-groomed ❏ Disheveled ❏ Bizarre ❏ Inappropriate

Attitude: . . . . ☒ Cooperative ❏ Guarded ❏ Suspicious ❏ Uncooperative ❏ Belligerent

Motor Activity: . . ❏ Lethargic ☒ Calm ❏ Hyperactive ❏ Agitated ❏ Tremor/Tic ❏ Muscle Spasms

Affect: . . . . ☒ Appropriate ❏ Labile ❏ Expansive ❏ Constricted ❏ Blunted ❏ Flat

Mood: . . . . ☒ Normal ❏ Depressed ❏ Anxious ❏ Euphoric

Speech:

☒ Normal ❏ Soft ❏ Slurred ❏ Pressured ❏ Incoherent ❏ Poverty of
❏ Delayed ❏ Loud ❏ Excessive ❏ Perseverating Speech

Thought Process: . . ☒ Intact ❏ Circumstantial ❏ Loose Associations ❏ Tangential ❏ Flight of Ideas

Hallucinations: . . . . ☒ Not Present ❏ Auditory ❏ Visual ❏ Tactile ❏ Olfactory

Delusions:

☒ Not Present ❏ Being Controlled ❏ Ideas of Reference ❏ Thought
❏ Persecutory ❏ Bizarre ❏ Grandiose insertion/deletion

Orientation: . . . . ☒ Fully oriented x3 ❏ Partially oriented ❏ Disoriented

Insight: . . . . ☒ Intact ❏ Impaired

Describe impairment: _____

Judgment: . . . . ☒ Intact ❏ Impaired

Describe impairment: _____

Memory: Immediate . . . . ☒ *Intact* ☐ *Impaired*

Memory: Recent . . . . ☒ *Intact* ☐ *Impaired*

Memory: Remote . . . . ☒ *Intact* ☐ *Impaired*

AXIS II: THE PROBLEM

Psychiatric History:

Does the client have a history with any of the following problems?

☐ *None by Client Report*
☒ *Depression*
☐ *Anger*
☐ *Mania*
☒ *Anxiety*
☒ *Somatic symptoms*
☐ *Suicidal ideation*
☐ *Homicidal ideation*

☐ *Suicide attempts*
☐ *Psychosis*
☒ *Sleep problems*
☐ *Memory*
☒ *Repetitive thoughts/behaviors*
☒ *Dissociation*
☐ *Personality disorder*
☐ *Substance abuse*

☒ *Inattention*
☒ *Irritability*
☐ *Impulsive*
   (gambling/sex/shopping)
☐ *Trauma/Abuse*
☐ *Sexual/Physical/Emotional Abuse*

Symptom Specifics: ___OCD - handwashing___

Has the client experienced any of the following interventions?

☐ *Inpatient Psych/Substance Abuse*
   TX
☐ *ER Visits or Crisis Episode prior*
   12 months

☐ *Outpatient Psych/Substance*
   Abuse TX
☒ *Psychiatric Medication*
☐ *Arrested*

☐ *Incarcerated*
☐ *Family History of Treatment*
☐ *No Previous Treatment*

Treatment Specifics: ___Luvox, Klonazepan, Methylphenidate___

Presenting Complaints:

Indicate the client's presenting problems:

☐ *None by Client Report*
☒ *Depression*
☐ *Anger*
☐ *Mania*
☒ *Anxiety*
☒ *Somatic symptoms*
☐ *Suicidal ideation*
☐ *Homicidal ideation*

☐ *Suicide attempts*
☐ *Psychosis*
☒ *Sleep problems*
☐ *Memory*
☒ *Repetitive thoughts/behaviors*
☐ *Dissociation*
☐ *Personality disorder*
☐ *Substance abuse*

☐ *Inattention*
☐ *Irritability*
☐ *Impulsive*
   (gambling/sex/shopping)
☐ *Trauma/Abuse*
☐ *Sexual/Physical/Emotional Abuse*

Symptom Specifics: ___Pt reports that excessive handwashing & contamination fears interfere w/- occupational functioning___

List Relevant Z-codes: ___F42.2___

List All Current Medications: ___Luvox, Klonazepan, Methylphenidate___

Indicate health-related issues currently affecting the client:

☐ *Cancer,*
   type:___
☐ *Diabetes*
☐ *Cardiovascular*
☐ *Hepatitis*
☐ *High blood pressure*
☐ *Epilepsy*
☐ *Other:___*

☒ *Digestive issues*
☒ *Stomach issues*
☐ *Neurological condition,*
   type:___
☒ *Sleep disturbances*
☒ *Weight management*
☐ *Vision-related problems*

☐ *Kidney/bladder*
☐ *Reproductive issues*
☐ *Head trauma/injury*
☒ *Asthma*
☐ *Hearing-related problems*
☒ *Allergies,*
   type: Seasonal
   bee stings

Page 2 of 5. Client Name:

Current Support Systems:

☑ Family   ☑ Spouse/Significant Other   *fishing*
☑ Faith Group   ☑ Work   ☑ Hobbies/Interests
☑ Friends   ☐ Recreation   ☐ Living Context
☐ Other:

Barriers To Treatment:

☐ Homelessness   ☐ Safety   ☐ Motivation
☐ Transportation Issues   ☐ Health   ☐ Financial
☐ Food   ☐ Disability   ☐ Insurance
☐ Other:

Please rate the client on the following dimensions using the scale provided.

Degree of personal dysphoria	☑ None	☐ Mild	☐ Moderate	☐ Severe	☐ Extreme
Degree of psychosocial impairment	☐ None	☐ Mild	☑ Moderate	☐ Severe	☐ Extreme
Degree of perceptual aberration	☑ None	☐ Mild	☐ Moderate	☐ Severe	☐ Extreme
Degree of cognitive distortion	☑ None	☐ Mild	☐ Moderate	☐ Severe	☐ Extreme

AXIS III: THE PERSON

This section assesses stable attributes of the client. As such, your responses should indicate how the client is generally or usually. What is his/her overall level of each of these qualities?

Coping Ability	☑ Strong	☐ Average	☐ Weak	☐ Impaired
Self-Esteem	☑ Strong	☐ Average	☐ Weak	☐ Impaired
Ability to Tolerate Frustration	☐ Strong	☑ Average	☐ Weak	☐ Impaired
Ability to Control Cravings	☐ Strong	☐ Average	☑ Weak	☐ Impaired
Level of Negative Affect (e.g., depression, sadness, anxiety)	☐ None	☑ Some	☐ Moderate	☐ High

Sociability	☐ Gregarious	☑ Approachable	☐ Loner	☐ Detached
Personal Energy Level	☐ Energetic	☑ Active	☐ Relaxed	☐ Sluggish
Level of Positive Affect (e.g., joy, enthusiasm)	☐ High	☑ Moderate	☐ Some	☐ None

Level of Personal Rigidity	☐ None	☑ Some	☐ Moderate	☐ High
Need for Structure	☐ None	☑ Some	☐ Moderate	☐ High
Level of Personal Insight	☑ High	☐ Moderate	☐ Some	☐ None

Orientation to Others	☑ Caring	☐ Considerate	☐ Manipulative	☐ Disingenuous
Interpersonal Orientation	☑ Other-oriented	☐ Responds to Appeals	☐ Self-focused	☐ Uninterested in Others

Self-Discipline	☑ Strong	☐ Average	☐ Weak	☐ Impaired
Personal Organization	☑ Strong	☐ Average	☐ Weak	☐ Impaired
Personal Competence	☑ Strong	☐ Average	☐ Weak	☐ Impaired

Please evaluate the level of clinical impairment the client exhibits on each of the following aspects of personality functioning.

Identity: Ability to experience oneself as unique, with clear boundaries between self and others; stability of self-esteem and accuracy of self-appraisal; capacity for, and ability to regulate, a range of emotional experiences

☒ *Little or no impairment* ☐ *Some impairment* ☐ *Moderate impairment* ☐ *Severe impairment*

Self-Direction: Ability to pursue a coherent and meaningful set of short-term and life goals; utilization of constructive and prosocial internal standards of behavior; ability to self-reflect productively

☒ *Little or no impairment* ☐ *Some impairment* ☐ *Moderate impairment* ☐ *Severe impairment*

Empathy: Ability to comprehend and appreciate other's experiences and motivations; tolerance of different perspectives; understands the effects of one's own behavior on others.

☒ *Little or no impairment* ☐ *Some impairment* ☐ *Moderate impairment* ☐ *Severe impairment*

Intimacy: The depth and duration of connection with others; desire and capacity for closeness; mutuality of regard reflected in interpersonal behavior.

☒ *Little or no impairment* ☐ *Some impairment* ☐ *Moderate impairment* ☐ *Severe impairment*

AXIS IV: THE PREDICAMENT

How frequently is the client involved in the practice of his/her faith tradition (this includes any aspect, attending services, reading religious literature, involvement in faith groups).

☐ *Never* ☐ *Rarely* ☐ *Occasionally* ☐ *Often* ☒ *Quite Often* ☐ *N/A*

How important are the client's RELIGIOUS beliefs?

☐ *Not at all important* ☐ *Somewhat unimportant* ☐ *Fairly important* ☒ *Extremely important* ☐ *N/A*

How important are the client's SPIRITUAL beliefs?

☐ *Not at all important* ☐ *Somewhat unimportant* ☐ *Fairly important* ☒ *Extremely important* ☐ *N/A*

Over the past 12 months, has the client's religious and/or spiritual interests and involvements:

☐ *Decreased* ☒ *Stayed the Same* ☐ *Increased*

To what extent does the client have a personal, unique, close relationship with a Transcendent Reality and/or God?

☐ *Not at all* ☐ *Slight* ☐ *Moderate* ☐ *Strong* ☒ *Very Strong*

To what extent does the client feel a union with a Transcendent Reality and/or God that provides him/her with spiritual truth?

☐ *Not at all* ☐ *Slight* ☐ *Moderate* ☐ *Strong* ☒ *Very Strong*

To what extent does the client feel that God is punishing him/her?

☐ *Not at all* ☒ *Slight* ☐ *Moderate* ☐ *Strong* ☐ *Very Strong*

To what extent does the client believe he/she has been abandoned by God?

☒ *Not at all* ☐ *Slight* ☐ *Moderate* ☐ *Strong* ☐ *Very Strong*

To what extent does the client feel rejected by God?

☒ *Not at all* ☐ *Slight* ☐ *Moderate* ☐ *Strong* ☐ *Very Strong*

Page 4 of 5. Client Name:

Overall meaning-making orientation of client:

❏ *Materialistic:Very self-focused, narcissistic, distrusts others, cut-off from nurturance of others, oriented towards short-term goals*

❏ *Humanistic: Concerned with own needs and realities that are experienced through senses; is socially responsible and civic minded, socially generative*

❏ *Self-Directing: Concerned about personal meaning and transcendence, however focus is on self; relationship to transcendent is personal/singular*

☒ *Spiritual/Transpersonal: Broad sense of personal meaning that is expressed within defined community; Relationship with transcendent defined in/with/by connection to community*

PASTORAL THEMES:

Personal Durability and Infinitude Themes (check all that apply):

☒ Adoration
☒ Benevolence
⇒ ❏ Creating/Continuance
☒ Determination
☒ Development
☒ Endurance
☒ Eternal Perspective
❏ Fear of Death
☒ Finding Wisdom in Past
❏ Greed to Feel Secure

☒ Growth
❏ Initiative
☒ Loyalty to Ideals
☒ Miracles
☒ Mourning
☒ Mysticism
☒ Need for Certainty
❏ Patience
☒ Perserverence in Face of Fear
☒ Prayer

☒ Protection
☒ Ressurection
❏ Securing a Legacy
☒ Sense of Personal Abundance
❏ Shepherd
❏ Stewardship
❏ Transform for Lasting Change
❏ Trust in Ultimate Reality
❏ Vision

Meaning Themes (check all that apply):

❏ Ambiguity
☒ Care-giving
❏ Conformity
❏ Contemplation
☒ Discernment
☒ Disillusionment
☒ Exploring the Shadow
☒ Faith
☒ Feeling Blessed
❏ Grief/Loss

❏ Identity
❏ Justice
❏ Meditation
❏ Mission
☒ Morality
❏ Nature
❏ Order
❏ Purpose
❏ Quest
❏ Rebirth

❏ Reverence
❏ Risk
❏ Sacrifice
☒ Self-Identity/Purpose
❏ Simplicity
❏ Surrender
❏ Temptation
☒ Thanksgiving
❏ Wisdom

Worthiness Themes (check all that apply):

❏ Abandonment
❏ Alienation
❏ Betrayal
❏ Brokenness, Unfixable
❏ Despair over Lack of Self-worth
❏ Discipleship
❏ Envy
❏ Evil
❏ False Self
❏ Genuineness
❏ Gluttony
❏ God Forgiveness
❏ Goodness
❏ Guilt

❏ Humiliation
❏ Isolation
❏ Judgment
❏ Loneliness
❏ Mercy
❏ Obedience
❏ Penitence
❏ Perfection
❏ Personal Brokenness
❏ Personal Suffering
❏ Prodigal: Hope Despite Failure
❏ Reconciliation
❏ Redemption
❏ Repentence

☒ Sanctification
☒ Self-Acceptance
❏ Self-Compassion
☒ Self-Condemnation
❏ Selflessness
❏ Shame
❏ Sin
❏ Sloth
❏ Social Isolation
❏ Superiority
❏ Supplication
❏ Woundedness

Other Relevant Observations:

_____

_____

_____

_____

Page 5 of 5. Client Name:

9 Recommendations for Developing the Science of the Numinous

This volume has presented a comprehensive paradigm for conceptualizing, developing, and applying numinous constructs as organismic qualities. We believe that this paradigm can be very useful for anyone interested in scientifically understanding religiousness/spirituality (R/S) concepts. It provides a solid foundation for creating a psychologically based platform for grasping the origin of numinous motivations and the intrapsychic functions they serve. Each of us has a deep-seated need to feel a personal sense of abundance, purpose, and acceptance, the essential elements for creating a sound sense of self. The numinous lies at the core of our humanity and serves to focus and direct the tremendous capacities of people to bring value to life. Understanding what the numinous represents enables the development of an empirical framework for developing, testing, validating, and applying constructs that capture these unique drivers of behavior. It is fortuitous that the field has come to a point where it has been able to construct a relatively comprehensive taxonomy of temperamental traits that can serve as the scaffolding for the development of numinous constructs. Without such a taxonomy, this type of work would be much more difficult to accomplish, if it could be done at all.

Having both a psychological ontogeny for understanding the underlying nature of R/S concepts and an empirical epistemology for developing and validating numinous constructs creates new potentials for the field. The development of measures that capture these motivations helps to expand our understanding of human striving and adds an additional explanatory construct to any developing model of the mind. A consideration of the numinous will provide new hypotheses surrounding human development and activity. Measures like the ASPIRES (see Chapter 5) will help to organize the wide literature on R/S constructs because of its universal applicability. The potential exists for the establishment of a cumulative base of knowledge in this area. Research findings across diverse groups (e.g., faith status, religious affiliation, culture, language) can now be systematically compared on a common set of constructs, allowing for the identification of deeper insights and the recognition of new, broad patterns operating across different psychological processes. The CPSCI (see Chapter 7) now provides professionals with a systematic method for assessing clients in an efficient manner and also ensures that the numinous is addressed in this evaluation. It will be interesting to note whether the inclusion of numinous information will help to identify new types of pathology heretofore unrecognized as contributing to dysfunction.

We hope that the information presented in this volume will stimulate researchers and practitioners from across the professional spectrum to think about the numinous in new ways and to gain an appreciation for just how important these constructs are for understanding what it means for us to be human. Because the numinous represents the highest aspects of our personality system, investigating these qualities ought to expand our view of human nature and to highlight the possibilities for human achievement. It can also provide insights into the existential darkness that impairment on this level may hold for those who have not managed to adaptively deploy these psychological resources.

While we believe, and hope, that this book represents an important resource for professionals interested in R/S issues, we recognize that the work is just beginning. What has been presented herein represents over 25 years of systematic research in this area, yet there is still much more that needs to be done. The focus of this chapter is to touch on some of the more salient topics to be addressed as we move forward (although we do not consider this list to be exhaustive). There are six areas that will each be discussed in turn: a) core issues for training; b) development of better numinous measures; c) CPSCI development; d) Logoplex development; e) numinous interventions, and f) developing the psychological implications for Religious Crisis/Worthiness.

Core Issues for Training

Back in the 1980s and 1990s, it would be very difficult to find a licensed, mental health therapist who actively included R/S content in treatment. Today, one would be hard pressed to find such a professional who avoids such material. Many major professional associations have developed guidelines and competencies for their members in addressing these types of subjects and any examination of book lists and research articles will clearly show the tremendous interest in R/S topics in the clinical context. It is exciting to see such a radical shift in focus in the professions over a relatively brief time period. One subject fueling such a shift is the results of survey research that shows how the majority of those living in the US believe in a God (96%), that over 90% pray, and that 69% are church members of some type (Princeton Religion Research Center, 2000). When such individuals enter therapy, there is no doubt that some will present these issues as involved in whatever problems they have come to address.

We have noted in Chapter 3 just how the professional field has changed itself in this time frame, moving from mostly a clergy-dominated set of therapists to a secular-dominated set of professionals. While these experts are amenable to managing such matters in treatment, there still exists a quite varied menu of techniques for how to include and use such material. The model that we presented helps to organize the clinical focus of therapy and provide a strictly social science paradigm for acquiring and engaging R/S content. There are two points of interest that need to be drawn out.

First, our model is firmly oriented towards the scientific. Yet, it does not explicitly rule out any particular types of interventions or strategies that one may use to manage R/S material. Therapists may find it important to pray with their clients, or assign biblically based reading assignments that address specific issues, or discuss denomination-specific issues related to the presenting problems. Our paradigm does not eliminate any of these techniques or methods. Therapists need to be free to pursue any strategy that is appropriate to the client. However, what we do argue as essential is the interpretation and goal of such interventions. Licensed mental health professionals need always to stay within the scope of practice as defined by their oversight boards. Their work must be related to addressing the psychosocial problems in adaptation affecting their clients. The goal of treatment is improved mental health and psychological functioning. Thus, all R/S material needs to be interpreted from this perspective.

Helping professionals need to be trained in various religious traditions/models in a manner that highlights issues of Infinitude, Meaning, and Worthiness: the essential numinous motivations. They need to become conversant in how various belief systems understand and present the numinous. We assert that the great value of religious traditions is that they provide accessible, understandable answers to complex existential questions. The languages used by the various Wisdom Traditions provide a venue for ordinary people to discuss and engage in such deeper issues of living. Therapists need to be able to translate the specifics of any given tradition into the larger meanings afforded by our numinous ontology. They need to understand how these numinous motivations impact real-life outcomes in clients' lives. The CPSCI can be helpful in making such translations. Therapists can discern areas where clients emphasize or neglect these motivations, and these evaluations can help direct the course of discussion around topics centering on ultimate meaning and self-understanding. A goal of such an intervention can be to balance out these motivations or to help clients address both the positive and negative aspects in an equable manner. The ultimate focus of such work is the improvement in clients' adaptation and resilience. Keeping a clear focus on the psychological goals of treatment is essential for licensed mental health workers operating in an ethically appropriate manner.

The second issue is the need to train all therapists in numinous issues. The numinous should not be seen as a subdiscipline, or specific content area, or theoretical orientation. As the data presented here indicated, the numinous represents the most fundamental aspect of human functioning that is universal to all people. The numinous does not emerge out of being a religiously committed individual, nor is it a consequence of being a person of faith. As we stated in Chapter 1, the numinous represents those psychological qualities that make religion and spirituality important to us. The numinous is the reason why all human societies and cultures have developed religious beliefs and traditions. These efforts at building cultural identity, law, art, and philosophy, among other endeavors, all find their primary motivations within the numinous. The numinous is a core defining quality of our species, so not to include it in the study of the psychological lives of people is to create an incomplete understanding of who we are and the ultimate goals we are pursuing.

The numinous needs to be considered a component of every other subdiscipline of the field, whether one is behaviorally, dynamically, existentially, or quantitatively oriented. Its impact can be felt in any study of human endeavor. As such, the study of the numinous should be a standard element to the training curricula of all social sciences. Its salient, universal presence will show itself in every human endeavor that addresses issues of human abundance, meaning, and personal value. The numinous is the psychological cloth we use to comfort and support us in the face of chaos and death. The history of humanity has been defined by these numinous motivations and our future will brighten as we harness our personal abundance and better appreciate the value our species offers nature. We hope that the information and data presented in this book have made a compelling case for the universal inclusion of numinous information and practices in the training curricula for all helping professionals

Development of Better Numinous Measures

The epistemology presented in Chapter 4 represents what we believe to be an essential paradigm for the development of numinous scales that are novel and independent of already established personality domains. The criteria presented will ensure that any developed scale will carry useful personological power and empirical robustness. Chapter 5 demonstrated the value of this paradigm by presenting the development and application of the ASPIRES, the first scale to capture the numinous as a trait-based, personality-oriented construct. The ASPIRES has been in use for over a decade and has found wide usage in the field, both domestically and internationally. The ASPIRES is one of only a very few R/S measures that have been abstracted in *Buros Mental Measurement Yearbook* (Carlson, Geisinger, & Jonson, 2014) as well in other reference works (e.g., Gregory, 2015; Piedmont & Toscano, 2016). As outlined in Chapter 5, the ASPIRES has a very large, and expanding, validity literature, which supports its use as a universal measure of the numinous.

For our purposes here, one of the more important aspects of the ASPIRES is its ability to serve as a taxonometric reference point in the development of new numinous measures. We have argued that the numinous represents the sixth dimension of personality, and the ASPIRES can serve as an empirical reference point for determining whether or not a new measure captures similar personological content. Measures that associate with it certainly represent similar qualities, while scales that are orthogonal to it cannot be considered numinous in nature. The process for developing new measures has become quite clear, direct, and empirically grounded. To be of ultimate use, any new measure of the numinous must not only associate with the ASPIRES (i.e., load significantly on the factor defined by the ASPIRES scales) but should ultimately be able to demonstrate incremental validity over both the FFM domains and the ASPIRES. In this way, the new scale demonstrates not only its category membership but also its unique contribution to defining the category.

When the ASPIRES was being developed in the late 1990s, we did not have our ontological model, with its clear specification of basic numinous motivations. As such, the development of the ASPIRES had to follow a different path. This process focused on bootstrapping a construct from the discussions of diverse theological experts on those aspects of spirituality they believed were universal. The facet scales of Prayer Fulfillment, Universality, and Connectedness were the results of this process. Developing these scales was inefficient in some ways because we did not have any clear exemplars of what constituted the numinous domain. As such, we needed to focus more on identifying content that was independent of the FFM domains yet correlated with our measures of religious involvement. The result of this somewhat cumbersome process was quite successful.

However, now that we have an ontological model for describing the numinous, the process of scale constructs should proceed more efficiently going forward. The model presented in Chapter 2 provides very clear definitions of what is considered to be numinous, and these definitions can serve as guidelines for item development. As such, the Numinous Assessment Group (NAG), described in Chapter 7, undertook the creation of what we labeled a *second-generation measure of the numinous*. Termed the Numinous Motivation Inventory (NMI), we underwent the development of items that captured the qualities defined in the model. These items were given to subjects, and responses were factor analyzed. Items were kept that loaded on factors containing ASPIRES facet scales and factors that were independent of the FFM and ASPIRES. After several iterations, the NMI emerged in its final form containing 22 items and reflecting the three domains of Infinitude,

Meaning, and Worthiness. Both a self-report and observer-rating versions were created. While still in its early testing stages, a preliminary manual has been developed, and normative information for both versions has been obtained (Piedmont, 2017b). The results emerging from this instrument are very exciting and encouraging. Specimen sets are available from the first author (RLP).

Table 9.1 presents the correlations between the NMI scales and the ASPIRES scales in the normative sample. This sample consists of 659 men and 959 women ages 18 to 81 years old. Individuals were recruited through MTurk and reflect a relatively representative group, coming from all 50 states and representing a diverse range of ethnic and religious backgrounds. These individuals completed the NMI for themselves and also provided a rating for someone they knew well. As can be seen, the NMI scales of I and M correlate with the ASPIRES scales, with values ranging from $r = -.15$ to $r = .74$, all $ps < .001$. The NMI scales of I and M correlate strongly with the Spiritual Transcendence Scales (STS) and Religious Involvement (RI); W appears more related to the Religious Crisis (RC) Scale. Clearly this scale is capturing elements of spiritual struggle and existential crisis. These associations do provide evidence of convergent validity for all of the NMI scales. They are reflecting similar content as the ASPIRES.

More importantly, it is necessary to evaluate the incremental validity of these new scales over both personality and the ASPIRES. Participants in the normative sample completed a number of relevant psychosocial measures. These included the Depression-Anxiety-Stress Scale-21 (DASS-21), Affect Balance Scale (ABS), Brief Resilience Scale (BRS), Self-Compassion Scale-Short Form (SCS-SF), a single item measure of

Table 9.1 Zero-Order Correlations between the NMI Self-Report Scales and the ASPIRES Scales

ASPIRES Scale	NMI Scale		
	Infinitude	*Worthiness*	*Meaning*
Prayer Fulfillment	.74***	.21***	.71***
Universality	.60***	.31***	.40***
Connectedness	.29***	.16***	.20***
Total STS	.74***	.28***	.63***
Religious Involvement	.63***	.17***	.72***
Religious Crisis	-.15***	-.43***	-.19***

$N = 1618$.

*** $p < .001$.

work satisfaction (WORK), and the Delighted-Terrible scale (DELITE). Also included in this series of analyses was the Religious Crisis scale from the ASPIRES. This scale was developed to capture aspects of existential dread, the belief by individuals that God has rejected them as worthy people. This scale has been shown to represent an independent predictor of psychopathology (Piedmont et al., 2007).

Each of the above scales served as the outcome variable in a series of hierarchical multiple regression analyses. On step 1 of each analysis, the gender and age were entered. This was done because raw scores for the NMI scales were included and, as discussed in Chapter 5, these variables need to be controlled for when examining the effects of the NMI scales. On step 2, the FFM personality dimensions were entered as a block. On step 3, the ST facet scales were entered simultaneously. Finally, on step 4, the NMI scales were entered using a forward entry method. Partial *F*-tests were conducted to determine whether a given block added a significant amount of additional explanatory variance in the outcomes measured. The results of these analyses are presented in Table 9.2.

Several points of interest emerge from Table 9.2. First, the FFM dimensions were the single strongest predictors of each outcome. Nevertheless,

Table 9.2 Incremental Validity of the Self-Report NMI Scales over Demographic Variables and the Five-Factor Model Domains in Predicting Psychosocial Outcomes.

Outcome	Demographic R^2	FFM ΔR^2	ASPIRES $\Delta\Delta R^2$	NMI $\Delta\Delta\Delta R^2$	NMI Predictors
DASS	.04*	.43*	.01*	.11*	W
Depression	.05*	.29*	.01*	.04*	W
Anxiety	.05*	.47*	.01*	.03*	W
Stress					
ABS	.04*	.31*	.01*	.01*	W/I
Negative Affect	.01*	.16*	.02*	.04*	W
Positive Affect					
Resilience	.01*	.32*	.00	.01*	W
Self-Compassion	.03*	.49*	.01*	.02*	W/I
Delighted-Terrible	.00	.33*	.02*	.08*	W
Work Satisfaction	.01*	.13*	.01*	.02*	W/M
Religious Crisis	.00	.14*	.02*	.07*	W/M/I

Note: DASS: Depression-Anxiety-Stress Scale; ABS: Affect Balance Scale. W = Worthiness, I = Infinitude, M = Meaning.

$N = 1618.$ * $p < .01$.

the numinous constructs provided significant incremental predictive power in every instance. Second, the NMI scales were significant, unique predictors of every outcome variable. Like the ASPIRES, numinous aspects of personality captured by the NMI have a broad range of predictive appeal. As a single domain, it is exciting to see that this construct relates to both negative aspects of functioning (e.g., stress and anxiety) and positive elements (e.g., resilience, compassion). Third, in this set of outcome variables, W emerged as the most robust predictor, being relevant to all of these outcomes.

Finally, it is important to note that not only were the NMI scales incrementally significant over the ASPIRES ST scales, but the magnitude of contribution for the NMI scales was larger than the ASPIRES' contribution in every instance. These findings support the contention that the NMI is a second-generation measure of the numinous. Building on the research findings from the ASPIRES, we have been successful in developing a measure that more clearly assesses numinous functioning, resulting in an instrument that incrementally predicts important psychosocial outcomes. It is hoped that the NMI will provide a more persuasive empirical demonstration of the importance of numinous constructs for understanding psychological functioning.

CPSCI Development

The CPSCI, which is presented in Chapter 7, is an important clinical tool for anyone interested in bringing numinous issues into the treatment process. This tool provides for a comprehensive examination of clients that also includes a relevant examination of numinous constructs, which is perhaps its greatest strength. As far as we are aware, there are no intake forms that provide such a complete coverage of this area. A second strength of this form is that it also includes scales that have normative data associated with them. This allows therapists to obtain inferential information about clients in the areas of symptom experience, treatment readiness, dysfunctional personality, spirituality, religiousness, religious crisis, and numinous concerns. Thus, one can determine how the current client compares to other treatment-seeking people. Because these scales also demonstrated evidence of construct validity, therapists can begin to draw personological inferences from information that is collected at intake. These features allow the CPSCI to make a tremendously positive contribution to the therapeutic process by providing therapists with important insights into temperament and dysfunctional experiences that can be useful in tailoring treatment specifically to the client. This information can also help clinicians to anticipate specific issues that are likely to emerge in the treatment process.

While we believe that the CPSCI is an important contribution to the field, there are still some issues that need to be addressed. We see four areas for research. First, having normed scales on this intake is an important innovation, but the current size of the norms group is quite small ($N = 65$). What makes this sample useful is that it includes only individuals who are currently receiving outpatient treatment. Certainly, more information is needed. It would be helpful to get over 300 individuals in the group. Such an increase would make it possible to expand the diversity of the group, including individuals with a variety of mental health issues, who are being seen in a diversity of treatment settings (e.g., private practices, community clinics, inner-city facilities). It would also be helpful if inpatient individuals' data could also be collected. They would represent an important client population to use with the CPSCI.

Second, more validity information on the current set of scales would be helpful. As was noted in Chapter 7, the outcome criterion scales were very selective and may not have included as broad an array of psychosocial constructs as hoped. It would be useful to have other indices that are more directly related to treatment-specific dynamics, such as counseling readiness, levels of defensiveness, and clinician ratings of treatment success. The more validity evidence for the scales, the greater the interpretive depth of the resulting scores. Relatedly, additional work may be needed on some of the scales. In particular, the Dysfunctional Openness scale may need to be modified so that the items are more clearly related to Openness to Experience. The Logoplex scales can use some additional developmental work as well. While there were clear differences between the lowest and highest meaning categories (i.e., Solipsism vs Spiritualism), there was little discriminating evidence between the two middle categories (i.e., Secular Humanism vs Asceticism). This may have been a consequence of the outcome criteria used to evaluate these dimensions, but there may also be room for developing crisper definitions of these categories, including better exemplars of the meaning styles they represent.

A third area for investigation concerns the items comprising the Pastoral Themes section. While the number of issues checked in these categories was meaningfully related to other psycho-social-numinous outcomes, a more detailed examination of the content of these elements may open new insights into client dynamics. As was noted, each section contains both positive and negative elements for each meaning-making theme. It would be of interest to examine whether the numbers of positive and negative items each have their own relations with the outcome criteria. It may be possible to determine whether a client has satisfactorily resolved a particular theme or is currently in crisis with that theme. This would be important information for treatment planning.

The final area for work on the CPSCI would be to determine whether new, relevant scales can be developed from those items not currently contained by a scale. Are there other neuropsychological scales that can be created from the Mental Status items? What implications for diagnosis, treatment, and outcome would they hold? Perhaps a factor analysis of all the items of the instrument ought to be conducted to determine the number and type of dimensions that appear to be represented in this item set. These larger item groupings may have other, unique insights into client functioning that are not observable through the current set of scales and items. It would also be of interest to determine if there are other important aspects of functioning that ought to be included in this scale. While every attempt was made in constructing the scale to be thorough, only through usage will the adequacy of the instrument's clinical utility and comprehensiveness be evaluated.

Logoplex Development

The Logoplex was developed in an effort to differentiate among the various types of meaning people make. Meaning is an essential element to spiritual strivings, so having a structure for understanding how and in which ways individuals create meaning for themselves would be a clinical asset. While we believe there is great heuristic value to the Logoplex model, more work needs to be done to assess the putative qualities that are represented. As we noted in Chapter 6, given the circumplical nature of the model, special analytical techniques need to be applied in order to identify useful scales that assess the portrayed qualities at specific intervals around the circle. Usually eight scales (referred to as octants) are formed to map the circular ordering of qualities.

Another aspect of the Logoplex to be examined is the component that is included on the CPSCI. As it stands, it represents only a single question where clinicians are to select, given the provided definitions, the particular category into which they believe the client falls. This is a very broad conceptualization of the Logoplex, leaving much room for further improvement. Perhaps more specific definitions can be created or more options provided. More research needs to be devoted to examining various assessment options and their practical utility. Perhaps each category can receive its own Likert-type rating, allowing for a multidimensional assessment. Clients can be assessed in terms of how much of their meaning-making centers in each of the four quadrants. Or, perhaps multiple assessments can be made across different aspects of the client's life space (e.g., relationships, vocation, personal goal setting, etc.). There are numerous possibilities to consider, each with its own advantages. However, research will need to determine what works best in the clinical context.

Developing New Interventions

As we have noted throughout this book, there are numerous textbooks devoted to the clinical issues associated with the application of R/S material in the therapeutic context. Multiple techniques already exist, such as mindfulness, gratitude, and prayer, to name a few. Some of these techniques have emerged directly from various spiritual practices associated with several religious groups. Our model is not concerned so much with specific techniques as it is with the reason behind their deployment and the clinical goals being addressed. However, having an ontological model that identifies specific numinous motivations opens the door for the development of new techniques that are aimed at addressing these intrinsic qualities. There are two components to this.

The first component would address the development of techniques that are designed to harness these motivations and use them to attain specific clinical outcomes. What types of interventions would be based on motives surrounding I? Or Worthiness? How can these motivations be stimulated so that they may have a more direct influence on behavior? We do not have, as yet, any answers to these questions, unfortunately. We hope that by articulating their presence and significance, others may be intrigued enough to seek out methods for addressing them. The numinous motivations are very powerful and gripping; their presence can create strong feelings in people and attract their attention and involvement. It is interesting to note how these motivations are routinely portrayed in movies and other art modalities, leading to profound reactions from those who view them.

We have a working hypothesis that movies engaging story content around the numinous motivations experience more success than those films that do not include such content. For example, consider the movie *Avatar* (Cameron & Landau, 2009). It was a blockbuster of a film generating quite a response from audiences. When closely examined, it is evident that this movie stressed themes associated with all three numinous motivations. There was much on infinitude, with its focus on the spiritual beliefs of the alien culture and how these forces ultimately came to the assistance of the Na'vi, the people indigenous to Pandora, the world earthlings were eager to colonize. The human protagonist and hero in this film, Jake, was a physically handicapped former military soldier who was struggling with many personal demons. Issues of meaning and worthiness were thoroughly infused in the film as Jake inhabited an avatar (the physical representation of Jake's persona into a physical form that would interact with the Na'vi) and strove to find safety for these indigenous peoples and protect them from the humans who wanted to exploit the planet for their own purposes. At the end, the spiritual forces existing in the Tree of Souls eventually redeemed Jake and saved the Na'vi from annihilation. The depths of numinous meaning were explored in detail, and the supporting psychological effects of their cultural values clearly demonstrated. Viewers were treated to a moral tale about how all time folds into a single point of existence, and all life embraces itself, past and present, creating a universal sense of unity and goodness that redeems, renews, and embraces. It is no wonder this movie broke all records at the box office! We are all drawn, like moths to the fire, to those ineluctable qualities that the numinous calls forth from us. Thus, identifying ways in which these motivations can be accessed during the clinical session would add much value to the treatment. It remains to be seen how the numinous can potentiate positive treatment effects.

The second component would be to develop intervention strategies that are designed to address conflict within each of these numinous motivations. How does one manage a client who is struggling with W issues? What steps would need to be taken to address the deep levels of existential dread and emptiness that such conflicts may create? It is not known how amenable these motivations are to change; they are situated at the core of being and are linked to many other psychological systems. Being able to access these motivations directly and to work with their content, which may be infused in many aspects of character and behavior, in ways that can embrace and influence other psychological self-systems needs to be explored.

Certainly, the Wisdom Traditions provide a point of departure in the search for potential tools for accessing and developing these core motivations. Every religious tradition has its own spiritual formation process for guiding and developing the spiritual sentiments of believers. Techniques such as fasting, tithing, reading religious literature, involvement in special rituals, prayer, meditation, and retreats are some of the many potential interventions to be explored. Of course, in evaluating these various techniques, it would be important that the specific theological material is removed and some determination of their psychological impact be used as criteria for evaluating their utility for general clinical practice. These would be good places to start the search for new treatment domains. We hope that, with time, systematic reviews of these methods would be able to identify the active elements responsible for driving change, with the consequent development and standardization of these processes.

Developing the Psychological Implications for Religious Crisis and Worthiness

As we have noted throughout this book, the value of the numinous is that it represents a new dimension of personality. One consequence of this is that the construct may contain new personological implications that cast light onto issues of both resilience and pathology. It is this last potential that needs to be further developed. As we have shown, Religious Crisis (RC) and W represent aspects of functioning that address the core ability of individuals to find a sense of acceptance and value from their perceived existential world view. In Chapter 5, we discussed how individuals who are unable to find this acceptance and come to believe that they are unworthy and inadequate experience a deep sense of personal dread and emptiness that is inconsolable by any other personal, social, or institutional agency. Such individuals may experience high levels of emotional distress and may be prone to suicidal ideations and actions. We believe that a deeper examination of this construct holds the possibility for redefining our knowledge of mental impairment in directions that enhance and expand clinical understanding and intervening.

In our overview of the NMI, we presented data suggesting that the dimension of W may represent an entirely new pathway for the development of emotional distress and pathology creation (see also Piedmont et al., 2007). It has already been shown in the research literature that the personality dimension of Neuroticism (N) underlies the experience of most of the categories of distress that are represented in the current diagnostic manuals. Syndromes related to trauma and stress, phobias, impulse disorders, and the personality disorders, among others, have been shown to be linked to high levels of this domain (Miller, Lynam, Widiger, & Leukefeld, 2001; Zonderman, Herbst, Schmidt, Costa, & McCrae, 1993). It is easy to see the connection between affective lability and impaired psychological functioning. However, RC and W are independent of N yet are also significantly related to psychological impairment. Future work needs to identify the underlying pathways by which these qualities either create fundamental vulnerabilities to experience impairment or serve as direct predictors of pathology. How do RC and W operate in tandem with N in the expression of current psychological disorders? Do these numinous qualities underlie their own, unique domain of mental impairment that is currently uncharted?

These are important questions that need immediate attention. We believe that the data presented on the dimensions of RC and W provide the most compelling argument for the inclusion of the numinous in the sciences. Their empirical relations to pathology raise serious concerns about the comprehensiveness of current psychological models. The numinous aspects of distress offer the potential for significantly redefining current clinical paradigms for assessment, diagnosis, and treatment. They hold out the possibility of expanding our knowledge of psychological functioning. This is what we find as the most exciting aspect of work with numinous: These constructs stand at the cusp of what is known and what may be the next great discoveries in the social sciences.

Final Comments

There is certainly much more work to be done in the scientific study of the numinous. We hope that this volume will help stimulate thinking and motivate new research endeavors. We believe that the models presented here provide a very useful approach to organizing our understanding of numinous constructs and for providing a platform for developing new sets of questions that will help organize the field and direct it to goals that are scientifically valid and clinically useful. Our hope is that the book will now help change the focus of action from rational discourse to empirical study for engaging with numinous material.

While there is still much work yet to be done, we believe that this book has provided the field with a set of excellent tools to help direct these future efforts. Included in this volume is what we see as a complete, "soup to nuts" integrated package of theories, paradigms, methodologies, and applications: a complete working model for understanding and engaging the numinous. This rubric should provide direction and consistency to research and clinical activities, all of which have now been clearly situated within a social science context. Scientifically oriented professionals should feel comfortable discussing, describing, and using any aspect of this model. Students should be able to find clarity and structure to this field, making it more understandable and accessible. Clinicians now have tools for engaging and assessing clients in ways that are consistent with their training and scope of practice requirements. One does not have to be theologically trained or informed in order to fully understand and apply this material. Further, because of its psychological nature, information about the numinous is relevant for all clients, regardless of whether they are religious or not, believe in a transcendent reality or not, or come from different cultures and backgrounds. The numinous represents universal aspects of human functioning. Researchers should be able to find the type of methodological clarity and direction that can contribute to the conducting of efficient research endeavors that have the necessary power to demonstrate their intended effects.

A few years ago, I (RLP) was invited to contribute a paper to *Spirituality in Clinical Practice* describing those events and experiences that contributed to my becoming involved in this area of work (Piedmont, 2017a). In that piece, I recounted how, as an undergraduate psychology major in the 1970s, I had this very interesting conversation with an older friend of mine who was working on his doctorate in psychology at the time. This person, Randy as I named him in the article, was a staunch atheist. He had great contempt for religion and was highly motivated to get me to recant my religious faith. His major point was how I could claim to be a "social scientist" and yet still be a person of faith. The two positions, from his perspective, seemed incompatible. While I knew that physical and meta-physical phenomena were completely different types of realities, they were never in conflict in my mind. To me, they were complementary experiences. Nonetheless, the evening was long, and Randy was tireless in his harangue. I came away from this encounter feeling that I did not do a good job in arguing my point of view. Randy wanted data and facts, things that our spiritual world always seemed short on. I remembered driving home that night thinking, wishing, that someday I would get the chance to show scientifically the importance and value of spirituality for human life. Now, over 40 years later, I finally have my response to Randy. Thanks, Randy for stimulating my numinous motivations!

References

Cameron, J. (Producer & Director), & Landau, J. (Producer). (2009). *Avatar* [Motion picture]. US: Lightstorm Entertainment.

Carlson, J. F., Geisinger, K. F., & Jonson, J. L. (Eds.). (2014). *The nineteenth mental measurements yearbook* (pp. 24–28). Lincoln, NE: The University of Nebraska Press.

Gregory, R. J. (2015). *Psychological testing: History, principles, and applications* (7th ed.). Boston, MA: Pearson.

Miller, J. D., Lynam, D. R., Widiger, T. A., Leukefeld, C. (2001). Personality disorders as extreme variants of common personality dimensions: Can the Five-Factor Model adequately represent pathology? *Journal of Personality, 69*, 253–276.

Piedmont, R. L. (2017a). Knowing and understanding: A personal integration. *Spirituality in Clinical Practice, 4*, 288–291.

Piedmont, R. L. (2017b). *Numinous Motivation Inventory: Preliminary technical manual.* Timonium, MD: Author.

Piedmont, R. L., Hassinger, C. J., Rhorer, J., Sherman, M. F., Sherman, N. C., & Williams, J. E. G. (2007). The relations among spirituality and religiosity and Axis II functioning in two college samples. *Research in the Social Scientific Study of Religion, 18*, 53–73.

Piedmont, R. L., & Toscano, M. E. (2016). The Assessment of Spirituality and Religious Sentiments (ASPIRES) scale. In V. Zeigler & T. K. Shackelford (Eds.). *Encyclopedia of Personality and Individual Differences.* New York, NY: Meteor-Springer.

Princeton Religion Research Center. (2000). Americans remain very religious, but not necessarily in conventional ways. *Emerging Trends, 22*(1), 2–3.

Zonderman, A. B., Herbst, J. H., Schmidt, C., Jr., Costa, P. T., Jr., & McCrae, R. R. (1993). Depressive symptoms as a nonspecific graded risk for psychiatric diagnosis. *Journal of Abnormal Psychology, 102*, 544–552.

Author Index

Subject Index

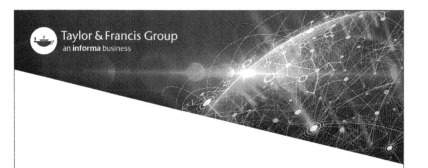